*Fun was my living*

QUINNY

*Quintin Gilbey*

# FUN WAS MY LIVING

HUTCHINSON OF LONDON

HUTCHINSON & CO (*Publishers*) LTD
*178–202 Great Portland Street, London W1*
London Melbourne Sydney Auckland
Bombay Toronto Johannesburg New York

*First published February 1970*
*Second impression March 1970*
*Third impression May 1970*



*Printed in Great Britain by litho on Antique Wove paper*
*by Anchor Press, and bound by Wm. Brendon,*
*both of Tiptree, Essex*
ISBN 0 09 100780 1

*To Zoë*

# *Contents*

# 1 *An Edwardian childhood*

'The parents were largely to blame', is the almost universal verdict when someone under the age of thirty perpetrates some particularly revolting crime against society. Magistrates, judges and the popular press share the view that the young criminal could not resist the temptation to cosh some unfortunate old woman because his childish illusions had been shattered by the discovery that Mum and Dad weren't hitting it off too well. Passing the buck to the parents is a common, and more often than not successful, line of defence on the part of learned counsel, but as most of us have disobeyed our parents from the moment we could walk it seems a little unfair to hold them responsible for our grown-up misdemeanours.

I believe, however, that I am an exception; I believe my parents did unwittingly decide my destiny.

My father, like most well-to-do men of his day, was a paradoxical figure: he loved animals; yet he was never so happy as when killing them. As he was a Master of Foxhounds, a first-class shot and an expert fisherman, he led a very enjoyable life.

Having established the Guv'nor as a fine sportsman, I must add that he disapproved of racing so heartily that we were forbidden to discuss it in his presence.

I have never discovered the reason for this, but I imagine he was mortally afraid that his sons might gamble away the fortunes accumulated in the latter half of the nineteenth century by his father and his uncles.

The history of the firm of W. and A. Gilbey has been chronicled by such famous authors as Alec Waugh and the late Sir Herbert Maxwell; it is a story of which I am immensely proud. As a younger son I have at no time been a member of the firm, but it has given me many of the things I have enjoyed most in life even after I was able to earn my own living.

It was my father's horror of racing – plus the intense interest it held for my four elder brothers, whose likes and dislikes I accepted without question – that nurtured my love of it. Racing started as my hobby, proved to be my source of livelihood and, at the end of 1966, once again became my hobby.

Although my father believed that the Turf was largely peopled by thieves and vagabonds he admitted there were exceptions. Being handy with a gun himself, he was invited to many great houses from which, as only one generation removed from a parvenu, he would otherwise have been debarred.

In this way he became on friendly terms with King Edward, who as Prince of Wales had won the Derby and the St Leger with Persimmon, and the triple crown with Persimmon's full brother, Diamond Jubilee. One of my father's closest friends was Waldorf Astor, whose Cliveden estate and stud were only a couple of miles from Wooburn House, where we lived till just after my eleventh birthday. In the eyes of a Royalist like my father, kings were laws unto themselves and could do no wrong. Waldorf Astor, on the other hand, did not bet and he therefore considered him an excellent example to his sons. Another near neighbour was Lord Burnham who raised thousands of pheasants annually on his Hall Barn estate. They were so many and so tame that their destruction called for no great skill, and this delighted the King, who, unlike his son King George V, was only a moderate shot.

On one occasion, between drives, the King asked my father to walk with him to the next stand. They were wearing similar capes, voluminous garments giving free play to the arms. In the distance they might have been mistaken for one another, though my father had a large moustache and no beard. On reaching the stand, the King said, 'I am getting tired, Gilbey, you shoot this drive.' As always, flocks of birds flew over the Royal gun, but it was my father who brought them down. At the end of the drive His Majesty was warmly congratulated on his skill; without the hint of a conspiratorial wink at my father, he cheerfully agreed that he had shot pretty well. In my limited experience of Royalty I have noticed that while they are prepared to laugh uproariously at someone else's discomfiture, any joke remotely at their own expense is quite unfunny.

King Edward VII was the only subject on which my Victorian parents did not agree. My father believed in the Divine Right of Kings; my mother, although an ardent Royalist, took grave exception to the King's morals. My father's antagonism to racing had made it appear in my eyes the most glamorous of amusements, while my mother's preoccupation with the private life of Royalty gave me a strong suspicion that the Seventh Commandment would be a whole lot of fun to break. Forbidden fruits are the sweetest, and my life might well have been very different had my father been a racing man and my mother had a lover.

My great-grandfather Henry Gilbey, who was born in 1790, owned the stage coaches which ran between London and Bishop's Stortford, and he dismissed the first railway trains as a nine days' wonder; of course they could never take the place of horses. His mistake cost him dearly, and when he died in 1842 he had little to leave his six sons, and a like number of daughters, except his good name.

He also had talked with kings, having often driven the Prince Regent from Bishop's Stortford in his coach, after he had changed coaches there on his way home from Newmarket. The 'First Gentleman' made up for his many shortcomings with an open-handed disposition, and once after a particularly good day at Newmarket he made Great-grandfather the present of a horse.

My great-uncle, Henry Parry Gilbey, was already established in a firm of wine merchants, but his younger brothers Walter and Alfred (my grandfather) started life as clerks. During the Crimean War they became clerks in the Army Pay Department, and spent two very uncomfortable years working in an army convalescent home near Gallipoli.

At the end of the war Walter was twenty-six and my grandfather twenty-four, and they hadn't a ha'p'orth of capital between them. In 1857, however, on the advice and with the financial assistance of their elder brother Henry, they rented cellars at the corner of Berwick Street and Oxford Street as retail merchants under the name of W. and A. Gilbey.

The business prospered from the start, as they dealt in Colonial wines; but their great stroke of luck came about in 1860 when the Cobden treaty with France brought about a fiscal revolution. At first, this looked as much of a threat to the young Gilbeys' business as the trains had been to their father's. Colonial preference was swept away by Mr Gladstone's budget of 1860, which reduced the duty on French wines from twelve shillings to two shillings a dozen, dealing a death blow to the popularity of the Cape wines, and opening the market to the wines of Bordeaux and Burgundy, hitherto excluded from all but the well-to-do.

The young Gilbeys observed that the old established firms were not lowering their prices for French wines. Thereupon this upstart firm, scarcely four years old, announced that they would allow their customers the full benefit accruing from the reduction of the duty by 70 per cent. It was a gamble but they deserved to win. They did win and became rich men overnight.

I tell this story, firstly because I am proud to be descended from men of such courage, business acumen and integrity; and secondly to establish beyond doubt that we owe the amassing of our family fortunes to Free Trade.

Alfred Gilbey, sen., died in 1879 at Wooburn House, where twenty years later I was born. Alec Waugh, in his admirable book *Merchants of Wine*, describes my grandfather as 'a typical Victorian philanthropist, the poor man who has made money quickly, who is conscious of his debt to the community, and who devoted his leisure to good works'. He left my grandmother amply provided for, which was just as well as she was the mother of eleven children, the eldest being my father, then aged twenty.

My grandmother came from humble Scottish stock; but she often told me how, when she was a little girl, living over her parents' coffee shop, a fortune-teller told her that she would one day have her own carriage and pair, and how her brothers and sisters teased her about it. This wasn't one of my father's favourite stories, and once, when I began to tell it in the presence of important guests, my mother said it was high time I ran upstairs to Nannie.

About the same time, when I was about seven, I made an even worse *faux pas*, and the words were out before I could be shut up. The conversation concerned Mr Solly Joel, whose South African business interests were very much in the news. One of the guests wondered whether he had been christened Solly or whether it was short for Solomon, to which I piped up, 'As he's a Jew I don't expect he was christened at all, just circumcised.' For once, my bible learning, of which my mother was so proud, proved an embarrassment.

My father, as head of a family of eleven and the eldest of the new generation of this rapidly expanding firm of wine merchants, had a heavy load of responsibility at an age when most young men are sowing their wild oats. He was under no illusions and he immediately set out to make it clear, not only to his brothers and sisters but also to his generation of wine merchants, that he intended to be the boss. In this he was supported by my grandmother. Although he did not care much for stories about Granny's childhood he loved her dearly and they were staunch allies.

Of all the members of the vast family of Gilbeys and their cousins the Golds, the Blyths and the Grinlings, with whom they intermarried so freely, my grandmother stood out among a host of mediocrities. She outlived her husband by over forty years and at her death shortly after World War One she was well into her eighties. Her back was always as straight as a ramrod, and this was symbolic of her character. Rich and poor alike loved her, and she can never have known what it was to be lonely. On Sundays it was in no way exceptional for her to be visited by as many as twenty members of the family.

My uncles and aunts used to say that my father had never been a young man. I can well believe it. Though I was the youngest by far of his five sons, yet he was no more than forty-six when I first remember him clearly; but even then his demeanour was that of a much older man. He had a pronounced stoop; on the rare occasions when he played cricket he insisted on having a runner, and he always mounted his horse from a mounting-block. One of my earliest recollections of the hunting field is watching him 'spend a penny' without dismounting.

I have said that the Gilbey fortune was the outcome of Free Trade and if any family ever owed a debt of gratitude to the Liberals it was the Gilbeys. As a young man, in accordance with the family tradition, my father stood as a Liberal for South Bucks. He was defeated, and later, by the time I was old enough to take notice, he had become a Conservative and a Tariff Reformer. His association with the Liberal Party was never mentioned, and I had a terrific shock when one of the masters at my private school let the cat out of the bag, with the result that the cry went up 'Gilbey's a stinking Liberal, his pater stood for Parliament and got licked, jolly well serves him right.' The truth was that from my earliest years I had been told I was Oxford and Conservative and had been given a dark blue rosette, which I had worn, pinned on the collar of my sailor suit, for two boat races and one general election. So I sent an S O S to my mother for my rosette, and thereby established myself as a member of the party in favour, though at the time not in office.

In the eyes of all my family, with the exception of my grandmother and a couple of aunts who married impecunious clergymen, the world was divided into two categories – the haves and the have-nots. The haves were concerned with preserving the *status quo*, and naturally voted Conservative; the idea that a more equal distribution of the country's wealth would benefit mankind had never entered their heads.

My parents were typical of their time, and no more honourable people ever lived. They went to church on Sundays, and never owed a penny for more than a day, which could not be said for some members of the aristocracy who could trace their ancestors back into the mists of time.

The only man my father ever deceived was himself, and it is now hard to believe that a man who had inherited a fortune derived from a successful gamble that he himself would never have taken, should have thought himself to be so infinitely superior to those whose forebears had been less fortunate. Had the established wine merchants been less greedy, and the young Gilbeys less venturesome, my father would have been a have-not, while I should have left school and gone out to work for my living instead of going to Eton. So far to the right was this one-time unsuccessful Liberal candidate that he might well in due course have become a Fascist; he certainly admired Mussolini for getting the Italian trains running on time, and 'standing no damn' nonsense from the left wing'. But he was a very humane man and would have been as shocked as was the rest of the world at the atrocities committed by the Nazis.

My father was undoubtedly a great patriot, though I have never been quite clear where patriotism ends and chauvinism begins. Although I never heard him say that niggers began at Calais or 'abroad is bloody' like Nancy Mitford's Uncle Matthew, I think this reflected his views. He disliked Jews, except for a few very rich ones whose wealth had bought them access to the most exclusive households and to the friendship of King Edward VII. My father was a firm believer in Kipling's philosophy that 'East is East and West is West and never the twain shall meet', and he also had the most profound distrust of all men whose colour was different from his own; he would even refer to the immortal Ranjitsinjhi as that 'infernal black man they can't get out'.

Though a poor performer himself, my father was tremendously keen on cricket, and I shall never forget the day he first took me into the pavilion at Lords and introduced me to Pelham (later Sir Pelham) Warner, captain of Middlesex. 'Plum' had married Agnes Blyth, a cousin of ours, and was one of my boyhood heroes; but Middlesex were playing Kent, and Kent was my county, champion county for the previous two years, and in my eyes every member of the Kent team was a God from Olympus. I was only eleven years old, but I can still recall the scores of all the Kent side without looking it up in *Wisden*, which was my bible. Yes, I know 'Plum' Warner made 109 that day in the second innings, but my beloved Kent won comfortably.

A love of cricket was the only characteristic I had inherited from my father, as I loathed shooting, I was bored by fishing, and although I hunted occasionally until the outbreak of World War Two, I never enjoyed it much after I grew up. Like so many followers of the chase, however, I was too much of a moral coward to admit that I looked forward to the moment when I could head for home without ignominy.

In my childhood the killing of animals was all part of the daily routine and hunting was the sport *par excellence*. But I also enjoyed the thrill of chasing rabbits with our four dachshunds. A dachshund would not stand a 100–1 chance of killing a rabbit in the open, but the unfortunate bunny, having burrowed its way into the garden under the wire netting, could seldom find its way out again, with the result that hardly a week passed without my proudly carrying a still warm corpse into the kitchen to a chorus of 'That Master Quintin's a proper little hunter, just like his Dad.'

But imperceptibly my unwillingness to participate in the act of killing grew with the years, and it came as a shock to me when I realised that I could no longer take part in blood sports though I still consider it an impertinence to try to convert those who do not share my feelings.

Cricket therefore was the only bond between my father and myself, though I loved him in a somewhat impersonal manner, as I did my mother. They were admirable parents, according to their lights, and did everything in their power to fit me for a successful career. They gave me a happy childhood and provided me with social and material advantages that helped me to make my own way in the world.

I wish we had been as close to one another as most of my contemporaries were to their parents but, after all, I was their fifth son, born sixteen years after their marriage, and they had dearly wanted a daughter. My father had become old before his time and was much concerned with his business affairs and politics, while my mother was too shy and reserved to be able to show her true feelings.

Most of my time, therefore, was spent with Nannie. It is the fashion for many people who grew up in the Edwardian era to vilify their nurses, depicting them as stony-faced disciplinarians determined to impose their will on their innocent charges, but Nannie Crush was not that kind. She came to look after my elder brothers ten years before I was born and she never had another job. Having nursed me through a series of illnesses, she looked after my brother Ronald's children till she retired more than sixty years after entering service with the Gilbeys. Even then her years of toil were not over. Shortly after her retirement her sister took to her bed and had to be waited on hand and foot till she died six months after her hundredth birthday. Nannie died at the age of eighty-nine.

I still look back on the days of 'the Hay' as the happiest of my life. 'The Hay' was the week in which Mr Reeves, our tenant farmer, cut the hay in a wide expanse of grass-land known as 'the Park'. Year after year this went on without incident, but one evening just before my eighth birthday, there were a few brief moments when all hell seemed to have been let loose.

Lessons were mercifully curtailed during 'the Hay' and from the moment the green grass was felled until the day it was carted to the ricks in the farm, silvery grey and warm with the sunshine, I was a member of that glamorous throng of men and boys who cut and gathered it in for sums varying from five to eighteen shillings a week. That year I was to help 14-year-old Joe lead the trace horses and I felt I should never know such happiness again. The shadows lengthened, and every moment I thought that Nannie would arrive and summon me to bed. It must have been after seven and I had never been out so late.

The children of Wooburn Green were usually well-behaved, but maybe they too sensed the intoxication of that evening. Perhaps in their immature minds there was born a feeling that there was something a trifle unfair in a little boy in a sailor suit having that lovely park, with its sweet-smelling hay, all to himself, while they had to make do with the scant grass at the side of the dusty road. In those 'good old days' it did not do for common folk to talk about things like equal rights, those who were foolish enough to do so lost their jobs and might well end up in the workhouse.

A paling in the shrubbery fence yielded to a kick, and in a matter of moments the shrubbery was a seething mass of young life. They leapt across the shallow stream and into 'the Park'. The hay was now in well ordered rows, made even tidier by my efforts with a hand-rake, but the children were not concerned with that. They dashed into the rows throwing the hay high in the air, running in it and gambolling like puppies. For a moment I was tempted to join them. There was something infectious in their joyous abandon.

But their happiness was short-lived; out of nowhere came gardeners armed with pitchforks, together with the odd stableman. Before the rebellion had been quelled my father appeared, followed as usual by the dachshunds and shaking his head as he always did when he was much provoked. 'Who's let these damned children into the Park?' he shouted, and when no one answered he threatened to have the law on the lot of them.

When the lamp was turned out that night I wondered whether God the Father would be as angry with those children as my own father had been. Was it not through God's grace that the rains fell, the sun shone and the grass grew tall? With the coming of another day, however, and the arrival of the hay wagons, some harnessed with two and some with three horses, I fear that my heart-searching was quickly pushed into the background. To my shame, it remained there for many years.

# 2 *Prep school*

Nannie's loving care had one disadvantage in that it was not the best training for the spartan life of a preparatory school in 1909. Cothill, near Abingdon, was as rough and ready as most schools were nearly sixty years ago. The Easter term was only nine weeks long, but to a little boy leaving home for the first time it seemed like a hundred years. I was not the pluckiest of little boys, and having lain awake most of the night on the first really hard bed I had ever come across, I wept on the way to early morning prayers at the thought that there were sixty-three more days before the end of the term.

The worst part about Cothill were the lavatories, situated in a tumbledown shed across the freezing playground from the main building. There was no plumbing, and the buckets were emptied, or supposed to be emptied, once a day. The stench was appalling, and to make matters worse the only light there was filtered through the cracks of ill-fitting doors. Several boys, including myself, became ill simply because we couldn't face the cold, the stench and the darkness of these hideous contraptions.

In the summer term of 1910 I had measles very badly, and in the summer holiday I developed rheumatic fever, which affected my heart. For many months I had to lie flat on my back and I earned an entirely false reputation for courage in the face of adversity. With Nannie to fuss over me, and the dachshunds lying under the eiderdown, life was heaven compared with Cothill. I would like to emphasise that these remarks cast no reflection on the magnificent modern school Cothill is today.

Everyone was wonderful to me and I was closer to my father during those months in bed than at any time before or since. On his return from London he would wrap himself in a couple of blankets – there was no electric light or central heating in Wooburn House – and read aloud to me till it was time for him to dress for dinner. *Treasure Island*, *The Pickwick Papers*, most of the works of Conan Doyle and Whyte Melville were the books he read to me, and we spent much time dicussing cricket.

My interest in racing was already some two years old, but my first bet was in the 1910 Derby, when I was convalescing from measles. We were not allowed to read the daily papers at Cothill, but my mother used to post me the *Sporting and Dramatic* every week, and the first article I always turned to was the one written by Rapier. Rapier had written a graphic description of that year's Two Thousand Guineas, which Lord Rosebery's Neil Gow, ridden by the great Danny Maher, won by a short head from Lemberg, ridden by Bernard Dillon. Rapier wrote that Lemberg had sweated more than Neil Gow, and had given him the impression that he would derive the greater benefit from the race. The captain of the cricket eleven at Cothill pinned his faith on the genius of Danny Maher and was prepared to accommodate me. My bet was a level half-crown that Lemberg would beat Neil Gow, and Lemberg won by a neck.

The factors which helped to make my life bearable during the winter months at Cothill were the catechism and the choir. A few days after my arrival we assembled in our various classes for instruction in the Scriptures. I was of course in the bottom form and, to my amazement, they had only got as far in the catechism as 'What did your Godfathers and Godmothers then for you?', the answer to which I had learned from my mother years before. So when I piped up, 'They did promise and vow three things in my name. First that I renounce the devil and all his works, the pomps and vanity of this wicked world and all the sinful lusts of the flesh', it was evident I was much too low in the handicap. As pleased as Punch with myself, I was moved up two forms to where they had got as far as 'My duty towards my Neighbour'. But once again I was able to inform them: 'My duty towards my neighbour is to love him as myself and to do to all men as I would they should do unto me', etc., etc., to the end of it, without once pausing for breath.

Once again young Gilbey was on the move, this time to the top form, where boys four-and-a-half years my senior were being instructed in the Sacraments. But there was no stopping Gilbey on this bright winter's morning, and when in reply to 'What is the inward and spiritual grace?' I answered without a moment's hesitation, 'A death unto sin, and a new birth unto righteousness: for being by nature born in sin, and the children of wrath, we are hereby made the children of grace', a gasp of astonishment went up from master and boys alike.

'Is there any part of the Scriptures you don't know by heart?' the master asked me, somewhat nervously, and I replied that I was a bit shaky on the Nicene Creed, and that I hadn't even started the Athanasian variety. 'Thank goodness for that,' he said, and told me to get cracking on the two creeds I didn't know.

My triumph was an ephemeral affair; in all other subjects, except reading, my knowledge was that of the average new boy. My mother had taught me the catechism, and like so many small boys possessed of a photographic memory, I had no difficulty in learning large portions of the Scriptures perfectly, though I did not understand a word of what I was gabbling.

I had a not unpleasing treble voice, and on my eighth birthday the vicar of Wooburn Green had asked my parents in my presence if they would allow me to join the village choir. Memories of the invasion of the village children still rankled, and I am quite sure that, had I not been present, they would have said No. 'Yes, yes, I'd love to', I told the vicar; 'please, please let me', I besought my parents, who reluctantly agreed. The prospect of praising God, wearing a white surplice over a black cassock, and taking part in the processions, was glamorous beyond words; what was even better was that I should be able to mix with boys older than myself, with good common names like Tommy, Harry and Jack, and not a silly name like Quintin, of which I was heartily ashamed.

My constant companion was my cousin Georgina, my mother's niece. Her father was very hard up, and they lived in one of the lodges on the estate. Georgina was eighteen months older than I was; we did lessons together, and though I was fond of her, she was only a girl. Now I was going to meet a lot of boys who dropped their H's! Incidentally, it was while playing tents with Georgina that I made the discovery that there was a certain fundamental difference between the two sexes.

The choir boys understandably eyed me with suspicion, but at the end of a month I asked my parents if I could invite them to tea, and to my astonishment they agreed. Mrs Henderson, the cook, provided a scrumptious feast, and from that day they accepted me as one of themselves, and I enjoyed Sundays more than ever before.

Always a bit of a show-off, I thought it smart to drop an H or two here and there in front of Nannie, who would never split on me, but my governess, Miss Toovey, had no scruples about complaining to my mother when I left out both the t's in 'little' in 'There's a friend for little children'. It was of course pure affectation, but it nearly cost me my place in the choir, as my parents feared I was catching 'their dreadful way of talking'.

I attended two services on Sundays and any choral service on weekdays, in addition to which there was choir practice on Tuesdays.

By the time I went to Cothill, therefore, it was not surprising that I not only knew the catechism by heart but also the Venite, Te Deum, Benedictus, Jubilate Deo, Magnificat, Nunc Dimittis and at least half a dozen hymns. I was immediately made a member of the school choir, and the smell of a freshly laundered surplice brought memories of home. I was by far the youngest member of the choir, and though I was the envy of the non-members – choirboys had sausages for tea – I did not altogether endear myself to my fellow choristers as when we were about to sing something I knew I would ostentatiously close my psalter or hymn-book, thrust my hands into the pockets of my cassock, throw my head back, and sing at the top of my voice.

# 3 *The silver spoon*

My father had for some time been contemplating leaving Wooburn House, and Lloyd George's series of budgets provided him with the opportunity to tell his neighbours, tenants and employees that as the result of the blows dealt him by that 'rascally little Welshman', he could no longer afford to live in his ancestral home.

He chose a political platform in order to acquaint the interested parties that he had been 'driven out by the budget'. This was a gross piece of self-deception and was received with ridicule by the Liberal press, who pointed out that he and his family had become rich as a result of Free Trade, and that now he was advocating Tariff Reform and crying before he was hurt. He was described as an opportunist, a prophet of expedience and a hypocrite.

He was speaking almost daily in support of Sir Alfred Cripps, the Conservative candidate for South Bucks at the forthcoming election, and perhaps he was tired when he made this unfortunate speech, as it was not at all like him to make an emotional speech which played into the enemy's hands.

His real reason for leaving Wooburn was that, with only one son still at home, the house was too big for his needs, and he and my mother no longer wished to entertain on the scale of former years. The partridge shooting was now non-existent, and all the fish in our little river Wye had been poisoned by the drainage from the paper mills. Moreover he had heard of a smaller house at Twyford near Winchester with first-class trout fishing on the Itchen, good partridge shooting on the downs, and snipe in the water meadows.

Wooburn was a large house by most standards, but Hall Barn and Cliveden, within a radius of three miles, were far bigger. Nevertheless, in the years between 1906 and 1911 my father employed a staff of thirty-six. In the house there was a butler, two liveried footmen and a boy who cleaned the boots and knives and filled the numerous oil lamps. The female staff consisted of a housekeeper, three housemaids, a nurse and undernurse, cook, kitchenmaid and scullerymaid, making a total of thirteen. In the garden there was the head gardener, who had a house of his own, two senior gardeners, who lived in the bothy adjoining the greenhouses, five working gardeners and a boy who led the horse which drew the lawnmower, and the estate carpenter and his mate. In the stables there were the head coachman, first coachman and second coachman and never less than three stablemen. There were two gamekeepers and the groundsman 'Moses', so called because he was alleged to have been found in the bulrushes. Although the large farm was sub-let, my father kept the home farm, consisting of about a dozen cows, twice that number of sheep and innumerable chickens, ducks and guinea fowl. These were cared for by the cowman and his mate, while a stout matron called Mrs Squibb presided over the dairy.

Although the garden of Wooburn House was one of the most spacious and beautiful in the county of Buckinghamshire the indoor staff was confined to a patch about 30 yards square concealed behind some bushes on which the sun never shone and the grass never grew. Any luckless under-housemaid or member of the kitchen staff who was seen by the 'gentry' in any other part of the garden would have been instantly dismissed, probably without a reference, the worst fate that could befall a girl whose parents had decided that her future lay in 'service', though servitude would have been a more apt description.

The scullerymaid and the most junior housemaid were each paid £15 per annum and shared a minute room under the eaves. The furniture consisted of two iron bedsteads, dressing table and washstand, a wooden kitchen chair, but no carpet. It was stiflingly hot in summer and freezingly cold in winter. They were not permitted to use one of the three bathrooms and were expected to immerse themselves once a week in a tin tub, the water for which had to be carried up a narrow well-nigh perpendicular staircase.

Should a member of the 'gentry' appear at the end of a long

carpeted passage while one of these unfortunate girls was on her knees with brush and dustpan she would scramble to her feet and stand with her back pressed against the wall in an attitude of the utmost humility until her social superior had passed. All the carpets in this large house were cleaned daily with brush and dust-pan, and as the only relief to the monotony of their lives consisted in attendance at the local church, housemaid's knee, which for some unaccountable reason became a music-hall joke, was a very real and painful occupational hazard.

Their chief oppressors were the non-commissioned officers, i.e. the housekeeper, a martinet if ever there was one, the cook and the head housemaid.

Meals were taken in the servants' hall, a bleak barely furnished room. Complete silence was enforced, at any rate at luncheon, which was presided over by the housekeeper at one end of the table and the butler at the other. The senior servants partook of their other meals in the comfortably furnished housekeeper's room, to the relief, no doubt, of the unfortunate girls over whom they ruled so despotically. The only rooms available to these unfortun-ate girls in this very large house were the attics in which they slept and the servants' hall which was devoid of a single armchair or sofa. They had no forms of diversion whatsoever and were expected to spend their leisure hours sewing. Newspapers were the sole prerogative of the gentry, and book-reading was not encouraged lest it should give them ideas above their station. The idea that a girl between the ages of 14 and 20 should associate with the opposite sex was too horrible to contemplate.

This description of the existence led by the lower orders in my father's house during my childhood is not meant as an indictment of my parents' attitude towards those who served them, as it was typical of that which prevailed in all the large houses throughout the length and breadth of the country prior to the first world war. Had my father and mother been more enlightened it might have dawned on them that they were treating adolescents as if they were less than human beings, but in those days the most important function of the well-to-do was to preserve the *status quo*. From time immemorial those who could afford servants had treated the youngest members of their staffs as if they were little (£15 a year, in fact) better than slaves, and only political agitators and Radicals held the view that domestic servants had the right to freedom and the pursuit of happiness.

One of the most shocking aspects of life in the early days of the century was the callous indifference on the part of members of the affluent society to the hideous poverty all around them. It would seem that the rich – and they were very rich in those days – were not only born without hearts, but were also devoid of any semblance of a social conscience. How could they vote solidly for the maintenance of the *status quo*, while barefooted, starving children begged in the streets of all our great cities, while their mothers, victims of sweated labour, sewed eighteen hours a day in the slums for a few pence? There was, of course, a number of Victorian philanthropists, like my grandfather, but even they would have opposed tooth and nail any form of social service or slum clearance scheme if they entailed even the smallest increase in taxation. One's name in *The Times* as the donor of a substantial sum to a hospital was money well spent, as it established one in the eyes of the world as a public-spirited individual of which the country could well be proud, but to have one's money taken from one by the Chancellor of the Exchequer, without so much as by your leave, in order to finance some damn fool scheme to build new houses for a lot of scallywags who would soon make them as dirty as their old ones, was quite another kettle of fish. Members of my family were often heard to say that if the poor were made less poor they would spend the additional money on gin, and on their return home from the public houses, would beat their children, so that they were better off as they were – a strange sentiment from those who had inherited a fortune largely from the manufacture and sale of alcohol. A notable exception was my brother Geoffrey, who spent much of his holidays in the East End of London and in the hop fields in an endeavour to bring a little happiness into the lives of those too poor to provide themselves with the barest necessities of food and clothing. Strangely enough, Geoffrey has remained completely aloof from politics, despite his first-hand experience of social injustice.

So great was the need for social reform that, had I been the eldest son and not the youngest, I should have become not only a socialist but a left-wing one at that. In, I fear, the unlikely event of my having had the guts to stand my ground in the continued face of parental wrath, I should doubtless have been disinherited. As a small boy, however, all I knew about politics was that Mr Balfour was a very good man and Lloyd George a very wicked one. Mr Asquith was also a bad man, but not as bad as Lloyd George. There were some even worse men, called Socialists, but my parents would not soil their lips by mentioning their names. 'Are they as wicked as Kruger?' I asked. 'Yes, just as wicked as Kruger,' I was told.

Fifty years later, I now believe that for the past hundred years the Left has been the refuge for all who felt they were not getting a square deal, and it is from that quarter that men and women looked for shelter from the rigours and injustices that flowed from the free play of economic forces. Keir Hardie, and those that came after him, championed the weak against the strong.

This does not mean that I shall necessarily vote Labour at the next election, as from past experience it would seem that some malady afflicts the body politic when Labour is in power. In my childhood days the Right and the Left were poles apart, but today their policies differ so little that personalities rather than policies are often the deciding factor as to which way we shall cast our votes.

I should be overjoyed to see a resurgence in the fortunes of the Liberals, but I fear the odds against it are considerable. The party has been so long in the wilderness that I am only one of thousands who regard a vote for the Liberals as a vote wasted. So we put our crosses against the name of either the Conservative or the Labour candidate, according to which party we find least distasteful at that particular moment.

My father's speeches helped to bring about the desired result in South Bucks as Sir Alfred Cripps was returned with a majority of over two thousand. One of my last memories of Wooburn was the visit of Sir Alfred after the result of the poll had been announced, when my father opened a bottle of champagne – a rare gesture.

Sir Alfred was a strange politician as he subsequently became a Liberal and ended up as a left-wing Socialist with the title of Lord Parmoor. He had two sons, Stafford Cripps, the famous Chancellor of the Exchequer, and Fred, a well-known man about town and popular clubman, who could hardly have been less like either his father or his younger brother.

We moved to Twyford in the summer of 1911, one of the hottest on record, and I immediately fell in love with our new home, which, although not as big as Wooburn, was much more modern and had electric light. This was an exciting year as in the spring I had been allowed to leave my bed for the first time for several months. It was great fun learning to walk again, and everybody made a fuss of me.

The carriage horses were replaced by a motor car before we moved to Twyford. Our first car was a 1910 Alldays and Onions, and I well remember the salesman arriving to see my father. Having expatiated on its numerous virtues, he said that it would go at forty miles an hour, to which my father replied, 'Good God, man, I don't want a fast car, I want a very slow one.' He got it.

I had loved the horses dearly, especially Watson, who had been the 'wheeler' in a coach before my father bought him cheaply. I cannot remember his ever paying more than seventy-five guineas for a horse and Watson cost only forty-five. Although he was apt to pull hard when he was fresh, he was the kindest of horses in the stable, and when still very small I used to go into his stall alone and feed him with carrots and apples. Having partaken of my gifts, like the great gentleman he was, he would grin at me – raising his lips and displaying his long yellow teeth. He was well over twenty years old when war broke out, and he was turned out in the meadow at the foot of the garden when men from the Remount Depot arrived with a Requisition Order. My mother's fervour on the outbreak of war would have done credit to an early Christian martyr, and before the requisitioners could open their mouths she exclaimed, 'Take all the horses we own, I give them gladly.' As a result of her outburst dear old Watson, who had served the family nobly for fifteen years, was led away to do his bit in defeating the Kaiser.

I was barely seven when I first went hunting with the Old Berkeley West and the Berks and Bucks Staghounds, and this opened up a fresh vista of horses. In a short while I knew the Masters' and the Hunt Servants' horses in addition to those ridden by the regular members of both packs.

I much preferred hunting the carted stag to the fox, as he always gave us a good gallop before he was apprehended and taken home again, which is more than could be said for the foxes in our part of the world. The country around Wooburn consisted of large woods and arable land, and there was very little grass. I shall never forget the meet at Gerrards Cross, when hounds ran almost to Ealing. This meant a sixteen-mile ride home on a tired pony, the last five miles in pitch dark.

All in all I must have known somewhere in the region of seventy horses well enough to identify them wherever I might encounter them, but sixty years later I can only recognise horses with distinctive markings, unless I see them several times.

Towards the end of that wonderful summer I was pronounced fit enough to attend school provided I took no violent exercise. This meant only one thing – a day school, and Twyford School, the oldest preparatory school in the country, and the one attended by Tom Brown before he went to Rugby, was a boarding school to which a day boy had never been admitted. My father, however, was a persuasive individual who usually got his own way, and he prevailed upon the headmaster, Mr H. C. McDonell, to break the rule in my favour.

My reception at Twyford School was similar to the one I got from the village choir at Wooburn. 'New boy Gilbey's a day boy' passed from lip to lip, and I could not have excited more curiosity had I been born with two heads. I appeared even stranger by reason of the fact that I was wearing a coloured tie, a black tie being *de rigueur* at Twyford.

I think the headmaster must have told them that it wasn't my fault that I was a day boy, and neither was it of my choosing that I had to lie down while the other boys played football. On the second day, when I arrived at school wearing a black tie, my reception was far more genial. I was even more popular when my parents allowed me to bring two or three new-found friends home to tea on Sundays. As a day boy I enjoyed the best of both worlds and I was as happy at Twyford as I had been unhappy at Cothill. Even had I not made many friends I should have been blissfully content as Mr McDonell was a first-class cricketer and therefore in my eyes a demigod. One of the best spin bowlers among the amateurs, he had been a Cambridge Blue, and still played regularly for Hampshire in the summer holidays. He was a very serious-minded, somewhat humourless man. He was very free with the cane, which was used as punishment for comparatively trivial offences. We were all frightened of him, but not for this reason. He was a man of remarkable personality.

On the outbreak of war my heart specialist joined up in the R.A.M.C. At once, my heart was magically cured. Later, at Eton, I was to run with the beagles and pass my medical for Sandhurst. At the age of forty, at the outset of World War Two, I was to pass A1 into the Army. At the age of sixty I underwent two major operations which I was told I might not have survived had I not been the possessor of an exceptionally strong heart.

Visits to London were always a great joy. London meant hansom cabs, and, unlike the elderly overworked horses which pulled four-wheelers, often laden with four passengers and heavy luggage, the hansom cab horses were well cared for and proceeded at a spanking trot.

Every commissionaire and manservant was provided with a whistle, with which he blew one blast for a four-wheeler, two for a hansom, and three for a taxi. I cannot have been more than five, and possibly less, when I saw my first taxi. It was standing at the corner of Portland Place and Park Crescent and I eyed it with as much suspicion as if it had been a flying saucer. Surely the grown-ups could not be right when they said that within a year or two there wouldn't be a hansom cab left on the streets.

My brothers exercised a considerable influence on my early days; Geoffrey's influence extended far beyond my childhood, and had it not been for him my life would have been very different.

I saw little of my second brother, Wilfrid, after my childhood.

He did not possess the mental equipment necessary for success in a highly competitive world, and like many people of little ability he was inclined to be self-assertive and was the worst judge of character I have ever met. This rendered him easy prey to the confidence trickster, and at the age of twenty-two he went bankrupt. My father paid his debts of honour, but rightly, in my view, declined to pay a penny of the money he was alleged to owe those responsible for his failure.

So Wilfrid was sent to Australia, to all intents and purposes a remittance man. He joined up in the ranks in Queensland in 1914 and fought at Gallipoli where he was slightly wounded. In 1916 he came to visit me at Eton, a rather scruffy private with untidy puttees, and a large Australian Forces hat. Every one of us has some things in his life of which he is bitterly ashamed, and I don't think I have committed throughout my life any sin worse than the way I received my brother Wilfrid. Here was a man with ten times more guts than I would ever have, who had never complained when he was banished to Queensland, fourteen thousand miles from everything he held most dear. He had joined up in the ranks and fought through one of the most horrifying campaigns of World War One. And here was I, a puffed-up little snob in a top hat, who had never done a hand's turn for anyone, feeling ashamed of him.

There was worse to come. After he had gone I was ragged by a number of boys who wanted to know who on earth my extraordinary visitor was. I replied that he was someone a friend of mine had met when he visited Australia, and I did not remember his name. I dare say other actions of mine might appear to many more blameworthy, but this is the action that I am most ashamed of, and with the passing of the years, increasingly so.

Wilfrid died alone and almost forgotten in Queensland in 1941. I was stationed in Iceland at the time, and news of his death did not reach me for many weeks. He had great courage and kindness, and would always do anything to help anyone.

It was entirely owing to my brother Geoffrey that I eventually went to Eton. The time for my taking the Common Entrance Exam coincided with one of those recurring crises when the doctors decreed that if I was not to be a permanent invalid I must spend several more weeks lying flat on my back.

It was a bitter blow when I realised that Eton was not for me; it had presented so glamorous a prospect for as long as I could remember. Three of my brothers had boarded at Somerville's, the house for which I was down, and my dark blue rosette was replaced by a pale blue one when Eton played Harrow at Lords and Winchester, either on Agars Plough at Eton or on Meads at Winchester.

I was almost the only Eton supporter at Twyford, which had strong Winchester connections. The headmaster was a Wykehamist, and nearly seventy per cent of the boys were bound for Winchester. Of the remainder, approximately ten per cent joined the Navy via Osborne and Dartmouth, having left Twyford at the age of twelve and a half.

Two boys who were at Twyford with me lost their lives as midshipmen at the battle of Jutland when fifteen years old. It seems unbelievable that only fifty years ago children were sent to fight in these terrifying battles at sea.

Having missed the bus for Eton as the result of these long periods of illness, I was now below the standard of boys of my age in all subjects with the exception, I need hardly say, of scripture. The headmaster therefore allowed me to stay on at Twyford for two more terms.

With the outbreak of war, over a hundred of the elder boys left Eton. Geoffrey, who was already in the Rifle Brigade, realised that there must now be vacancies at Eton; he jumped on his motor bike and rode over to see his former housemaster, Mr Somerville.

Geoffrey was in those days somewhat of a 'Walter Mitty' character: he could see himself in any number of roles. No profession that did not command an audience was ever considered, and no one has ever visualised Geoffrey as a back-room boy. He was the only one of us to take after my mother's side of the family; unlike Ronald, he was fired with ambition. He was a very good athlete, and at Eton he had won the Triple Crown – half-mile, mile and steeplechase.

He received a commission in the Rifle Brigade within a fortnight of war being declared, and in the summer of 1915 he went with the 20th Division to France, where he remained till the Armistice. One day, while I was at Eton, I received a letter from one of his brother officers saying, 'Geoffrey should get the V.C. for what he did last week'. He didn't get it; though he did get the Military Cross.

He had written a letter from the trenches to the *Daily Express* which they published, and when he was demobilised he joined the staff of Express Newspapers, and was an instantaneous success as Tattenham of the *Sunday Express*. Racing journalism has made great strides in the past fifty years, and Geoffrey approached his subject from an entirely new angle. He introduced the personal touch and was the first journalist to conduct a campaign against crooked racing. No racing journalist had ever made such an impact on racing as Geoffrey did in the early 'twenties.

# 4 *A wartime Eton*

On August Bank Holiday, as always, my father took me to Southampton for the Hants *v.* Middlesex match. It was a glorious day for cricket, but there was an air of unreality about the proceedings, and 'Plum' Warner, who had seldom thought of anything except cricket in his forty years, said that he had no heart for the game, adding, 'We ought to be fighting, not playing cricket.'

Everyone seemed to be striking attitudes and proclaiming what they would do to the Germans if war was declared and what they would do to the Government if it wasn't.

The declaration of war was responsible for an outburst of rejoicing, and one might have thought that we had won a glorious victory instead of having embarked on what was to be the bloodiest war in history. The papers described the jollifications on 4 August as reminiscent of those of Mafeking Night. No one seemed to consider what the cost in human life would be before Germany was defeated, but could they have envisaged even a hundredth part of the agony which the world was to suffer in the ensuing four years, they would have made it a day of mourning.

One day towards the end of August, my parents were out when a telegram arrived. Since the outbreak of war I had been authorised to open telegrams if no senior member of the family was present. I therefore opened it and read:

SOMERVILLE AGREES TO TAKE QUINNY PROVIDED HE PASSES ENTRANCE REASONABLY WELL GEOFFREY

Good news was rare to come by in the autumn of 1914, and Geoffrey's telegram was the most exciting news I had ever received. There was of course a distinct possibility that I should not get the requisite marks for I was much older than the average boy entering a public school, and if I didn't take a high enough form I should be eligible for superannuation before I even got there. However, I got high marks for French as the result of many hours spent in Winchester with a French governess, with whom I was slightly in love, and needless to say, I did well at Divinity. So although my Latin was below average and my mathematics almost non-existent, I scraped in. Mr Somerville was a friend of the family, and, being senior housemaster, had considerable pull with the authorities.

My career at Eton was completely lacking in distinction. I was not allowed to play football till I had been in the school a year, though I played cricket. I did the minimum work consistent with passing the end-of-half (term) exams known as Trials.

I have no doubt that Eton provided as good an education as there was to be had anywhere in the world, and I have never ceased to regret that I did not take full advantage of it. Geoffrey never stopped urging me to work hard and play hard, but the first friends I made at Eton were slack-bobs, boys who were determined not to exert themselves, either in the classrooms or on the playing fields.

This attitude conflicted with my love of cricket, but at that time my enthusiasm for all games was that of a spectator rather than of a participant. If I had really got down to it I might conceivably have got my 'twenty-two' (second eleven colours) in 1917, my last summer half at Eton. I think it improbable, but it would have been worth trying.

I was so much one of the crowd at Eton, with the instinct of a sheep, that I accepted other people's standards without question; but even I was shocked at the snobbish attitude of my schoolfellows at the public schools camp at Tidworth. The corps from approximately a dozen schools spent one of the wettest weeks of 1917 under canvas, but the Etonians only deigned to mix with the Harrovians, though they looked on them as bounders, and the Wykehamists, who were considered rather priggish. The others were thought to be beyond the pale. My greatest friend at Twyford had been Anthony Hill, who was now at Marlborough. He was a charming person and a fine cricketer, and for once in a way I defied public opinion by spending as much of my time as possible with him. He is still one of my greatest friends.

I enjoyed all my time at Eton, but I am appalled at the nasty bit of work I became as the result of my three years there. It is all too easy to put the blame on one's friends, but the fault of course lay in my inability to form my own set of values.

In one of my reports Mr Somerville described me as 'easily led', which I consider almost as damning a verdict as 'he means well'. At the age of seventeen I considered myself highly sophisticated, but I have since come to the conclusion that I was very young for my age, while my knowledge of any subjects other than first-class cricket, the contemporary theatre, and racing was negligible.

I had smoked surreptitiously for some years before I went to Eton, and by the time I arrived there I had acquired the taste for Turkish cigarettes. The fact that I was already a hardened smoker endeared me to my new-found friends, though in all other respects I was completely innocent, no one having acquainted me with the facts of life. I had a vague idea how animals produced their young, and I imagined that babies arrived in much the same way, but I was completely in the dark as to the part played by the male. I would not have confessed my ignorance for all the tea in China, and when the conversation went beyond my comprehension I used to smirk and try to give the impression that I had heard it all before.

At Eton, I was not left long in ignorance, and after a nocturnal visit from a boy slightly older than myself, I knew it all. I have lost count of the number of times that men and women, more often women than men, have lowered their voices as if we were participants in a great conspiracy, and asked me to tell them 'what went on at Eton'. My answer has always been the same – 'Surprisingly little.'

When one appreciates that at the age of fifteen a boy is physically mature and capable of reproducing his species, it is not to be wondered at that when twelve hundred boys are deprived of any feminine society for months on end they will look elsewhere to satisfy their normal sexual appetites. I am not in the least ashamed of my morals, either at Eton or at any other period of my life, and the trivial incidents which occur in the lives of perfectly normal boys would never happen if they were permitted an outlet to their pent-up emotions in the normal manner.

I have never met a homosexual who attributed his abnormality to practices he learnt at school, and the few boys at Eton with me who became homosexuals have assured me that at Eton they were as pure as the driven snow.

Two salient memories of my Eton days are the visit of Dame Clara Butt, and that of a couple of young officers in the Grenadier Guards. Dame Clara's visit had no far-reaching effect on my career, but I can still remember her magnificent rendering of Blake's 'Jerusalem', and 'Land of Hope and Glory'. These two songs are, of course, the highlights of the last night of the Proms, and as an elderly square I never hear them without getting a lump in my throat.

At the end of the concert, Dame Clara signed autographs for half-a-crown each in aid of war charities, and I eagerly bought one. I was a lower boy and this spending spree shocked a young friend who asked me if I realised that I could have bought two strawberry messes, an ice cream and a banana for the price of it. It was a sobering thought.

The two young guardsmen had been in the school with me, and having only recently passed out of Sandhurst, had not yet been to France. They had not been at m'tutors, and being very senior had never spoken to me. The gap dividing a Field Marshal from a private soldier is no wider than that which separates a boy in Pop from a lower boy at Eton, so you can imagine my pride when they stopped me in the street with a most genial 'Hullo, Gilbey, how are you?'

They were wearing the customary Foot Guards' brasshats and close-fitting grey overcoats, which reached almost to the ground, and they were smoking cigarettes, Turkish of course. To my way of thinking they constituted the personification of glamour, and it was inconceivable why they should bother to stop and talk to me. 'How much longer have you got in the school?' one of them asked. 'Two halves,' I replied. 'Any plans for the future?' 'No, not specially, but I suppose I'll get a commission somewhere or other, as I have been in the corps for over two years.' 'What about joining us? We could do with a few more like him, couldn't we, Tony?' 'Yes; well, what about it?' Tony replied. 'Do you mean as an officer?' I stammered. 'Of course, you silly mutt, provided you put your name down now, and pass out of Sandhurst.'

They went on to clinch matters with a description of a party they had been to the previous evening at which the females had all been glamorous figures from the other side of the footlights, whose names were household words.

I have no doubt that when they returned to barracks that evening they reported, with some glee, that, as the result of their visit to Eton, they had roped in some more cannon fodder.

That night I wrote to my father telling him that I would be granted a regular commission in the Grenadier Guards provided he would communicate with the Lieutenant-Colonel of the Regiment, who, I knew, was a friend of his.

He readily agreed, and from that moment I dreamed of wearing a brass hat and a long grey overcoat and escorting glamour girls to parties after the show. It seems hardly credible that I should not have spared a thought for the grim reality that we had been at war for nearly three years and looked like being at war for another three, and that a soldier's chief function was to fight in trenches, knee-deep in mud, and that an ensign's expectation of life in the Foot Guards at that time was a couple of months.

Never in the history of the theatre has the stage played so important a part in the life of the community as it did during the 1914–18 war. Even quite a moderate show played to capacity houses, and during our holidays I saw most of the shows which did so much to sustain the country's morale when men and boys were dying in thousands at Passchendaele, at Ypres or on the Somme.

I was still at Eton when I met the fabulously beautiful Lily Elsie. She was married to Ian Bullough who was stationed at Windsor, and his cousin Geordie Beech was in my div. Geordie was a friend of mine, and imagine my delight when he asked me to visit his cousin and his famous wife, 'after twelve'. Ten years earlier Lily Elsie had taken London by storm as the original Widow in Franz Lehar's musical comedy *The Merry Widow*.

Those who were present at the first night told me that never before or since was a show received with such enthusiasm. Lily Elsie was not only beautiful but was also possessed of great talent, and the few people who can remember her performance in *The Merry Widow* still regard her as the most glamorous musical comedy star of all time.

She greeted me most kindly, but I was so overawed by her beauty that even after a glass of sherry I was still tongue-tied. On our way back, Geordie said, 'What the hell's wrong with you? You never said a word.' 'She's so lovely Geordie, I just didn't know what to say.' 'Why in hell's name didn't you tell her so?' answered the worldly Geordie. 'All women like to hear that sort of thing, and she's no different from the rest.'

My father and four brothers were in the Army; Geoffrey by this time had been decorated, and boys who had been with me at Cothill, Twyford and Eton had been killed. But the only missile that had come my way had finished wide of its target; the Zeppelin responsible for it was poised above Leicester Square, and moving so slowly that its progress was barely perceptible.

I had been to see *Watch Your Step* at the Empire, and during the interval I had my first drink at a bar. It was a delicious pink concoction and must have been quite innocuous as it didn't make me feel the least bit tight. After the curtain had been lowered the stage manager announced that a Zeppelin was directly overhead and that we were advised not to leave the theatre.

This caused great excitement as it was the first time a Zeppelin had got as far as the West End. After a few minutes we decided we must have a look at it, and there it was over the Alhambra, heading in a north-easterly direction. We were no longer in the slightest danger from the airship, but quite a number of people were injured that night by our own shrapnel. I do not know what kind of bombs were dropped, but what seemed in those days to be very big fires broke out in several directions. The following morning we learned that the Zeppelin had been shot down at Cuffley in Essex. The crews in those dirigibles were certainly brave men, as a Zeppelin was a sitting target even for the primitive aeroplanes of fifty-odd years ago.

It was shortly before this memorable evening that I paid my first visit to a racing stable. Geoffrey was on leave and Atty Persse had asked him to tea and go round evening stables. By this time I was desperately keen on racing, though it was not till my last year at Eton that I got into the habit of betting regularly. I was therefore surprised when Geoffrey agreed to take me, provided I kept my mouth shut. The famous Chattis Hill stables were only about ten miles from Twyford, but I was so excited they seemed much farther. Atty had the reputation of being a bit of a tyrant who believed in corporal punishment for his apprentices, but on this occasion he was the very soul of geniality; in my eyes he was another God from Olympus, for had he not trained the spotted wonder known as The Tetrarch, the fastest horse that had ever lived?

But an even greater treat was in store as I espied an immaculately dressed little figure in a blue suit and shiny patent leather boots with cloth tops disembark from a car. 'It is, no it couldn't be, yes by Jove it is', and a moment later Atty Persse called out, 'Come on over, Steve, and meet the Gilbey brothers', and there I was shaking hands with the champion jockey, the great Steve Donoghue. In the space of half an hour I had met one of the greatest trainers and *the* greatest jockey in the world, and my cup of happiness was full. Little did I think that day that in the years to come both men would become friends of mine.

I first made the acquaintance of another famous man that summer, though he was only fourteen years old at the time. The occasion was a house match between C. M. Wells's house and m'tutor's, and a small boy, with broad shoulders and an outsize bottom, had already got a couple of wickets when I went in.

I took guard and faced up to him, but before my bat had begun its descent my middle stump was out of the ground. The fourteen-year-old's name was Gubby Allen.

My career at Sandhurst was as lacking in distinction as the three years I had spent at Eton, but nothing like so tranquil. Although I had wasted most of my opportunities at Eton, I was never in serious trouble if we overlook the time my cousin Dick Riviere and I overstayed long leave.

When we arrived at Paddington station on the Monday evening the fog was so thick that the porter thought it most unlikely that any more trains would run that night. That was good enough for Dick and me, and though we only had thirty shillings between us, we set off for the West End and the promenade of a music hall; which, I think, was the Holborn Empire.

We soon picked up a couple of tarts, and stood them each a glass of port. 'If only we had enough money,' Dick sighed. 'If only,' I echoed, at the same time thanking my lucky stars that we hadn't. The one I looked like being landed with was old enough to be my mother, with several years to spare, and I should have been scared to death had I been left alone in a room with her.

On leaving the theatre, we saw to our dismay that the fog had cleared, but instead of dashing back to Paddington to catch the last train, we decided to stay the night, to which my foolish Aunt Laura (Dick's mother) agreed, adding, 'Take it easy tomorrow morning, breakfast's not till 9.15.' When we were still absent at midday, m'tutor telephoned my father, who of course had no idea where I was but told him to request the headmaster to give me a damn' good hiding when I did turn up. He then wrote to his cousin, Dick's mother, calling her a silly old bitch for not sending us back to school. They never spoke again.

I have never seen a man as angry as Mr Somerville was when we strolled on to the football field without bothering to change. Our lower boy side was losing to a house whose tutor was his deadly enemy, so our arrival could not well have been worse timed.

Although we had both been tanned (beaten by either the Captain of the house or the Captain of the games) on a number of occasions, we had never been swiped by the headmaster, and those who had assured us it was a far more painful affair, in which the victim had to let down his trousers and kneel on a wooden block where he was held till the headmaster had given him what he considered a sufficient number of strokes. I was far from being one of the most courageous boys in the school, but there was a certain glamour attached to a swiping, especially if it was for something as dashing as overstaying leave and coming within a hair's breadth of losing one's virginity. Dick had been in favour of pretending we had really been and gone and done it, but although I was prepared to tell a whopping big lie to get myself out of a tight spot, I considered it unlucky to tell lies for one's self-glorification.

We adopted a devil-may-care attitude, promising to allow a few favoured friends to inspect the result of the headmaster's savagery. Lower boys were equally sadistically punished by the Lower Master, and afterwards earned the price of innumerable ice creams, by charging a tanner a look.

The following morning we were duly paraded before Dr Lyttelton, a solemn man with a deep voice. 'Your behaviour is a disgrace, and I shall punish you severely' was followed by a pause. 'Here it comes', I said to myself, and my knees began to knock, but contrary to my father's wishes, and those of my housemaster, the sentence was: 'You will each write out the fourth Georgic.' A swiping was undoubtedly a painful operation, but with every second after the first five minutes it would hurt less, and by the end of the day it wouldn't hurt at all so long as one didn't sit down abruptly. After it, one was also something of a hero, at any rate in one's own eyes. But there was no glamour attached to writing five hundred and sixty-six lines by that crashing bore, Virgil. Every spare moment of the ensuing forty-eight hours had to be devoted to this soul-destroying task, and with every line I cursed 'the bloody man' who had set me this humiliating punishment, comparable with the treadmill which in those days was still in operation in His Majesty's prisons.

Almost five years to the day after my father had purchased our first car, I was told that I was to have driving lessons, an announcement which gave rise to delight and surprise in equal proportions. If ever there were two law-abiding citizens they were my mother and father, and if I defied notices to Keep off the Grass and Trespassers will be Prosecuted, even for a couple of steps, I was told I should end up in prison. But at the age of sixteen, and too young to be granted a driving licence, I was being told I was to be taught to drive the Overland, an open car, and an Austin limousine which bore a marked resemblance to a sentry-box.

The subject of the licence was not mentioned, but subsequently, off her own bat, my mother told me that Butcher, the chauffeur, had procured me a licence to ride a motor bicycle, and that 'that would help'. Who or what it would help, in the event of my being apprehended, I had no idea, neither have I today. Their decision, out of character as it was, was even more surprising as I had never been allowed to touch the cars except to open the doors after ascertaining not only that the car had come to a standstill, but also that the engine had been switched off.

Edwardian children lived their lives to a chorus of 'Don't touch', which reached a crescendo with the arrival of the first car. When I protested that I could not do much harm by placing my hand on the mudguard my mother replied that meddling with things I didn't understand might cause a serious accident.

It was not to be expected that my Victorian parents would be *au fait* with the esoteric workings of the internal combustion engine, but as it required several minutes' frantic churning to evoke a protesting splutter I think that the most cautious bookmaker would have offered long odds against my starting the engine, putting it into gear (a feat in itself), to send it hurtling into the fishpond or the greenhouses, depending on which way it was facing.

My parents' astonishing decision was due to the fact that Butcher was going into the Army, and that there would be no one available to drive my mother from the clothing depot at Winchester to Southampton Docks, laden with supplies for the hospital ships. I should of course only be available during the holidays, but it was better than nothing.

I learned quite quickly to drive reasonably well, and as my mother was invariably my passenger I drove very slowly. I would arrange the bundles so as to obscure Mother's view of the speedometer, but none the less, her head would emerge like a ferret's, with the admonition, 'Not so fast; my head won't stand it.'

Docks in wartime are privileged places, and I felt immensely important as I produced my pass and was waved on towards the waiting ship with its red cross painted on its side. Sad to relate, the red cross did not provide immunity from the German submarines, and the ship, the *Asturias*, was torpedoed in the last year of the war.

Petrol being strictly rationed, there were few cars on the roads, and the bulk of the traffic consisted of military transport, drawn by horses. My proudest day of all was when I returned to Eton after being allowed forty-eight hours' leave as Geoffrey was on leave from the front. As luck would have it, there were about twenty boys outside m'tutor's as I drove up in the Overland. I was still only sixteen and this was something few boys of my age had done.

Although my father was fifty-five when war broke out, he was determined to do his bit. He had commanded a battalion of Volunteers (subsequently Territorials), and had been very disappointed when, by reason of the fact that he was the father of five children, he was not sent to South Africa to fight the Boers. My earliest memories concern stories of the wicked Boers, and for quite a long time I thought they were some sub-human species. This came about as the result of one of the old-fashioned copy books containing the sentence, 'Boars have tusks'. In our household, Kruger and De Wet were fiends incarnate, compared with whom Dr Crippen, who had been very much in the news following the discovery of his wife's dismembered body in the cellar, was a gentleman.

Having pulled the requisite strings, my father was informed that if he could raise a battalion as the result of his own eloquence, he could command it, and this he did. He had hoped to lead them into battle, but he was well over age, and his stamina had not been improved by his catching pneumonia a few weeks earlier.

Individual nursing was absolutely essential, so Nannie Crush was wired for. She was working in the Military Hospital at Winchester, but she arrived the same evening at High Wycombe, where my father lay gravely ill. Two weeks later he wrote to me at Eton that he was well on the way to recovery, 'thanks to the nursing of Nannie Crush, who never left my side for three days and nights. She is a wonderful woman.' So there was a subject, in addition to cricket, on which my father and I were in complete accord.

Ronald and Geoffrey had 'had their whips' at Eton, which meant that they had been permitted to run with the beagles, wearing a stock and a velvet jacket and white breeches, so it was expected that I should follow in their footsteps and plod wearily across the large expanse of arable land which in those days surrounded Eton College. This I did, which was a pity, as I was quite good at Fives, and both these activities take place in the Easter half. I am not sure whether I really enjoyed beagling but it was the nearest thing to hunting, and to admit you didn't like hunting in the Gilbey family would have been the equivalent of telling the Pope you were an atheist.

# 5 *Sandhurst*

I arrived at Sandhurst in the first week of January 1918, and throughout my junior term the situation was as critical as at any period of the war; it seemed doubtful whether the French and the British could hold out until the Americans arrived.

There were approximately nine hundred and fifty cadets in residence, and I think that I was the only one whose patriotism was ever suspect. We were on a tactical scheme, around Crowthorne, where there was a P.O.W. camp. As I was very bored I sauntered over to the wire and got into conversation with a German prisoner. He spoke good English but I can't remember what we talked about. No one criticised my action at the time, but the following morning I was up on a charge of 'fraternising with the enemy'.

I suppose the penalty for this offence is death, but my Company Commander presumably considered that a bit drastic, though, had it happened later in my career at the R.M.C., he might not have been so squeamish. I was therefore admonished and informed that soldiers shoot Germans, they don't talk to them.

However much one may dislike communal life and military discipline, one inevitably feels a glow of pride the first time one appears in uniform. It so happened that we were issued with our uniforms on the day I was due to go on forty-eight hours' leave to London to see one of my brothers who was on leave. On the Sunday I went for a walk in Hyde Park with my father, who was back in civilian life. Two private soldiers, not noticing that my uniform carried no pips, saluted me, and I returned their salutes as if I had been doing it all my life, much to the amusement of my father.

At Sandhurst drinking and going to London without a pass were the smart things to do in the set in which I moved; drink and how to get it became as universal a topic of conversation as it did in the United States during Prohibition. 'I was pretty tight, but old so-and-so was stinking' was a typical boast following a visit to London.

Except as an allayer of inhibitions, and therefore an indispensable ingredient for the enjoyment of a party, I have seldom felt the need for a drink, and I don't think I have had a drink by myself on more than a dozen occasions in my life. But anyone listening to our conversation during the summer and autumn of 1918 would have thought we were all confirmed alcoholics.

During my second term the flu epidemic which swept the country, killing thousands, reached Sandhurst. I was one of the large number of cadets to catch it, but I don't think I was very ill, and I have pleasant recollections of my convalescence, paddling a canoe about on the lake. As soon as we were strong enough to carry a rifle we were back again at work, but whether or not it was due to weakness following the flu, something happened to me which left its mark.

My P.T. squad was engaged in an exercise in which we had to grasp a bar about 4 feet 6 inches from the ground, and circle over it. Strain as I might, I could not get my legs anywhere near perpendicular on the other side of the bar. The instructor called me several rude names, and taunted me for my lack of guts. Suddenly, a pain like a knife went through me and I collapsed in a heap on the floor. 'Look at him taking a nice rest' shouted the instructor in his most sarcastic tone, but even he realised I wasn't shamming when I remained doubled up on the floor, and I was taken to hospital. The M.O. put me on light duty, which consisted of doing nothing except attend lectures.

I was soon all right again, but I began to suffer from indigestion, which grew more severe with the passing of the years. When I was over sixty I was discovered to have a hiatus hernia, and when I described the incident in the gym at Sandhurst, over forty years earlier, my surgeon told me that that was probably the cause of it.

My troubles were of my own making, but I was at a disadvantage in that I looked so young. I stood five foot seven, weighed eight stone, and might have been mistaken for fifteen, and this made me absurdly self-conscious when it was my turn to drill the squad. Instead of rapping out the words of command with frequent 'as you weres', I would stand with a self-deprecatory grin on my face, as if to say, 'I know I look a bloody fool'. Self-assurance and a loud voice are the only qualities necessary to drill a squad with reasonable efficiency, and I had neither.

Why could other cadets drill their fellows with all the assurance of a trained N.C.O. and appear to enjoy it, while to me it was such torture that I invariably made a complete bog of it?

The only occasion on which a cadet sees a battalion parade is when he is excused duty and the day on which I witnessed the battalion act as one man, I could hardly believe my eyes. 'We can't be as smart as that', I said to myself, but we were.

I subsequently served two years in the Grenadiers, during which, as an ensign, I frequently carried the colour at guard mounting at Buckingham Palace and St James's Palace, but I have never seen drill up to the standard at Sandhurst in 1918.

Saturday was the only half holiday, and on that day it was a simple matter to go to London and see a matinée, take a chorus girl to a *thé dansant* and cocktails at Murray's, and catch a train which got you back before 10 p.m., always provided you were prepared to take a chance.

Danger point No. 1 was Camberley station. All cadets on genuine leave travelled on vouchers, and the sight of a cadet in uniform buying a ticket would immediately have aroused suspicion, had there been a Nosey Parker hanging around.

Waterloo was another place which I was always glad to see the back of, as it was swarming with members of the A.P.M.'s staff, checking passes, looking for deserters, and generally making themselves officious. The theatre was pretty safe, but stage doors were scrutinised, while Murray's Club was under constant observation.

A matinée and *thé dansant*, even with a girl from the Gaiety, may sound pretty lukewarm entertainment, but in 1918 D.O.R.A. was all-powerful and a curfew having been imposed, all public places had to close by 10 p.m. If you wanted to dance, you had to do it at teatime.

The most sophisticated cadets were those who for one reason or another had left their public school somewhat earlier than had been intended, and had spent the intervening time at a crammer's. One such worldly young man was Raymond de Trafford. Even at that early stage it was apparent that Raymond's life would never be dull, whatever else it was. On joining the Coldstream, he was nicknamed the Borstal Boy, a name which has stuck to him ever since. An amusing companion, he introduced me to my first starting-price bookmaker, but he did not possess the understanding of racing of his elder brother Sir Humphrey, subsequently a prominent member of the Jockey Club.

Raymond made the headlines in both England and France in the early 'thirties when he was shot by his girl friend at the Gare du Nord. I was living in Paris at the time, and, running true to form, Raymond, leaning heavily on the arm of a friend, made his first public appearance after leaving hospital at the Ritz bar. Seeing me across the room, he shouted 'You always said these women would be the death of us', which only goes to show that you can't keep a good man down.

On one occasion I missed the last train back to Sandhurst and eventually arrived at 7 a.m., nine hours late, but mercifully the Sergeant of the Guard was a real sportsman, and in return for a pound note marked me in as only ten minutes late, for which I was awarded seven days' restriction.

Restriction at Sandhurst was the equivalent of C.B. in a regiment, and consisted of endless irritations and pinpricks, though by no stretch of the imagination could any of the various punishments have been considered inhuman.

When an eighteen-year-old has got away with a serious offence as lightly as I had done, he invariably pushes his luck. Hardly a Saturday passed without my boarding the 12.10 train to London.

It was my prowess as a cyclist which was responsible for my friendship with Eric Midwood, son of Walter Midwood, who subsequently won the Grand National with Shaun Goilin. The popular way of spending Sundays was to bicycle to Maidenhead and lunch at Skindles, where sometimes my girl friend Stella and some of her friends from the cast of *The Beauty Spot* at the Gaiety would join us. *The Beauty Spot* did not have a particularly long run, but I saw it four times, deriving a great kick from pointing out my friends in the chorus to anyone who might be with me, and my pride knew no bounds when one of the girls waved to me across the footlights. This was really living.

One Sunday, Eric Midwood, having stood several drinks all round, gave me an appraising look and told me I might be the chap he was looking for. 'You're light and you look willing, the very chap to pull his weight on my racing tandem. What about next Sunday?' I agreed, and the following Sunday we covered the eighteen miles between Camberley and Maidenhead in fifty minutes. Racing, as well as the tandem bicycle, was a bond between us, and by the time we went home for the fortnight's summer recess we had become firm friends.

No sooner had we returned for my senior term than there was a fresh outbreak of Spanish flu, and all leave was stopped.

The tandem remained in the bicycle shed, and one Sunday Eric announced that he could not think of a better way to while away the idle hours than by getting down to some serious drinking.

I have seldom met a young man with too much money who did not derive the maximum pleasure from getting his friends tight. I suppose it inflates his ego and gives him a feeling of power.

At about 4 p.m. Vernon Richards, who had joined us, fell over backwards, out to the world, and it was not long before I knew that it was only a matter of minutes before I'd pass out as Richards had done.

I got to my room unaided, but the next thing I remember was an officer waking me up to tell me I was under close arrest. When I awoke next morning there was a sergeant sitting outside my door, holding a rifle and fixed bayonet. We were remanded for the Commandant's Orderly Room on the charges of bringing liquor into the precincts of the Royal Military College, being drunk, and missing Mess Roll Call. White-moustached Commandant, Major General Stopford, announced that he could not deal with such serious offences himself, and he was referring our cases to the Army Council, with strong recommendations for our expulsion.

I had pushed my luck once too often. Forty-nine years have passed since I heard that awful sentence, but it remains to this day the worst moment of my life. How I managed to stumble back the three hundred yards across the parade grounds, under escort, with a sergeant shouting 'Left, Right' at my unheeding ears, I shall never know. My eyes were blinded with tears and I wished I was dead. The sergeant, whose job it was to guard this miserable young man who in the face of adversity had become a small frightened boy again, was most sympathetic. I was allowed to send a telegram to my father at his office saying: 'In serious trouble, please come at once.'

I had always been somewhat in awe of my father and, though I knew he was the only man in the world who could help me in my predicament, I dreaded his arrival. But there were no reproaches; one look at me convinced him that I had drunk the dregs, and that nothing he could say could increase my misery. He did not remain long with me and his final words were: 'I can't promise anything, but I'll see what I can do.' My closest friends were waiting for him as he left the New Buildings, and they told him what a good chap I was, certainly inventing a number of qualities I did not possess.

My father had a wide circle of acquaintances, and if he didn't know a man, he always had a friend who did. On his return to London he found out that my case would come up before Sir Ian MacPherson; he did not know Sir Ian himself but his friend Lord Burnham did, and within a matter of twenty-four hours my father was at the War Office, talking to the man who held his son's fate in his hands.

The only previous entry on my conduct sheet was seven days' restriction for being ten minutes late on my return from dining near by, and although he did not give Midwood away he convinced Sir Ian that I was shielding the man who supplied the liquor. The result was that my father left the War Office with the assurance that the Army Council would direct the Commandant himself to deal, not only with my case, but also with that of Vernon Richards.

That evening I received a telegram: 'KEEP IT TO YOURSELF, BUT NEITHER YOU NOR RICHARDS WILL BE DISMISSED.' Once again I wept, this time for joy. I was still under close arrest, but at the end of a week this was reduced to open arrest. We attended all parades and lectures, but another week had to go by before we were informed by the Staff Sergeant that we were for Commandant's Orderly Room.

I was not one of our Staff Sergeant's favourites, and there was a glint in his eye which seemed to say: 'You're for the high jump, and bloody well serves you right.' Only a few close friends had an inkling that the Army Council would not accede to the Commandant's recommendation, so many eyes were fixed on me as I was marched across the square on what was thought to be my last march as a Gentleman Cadet; by the end of the day I should be a private soldier, awaiting the next draft for France.

I thought I detected a look of disappointment in the ice-cold eyes of the ageing General seated behind his desk, holding in his hand a W.O. communication, as I stood rigidly to attention. Somewhat peevishly, he informed us that although he had recommended our removal the Army Council had instructed him to deal with the case himself. 'I therefore give you the most severe punishment I am permitted to award – twenty-eight days' restriction and stoppage of leave till the end of the term.'

A lecture in Military Law was in progress when I returned to the company, and as I saluted the lecturer, Major Galsworthy, and excused my lateness on the score of having to attend Commandant's Orderly Room, he replied: 'Judging from your expression I take it you won't be leaving us, and may I say how delighted I am.' Galsworthy was a grand chap, and on several occasions joined us at Company dinners in London, and once came to a party a friend and I gave in a private suite at the Savoy, to which Stella brought half a dozen girls from the Gaiety. At about 4 a.m., when he was slightly tight, Galsworthy said: 'I've always liked you, Gilbey, because you are exactly like I was at your age', something no superior officer ever said to me before or since.

I have already described what restriction entailed, but no cadet can ever have entered on twenty-eight days more light-heartedly than I did. I had, however, only completed about a week when I was informed I was up on a charge for having an untidy room. Although I was far from being a model soldier I had always got on well with the officers who remembered that they had been young and foolish themselves. But recently an officer was attached to us who I knew would be a pain in the neck from the moment I first saw him. He wore tartan trousers and spoke with a Scottish accent. So, of course, did a lot of magnificent men, but this individual had a prim and disapproving air about him which I immediately distrusted. By no stretch of the imagination could I visualise this horrible type drinking champagne, and enjoying himself with chorus girls in the way that Galsworthy did.

Sure enough, it was 'Tartan Trews' who had placed me under arrest, and while one couldn't blame him for that, I am quite sure Galsworthy would have said: 'Let the stupid little bastard sleep it off, and I'll give him hell in the morning.' When I didn't get the sack I am certain 'Tartan Trews' was determined to make my life as unpleasant as possible, and the easiest way to do that was to inspect my room at regular intervals.

Changing uniforms and equipment half a dozen times a day, it was impossible to hang up every item in the prescribed manner and still be in time for parades and, to his delight, the so-and-so found something out of place. My Company Commander, Jack Starkey, who had served with my brother Geoffrey in France, asked me if I had anything to say, but what was the use? So a further seven days' restriction was tacked on to my twenty-eight days and no one could recall anyone having done thirty-five days on the trot.

When the news reached us early on 11 November that an Armistice had been declared, I could not believe it till I read on the Company notice-board that all parades had been cancelled and would be replaced by a church parade. I am not suggesting that my heart, bursting with thankfulness, was in any way unique, but I do not suppose that many people were on restriction or C.B. on that joyous occasion, or that they became involved in a heated altercation with a belted Earl which would have come to blows if the latter had had his way.

I was incoherent with joy when ginger-haired Lord Shannon, his rubicund face, redder than ever, asked me what all the fuss was about. I gazed at him in astonishment as he went on to tell me that this was the blackest day of his life as it meant that he would not have the opportunity of avenging the death in action of some relative by killing a German. I called him a name, which had it been true, would have meant that he was not the Earl of Shannon. Things got rather heated, but taunts of cowardice left me unmoved, and I told him he must take me for a bloody fool if he thought that on the day that God had intervened on my behalf I should run the risk of being hurt by a part of the female anatomy like him.

It was not till the battalion knelt down in chapel that morning to thank God that a war, which had already destroyed civilisation, was at an end, that I could admit to myself the dread I had felt at the prospect of going to war.

My physical and moral cowardice have remained at war with one another throughout my life, and my moral cowardice has almost invariably proved the stronger. In the same way that I would jump a big fence out hunting for fear of being thought a funk if I went looking for a gap, I suppose I should have gone over the top with the rest of the cannon fodder, but thank you, God, a million times for not putting me to the test!

I do not regard physical courage, by itself, to be a virtue, as many of the worst men in history were incredibly brave. My heroes are those who stick to their guns in the face of opposition from friends and relatives. I sometimes like to kid myself that if I could have my time over again I should ignore 'the call' at the outbreak of war, that I should report for work and be sent to Coventry as a blackleg if I thought a strike unjustified, and that I should make an impassioned speech on the iniquity of all blood sports in the market place at Melton Mowbray, or marry a coloured girl if I was sure she was the girl for me. I have, however, been unable to convince myself that I should not follow the crowd as I have done since the first day I went to school sixty years ago. It takes a brave man to be different.

I left Sandhurst for good on 20 December 1918, and early in the new year I received a communication from the War Office to the effect that I had passed out. As my conduct sheet was unlikely to create a very favourable impression on any Commanding Officer, those in the know considered it most unlikely that I should make the Grenadiers. But once again they had reckoned without my father.

The same possibility had occurred to him, but fortunately he was on very friendly terms with the Hamilton family, and Lord Ernest Hamilton, uncle of Gilbert Hamilton, the Lieutenant-Colonel of the Grenadier Guards, was his best friend and a constant visitor to our house.

# 6 *Guards officer*

As the war was over we were not ordered to join the Regiment until the end of January, which we did, still wearing Sandhurst uniform, with one star on each shoulder denoting we were Ensigns, and a Sam Browne belt to which was attached a sword which was continually tripping me up. We must have looked rather strange parading on the square at Chelsea Barracks, where we had joined the Fifth (Reserve) Battalion, but newly joined officers were not considered capable of fitting themselves out in the correct uniform unless they were under the supervision of the Adjutant.

The prospect of walking down Bond Street in a long double-breasted grey overcoat with brass buttons had been one of the chief attractions in becoming an officer in the Brigade of Guards, but my hopes were shattered by an order from the Officer Commanding London District to the effect that while those already in possession of grey overcoats could continue to wear them, newly joined officers would purchase British warms. This singularly unglamorous garment had been worn by every officer in the British Army for the past four-and-a-half years, and it was a poor substitute for a coat which stamped you in the eyes of one and all as a Guards officer.

We carried swords at all times and the hilt of a sword always appeared out of place above the pocket of a British warm. One was ordered never to draw one's sword except when on duty, but of course it was impossible to remove one's overcoat without doing so, as the sword was passed into its scabbard through a slit in the overcoat. Cloakroom attendants sometimes ran for their lives when officers advanced on them with drawn swords.

Life in the Fifth Reserve Battalion at Chelsea was very pleasant. One attended Adjutant's Parade at 8.30 a.m. and one was usually finished for the day about 12.30. This was freedom hitherto undreamed of, but it had its disadvantages in that it provided more opportunities than ever before to spend money.

The East Room at the Criterion was the place for luncheon among theatre people, and in the space of a few weeks I had met Fay Compton, Phyllis Monkman, Jack Buchanan, Teddy Gerrard, Bea Lillie, and a whole lot more celebrities of that time whose names are now forgotten. All hero-worshippers are celebrity snobs and I had become one on the day my father introduced me to 'Plum' Warner eight years earlier. I must still have been very young for my age as I was so blissfully happy when in the company of actors and actresses that it seemed to me that life had nothing more glamorous to offer, no matter how long I lived.

I have described Stella as my girl friend, and that is exactly what she was – a friend of the opposite sex whom I found glamorous, simply and solely because she was on the stage, and would from time to time wave to me across the footlights. I do not pretend that I would not have liked our friendship to ripen into something more satisfying, but Stella seemed perfectly content with a platonic friendship, and I was far too timid to suggest otherwise.

Although I was nineteen I still looked only sixteen, and on the few occasions I had made tentative passes at girls I had been told to wait till I grew up. Unfortunately it was not till several years later, when I no longer looked like 'my baby boy', as Stella usually referred to me, that I heard that some women like very young boys. Although I was not normally in the least shy, my self-confidence deserted me when I found myself alone with a pretty girl, or on the parade ground when it was my turn to drill the squad, platoon or company as the case might be, and in both cases my lack of inches and juvenile appearance were largely responsible.

'On the Square' at Chelsea meant that for one-and-a-half hours each morning half a dozen newly joined officers took it in turns to shout words of command at guardsmen at a distance of seldom less than fifty yards and often a great deal farther. After three days of this my voice gave out, and I could only talk in a whisper.

The Adjutant, Major Teddy Simmons, a most delightful person, thought it a great joke and threatened to run me in for 'dumb insolence', the charge preferred against an unfortunate guardsman when he remained silent after being charged with some offence, having taken the sensible view that anything he could say might be taken down and used in evidence against him.

Although expensive, life was pleasant in this free and easy atmosphere, but there was, however, one black cloud hanging over me – I was still a virgin. My trouble was that owing to my youthful appearance my girl friends declined to take me seriously, while I found the tarts in Piccadilly and Leicester Square repellent.

I had been to the theatre with my mother, and having said goodnight to her, I decided to take the plunge. From Berkeley Street, as far as the Charing Cross Road, the pavements were crowded with prostitutes, who kept up a chorus of: 'Hullo dearie, who wants a good time with a naughty girl?' and other even more intimate invitations.

Outside the London Pavilion I was accosted by a blonde who didn't look too bad, so off I went with her to a flat off Regent Street, and from the moment I acceded to her request to 'put four pounds on the mantelpiece before you start undressing', I realised that this was going to be one of the less enjoyable episodes of my young life. So far from the black cloud being removed by the loss of my virginity it was ten times blacker as I realised on my way home that I had hated something which monopolised the conversations of my friends and was more highly esteemed even than fox hunting, racing or polo.

Could it be that I was queer? Surely not, as no one could have suffered from such unsatisfied longings as I did when in the company of my girl friends, and not be normal. It was something I couldn't possibly discuss with anyone unless it were a doctor, and he would lose all interest in me when he found I hadn't got venereal disease.

For several days I remained sunk in gloom, but my spirits soared as the result of a confession by another officer, on the parade ground of all places. From 8.25 till 8.30 the officers marched up and down in front of the company in pairs, and L., a great friend of mine, confided in me out of the corner of his mouth that he thought sex was grossly overrated. His experience had been almost identical with mine, but unlike me he was confident that all would be right with the right girl. This was very encouraging as L., who had stroked the Eton eight, was one of the most normal people I had ever met.

Rectors, in the Tottenham Court Road, was the place to dance after a show, now that the war was ended. Although it was frequented by young men with their girl friends, who had become bored at some deb dance, there were always a few lone girls on the pick-up, and some of them were quite attractive. I had never gone there unaccompanied before, but having dined with a friend on guard I went along, dressed in blue jacket with brass buttons, and blue trousers with a red stripe.

I immediately met an attractive and very amiable girl, who danced well, didn't demand very expensive drinks, and when I asked her if I could come home with her, answered: 'Why not?' I never met her again, but when I left her flat at 6.30 a.m. with just enough time to get changed and go on parade, there wasn't a happier nineteen-year-old throughout the length and breadth of the country.

It so happened that I was detailed that day to take a draft of a hundred and fifty men for demobilisation at Ripon in Yorkshire. No N.C.O.s had been detailed to accompany me, and the men were a bit of a handful as I marched them from Chelsea to King's Cross, but I too felt like singing that morning. There's one big advantage about a draft for demobilisation: they may be insubordinate, and they may whistle at every girl they see, though they're supposed to be marching at attention, but you can bet your life that not one of them will go absent.

When I joined the Regiment, like most young men of my age, I danced very indifferently. This wasn't particularly noticeable at a private dance, where the standard was very low, but chorus girls were highly critical, and when I asked them to dance they gave me the look they give the poor guy in the deodorant advertisement, before he used the product.

Unknown to my brother officers, I used to slink off to Miss Vacani, and after half a dozen lessons I became reasonably proficient at the quick-step, which was called the one-step in those days, and the slow fox-trot, which included steps known as the twinkle and the jelly-roll.

Stella and her friends were delighted with my improvement, and began to treat me less like a mentally retarded child of twelve. But you can't win. I attended as few private dances as possible, but after one of my rare appearances at one of these functions I was summoned before the Adjutant. 'Gentlemen,' I was told, 'dance up and down, but you were gliding around like a ponce.'

In the spring of 1919 the Second Battalion returned to Chelsea after four-and-a-half years' magnificent service in France where it had suffered ghastly casualties. The Fifth Battalion was wound up, and the Second Battalion took its place, the barracks being shared with the Third Coldstream. We young officers found life very different in the Second Battalion, and although I have no doubt that the Commanding Officer and Adjutant, Arthur Wiggins, had fought heroically throughout the war there seemed no reason why they should have treated the junior officers as if they had been conscientious objectors, by reason of the fact that, fortunately for them, they had been born a few weeks too late to run the risk of being killed.

We were told that discipline was appallingly slack and that the Battalion would be brought back to pre-war smartness in the shortest possible time. I had been determined to do well, or at any rate keep out of trouble, when I joined the Grenadiers, and I had worked hard in the Reserve Battalion. It was the least I could do in order to show my gratitude for the miracles my father had performed in getting me into the Regiment. In the Reserve Battalion I had appeared to satisfy my superior officers and the drill sergeants – the latter, though not of commissioned rank, can put the fear of God into young officers – and I had even shed some of my embarrassment when called upon to drill a company, provided I was left alone. Arthur Wiggins, however, would stand at one's shoulder, muttering criticisms; more often than not he would halt the company, and dress down the unfortunate officer in front of the men for 'incompetence and a sloppy word of command'.

One of his fiendish tricks was to order his victim to march the company on to a marker, a senseless manœuvre calculated to flummox a young officer, no matter how well he knew his drill, unless he was given time to work it out. On one occasion I completely lost my head and finished up with all four platoons facing one another, not having the faintest idea which were the front ranks and which the rear ranks.

Having told me exactly what he thought of me in a voice which could have been heard a mile away, he ordered me to run to the end of the barrack square and back again. The man who humiliates another demeans himself, and though I was not a vindictive young man I swore I would get my own back on the Adjutant for his unforgivable treatment of me in front of the men.

I was highly indignant when detailed to play cricket for my battalion against the Irish Guards at Warley on Royal Hunt Cup Day, and many friends thought that that was the reason for my sending in my papers, but though it was the last straw, it was the humiliations I received from the Adjutant which were the real reason for my taking a step which I have never regretted.

Away from the Regiment, Arthur Wiggins was a genial companion, and in later years we became very friendly. Many years after, over a drink in the Guards' Club, I said: 'Arthur, you have had a bigger influence on my career than any man living, and I have to thank you for what little success I have achieved.' 'How come?' he answered in amazement. 'I can't recall having helped you in any way.' 'Oh yes, you have, Arthur; if you hadn't been so utterly poisonous to me when I was an ensign in the Second Battalion I should have now reached retiring age as a senior captain, penniless and unemployable except perhaps as the assistant secretary of a Municipal Golf Club. Instead of which I am having a marvellous life; what about another drink?' 'After that I think I need one, old boy; on second thoughts make it a double.'

Troops had been arriving home in thousands, and by the middle of January 1919 over fifty per cent of those serving overseas had been repatriated, and had either been returned to civilian life or were awaiting demobilisation. It was therefore decided to hold a second Victory Ball at which those who had done the fighting could celebrate their survival.

Immediately this was announced, Stella begged me to take her and I readily agreed, though the tickets were three guineas each, a sizable sum in those days on an allowance of £400 a year. No junior officer saw a penny of his pay, this being swallowed up by messbills and other regimental expenses. I decided to see *The Beauty Spot* yet again, and pick up Stella at the stage door afterwards.

The Ball was already in full swing as we set foot on the huge dance floor, and almost immediately Stella shouted 'Alex!' to the youngest-looking Colonel I had ever seen. He was wearing the uniform of the Irish Guards, and asked me if he could have a dance with Stella, to which I of course agreed. That was the last I saw of Stella.

If you are stood up by a girl it is some consolation when it is for someone worth while, and the young Colonel subsequently became Field Marshal Earl Alexander of Tunis, K.G., P.C. (U.K. and Canada), G.C.B., O.M., G.C.M.G., C.S.I., D.S.O., M.C., though, as I saw neither him nor Stella again that evening, it may well be that they parted after one dance.

Stella had had it, I decided long before I left the Albert Hall, though had she rung up with some plausible excuse I expect I should have forgiven her; but she didn't.

I am not certain where I first met Gertrude Lawrence, but I think it must have been at Murray's as it was on a Sunday afternoon at a small party given at the flat of one of the members of the Versatile Four that I found myself sitting next to her.

I shudder to think what would have happened to me had it come to the ears of the Regiment that I had accepted the hospitality of coloured people, invariably referred to as 'niggers' or 'blackamoors'. Nothing short of imprisonment in the Tower, pending a court martial, as the result of which I should have been dismissed the service for behaviour unbecoming an officer and a gentleman, would have satisfied my superiors.

One of the principal reasons for the great success enjoyed by Murray's was the discovery by its white-haired owner Jack May of the Versatile Four, the first coloured dance band to make a hit in the West End of London. They were good musicians, and those who knew far more about dancing than I did declared that there was not a white band in the country to touch them. They were charming people and the pianist Palmer Jones was married to the night-club singer Florence, not to be confused with the Florence Mills who took London by storm when playing the lead in the all-coloured revue *Blackbirds* at the London Pavilion.

Every Sunday one of the four would invite a few friends to tea and cocktails at his flat, and they would play and sing to their guests. I felt very honoured to be invited, as most of their friends were either stage folk or people older and more important than myself. On this occasion I was indeed in luck to find myself sitting next to this marvellously friendly girl with a turned-up nose, who enjoyed the entertainment as much as I did. 'Rose of Washington Square' and the immortal 'A Pretty Girl is Like a Melody' were two of the numbers I remember we listened to in rapt attention, but in the intervals this wonderful girl and I gossiped away.

I eventually plucked up courage to ask her out to supper one evening; she accepted for the following Tuesday, and we made up a party of four with two mutual friends – Joan Emney, sister of the comedian Fred Emney, and Archie Grant, a brother officer.

I had made a resolution to go to bed early on that Tuesday as I was detailed for King's Guard for the first time on Wednesday, and as an ensign I would carry the King's Colour from Chelsea Barracks to Buckingham Palace, where the ceremony of Mounting the Guard takes place when the reigning monarch is in London, and then on to St James's Palace.

But any young man who was not prepared to risk a court martial for the privilege of taking Gertrude Lawrence out to supper would have been a very poor fellow indeed. We had an enjoyable supper, with a bottle of champagne, and when the club closed soon after midnight, none of us felt like going to bed. But the question was where we should go, as I had explained that I mustn't be all that late in view of what 'Lawrie' referred to as 'my first night'.

My parents had just taken a house in Upper Berkeley Street but were still living in the country, and the only room furnished was my bedroom. I explained this, and suggested we should take along a bottle of champagne and consume it there. This was considered an excellent idea, and with 'Lawrie' keeping us in fits of laughter with her stories, I could not believe it when I looked at my watch and saw it was 2 a.m.

Those who did not meet her until she was the brightest star in the theatrical firmament may be surprised at this abbreviation of her surname, but that was the name by which she was known to the boys and girls of her own age in 1919. I think that André Charlot and Bea Lillie called her 'Gee', but I am certain that no one called her Gertrude. She liked to hold the stage at a party and as a storyteller she was without an equal.

All Lawrie's stories were unprintable – and unrepeatable unless you knew your audience very well. Even if you had heard it before, a story told by Gertrude Lawrence, at the age of twenty, was a source of joy. When she realised how late it was she exclaimed: 'Let's put him to bed; if he doesn't get some sleep, he'll forget his routine and drop the ruddy flag.' As the party broke up I asked her to lunch with me one day soon, and she suggested a day on which she had a rehearsal at the Vaudeville.

She met me on the dot of 1 p.m. at the Savoy Grill. I had expected an hilarious meal, but Gertrude Lawrence at a party and Gertrude Lawrence tête-à-tête were two different people. It was nevertheless a most enjoyable meal, and while on the previous occasion no one else had been permitted to get a word in edgeways, she listened patiently while I told her of my aspirations to become a journalist, and gave me some sound advice into the bargain. 'From the little I have seen of you I think you're too damn' nice, and you let people push you around. If you want to write, it's no use going on sitting on your ass in Chelsea Barracks.' She was wrong in thinking me too nice, but I was a moral coward, which came to much the same thing. When she talked about herself she did not boast, but it was apparent that she had no doubt that she would get to the top of the tree, though I do not think that even she visualised the height of the tree she was destined to climb.

She already had her foot planted on one of the lower branches, and on Bea Lillie's meeting with an accident she had earned golden opinions when, as her understudy, she took over her role in *Some*, perhaps the most successful of all André Charlot's revues at the Vaudeville. 'And was I pregnant?' This astounded me as I knew nothing about her life, but she went on to tell me that she had married at seventeen and had a daughter called Pam, who was, I think, about six months old at the time.

Some people disapproved of her while others, of course, were just plain jealous. She spoke the truth too frankly and with an impish arrogance which antagonised those who do not appreciate plain speaking. A spade was a spade and I cannot believe that in all her fifty years she ever employed a euphemism.

As I left her at the stage door that afternoon she thanked me for lunch and a 'lovely gossip', and then said: 'I'm a bit short, have you got a quid?' I had, and after she had dashed away to her dressing room George, the stage-door keeper, remarked: 'That's the fourth she's had this week to my certain knowledge, but bless her I wish there was more like her.' As I had taken out other girls in the current show, I knew George well. A small man with a pointed beard, he was a great character, and was a keen racing man. We would discuss the next day's prospects while I waited for my date.

By the time I became a civilian the name 'Gertrude Lawrence' had become a household word, and she was also a great success socially. I would dearly have liked to ask her out again, but I could not believe that she would want to spend an evening with someone so insignificant, so I never did. I did not meet her again till 1930 when she was in *Private Lives*.

I had just returned from India and I had been to see the show with 'Smut' Sammut (subsequently Lady d'Erlanger). We had gone on to supper at the Embassy, and the star of the show came in with some people Smut knew, so we went over to have a word with them. I thought it unlikely she would remember me, and I was delighted when she greeted me as an old friend.

I met her again at the Derby a few months later, and she said: 'I see you've got where you wanted', to which I replied, quite truthfully, that my foot was poised somewhat insecurely on the bottom rung of the racing ladder.

I saw *Private Lives* four times, and foolishly went to a revival thirty-four years later, taking Smut with me. The principal parts were, I am sure, competently performed, but to me it was sheer torture, and had I been alone I should have left the theatre at the end of the first act.

The last occasion on which I saw Gertrude Lawrence was in *September Pride*. I only knew her for a short while, when we were both very young, but it is a friendship I look back on with pride.

Although guard mounting was a trifle nerve-racking, one felt the hell of a fellow as one marched into the forecourt of Buckingham Palace, and afterward down the Mall, carrying the Colour at the head of the Guard, with the crowd trying to get as close as possible.

I was leaving barracks one day when a brother officer asked me if I would help him out at a tea party that afternoon. When he told me that the hostess's name was Nora Swinburne I readily accepted as I had heard her name mentioned not only as a highly promising young actress, but also as one of the prettiest girls in London. I have described how, four years earlier, I had been rendered speechless by Lily Elsie's beauty, but whereas the 'Merry Widow' had been over twice my age, Nora was two years younger, and she immediately put me at my ease. Not only was she one of the loveliest, but also the friendliest girl I had ever known.

We were joined during tea by the juvenile lead, a young man called Noël – surnames are matters of small concern among the lesser lights of the theatre – and I thought him one of the most amusing young men I had met. He talked with a frantic urgency, never drawing a breath as he told us how the great Mr Bourchier had ticked him off three nights running for unprofessional conduct.

After he left us Nora confided in me that she was terribly worried about Noël. 'He's such a sweet person,' she told me, 'but he will play the fool, and Mr Bourchier is so furious with him that I am sure he will give him the sack. It's so awful, because he hasn't got a penny, and he'll starve.' A few weeks later Noël did get the sack, but fortunately for all lovers of the theatre he didn't starve – his second name being Coward.

I had never seen Nora look lovelier than when I called for her at the Strand Theatre to escort her to the Theatrical Garden Party at the Botanical Gardens, but it was apparent that she had other fish to fry, and when we arrived she announced that she had to meet someone. I had visions of a repetition of my Albert Hall experience, but at that moment the one girl appeared with whom I would have liked to spend the afternoon if I couldn't spend it with Nora. The previous week I had been to a musical comedy in which Bea Lillie played the lead. From the stalls I had seen a marvellous girl with huge dark blue eyes, and here she was. This was a great piece of luck, and luckier still that she and Nora had been together in *Theodore and Co.* at the Gaiety. So Nora introduced us. Her name was May Vivian, and I have never before or since met a girl like her. Everything was fun and her gaiety was infectious. Whenever I was with her I always felt that everything was happening for the best, and I hadn't a care in the world. After spending the afternoon together, I took her out to supper that night, the next night and the next, and on the Sunday we went on the river.

I continued to see Vivvy nearly every day till the Battalion went to Pirbright on a musketry course, and this was followed by a railway strike, the first of a number of strikes culminating in the General Strike of 1926. By the time I was back in London Vivvy's show had come off, and though I searched high and low for her she had vanished without a trace.

About two years later when I was living in Paris, I was at a party at the So Different in the rue Caumartin when she came in with some friends. My host was rather tight and had accused me of trying to get off with his wife. This was something I should very much like to have done, but although she was pretty bored with him, she had not given me the requisite encouragement to commit the offence I had been accused of. I went over and asked Vivvy for a dance, and on my return to my table my host was even more offensive, accusing me of dancing with a tart while in the company of his wife and other ladies.

When I saw that Vivvy's party was on the move, I rushed over and pleaded with her to stay. She had a word with her friends, and though one of them gave me a very dirty look she returned, and we flung our arms round each other's necks as we always had done when we met. Young people were much more demonstrative in those days than they are today, probably a legacy from the war when reunions were occasions of great joy, and 'goodbye' was a dreaded word. Her great ambition had been to become an exhibition ballroom dancer, and after the show had folded up she had gone to a dancing school and had met a man who had taught her all he knew and she was now his girl friend. But he was always making jealous scenes, though this was the first time she had given him cause for jealousy.

'But you were my first love, and I had to stay and talk to you,' she said, taking my hand and kissing it, a gesture I had always found enchanting during our short romance. Every movement she made was expressive of living and we talked and danced and drank champagne till I realised we were the only people left in the club. When I hailed a taxi and told the driver to go to the outskirts of Paris where Vivvy was staying, he spread his hands and shrugged his shoulders as Frenchmen do when they consider your request to be too foolish to merit a reply. He did not mind driving us to the rue Châteaubriand, off the Champs-Elysées where I occupied one room on the top floor, which went by the grandiose name of a 'garçonnière'.

Vivvy removed her dress, lay down on my bed, and in less than a minute was sound asleep. I lay down beside her and I too was soon asleep. The next day was Sunday and when the concierge brought my coffee at nine-thirty we were still asleep. Vivvy said she must leave at once, and it was evident that she was worried at the reception she would receive after being out all night.

I have always believed in keeping on the right side of the concierge, and anyone who antagonises him or her, as the case may be, is the equivalent of someone who calls a grand slam without an ace in his hand. The concierge is omnipotent, and has no counterpart anywhere in the world. America has her janitor, who can make life unpleasant if you get on the wrong side of him, and we have our hall porter, but neither has anything like the power of a concierge.

After seeing Vivvy into her taxi I popped my head into the holy of holies, where Madame Boulanger heard all and accumulated a vast store of knowledge concerning the habits and morals of the tenants. It was from here she pushed the button to open the front door if you arrived home after midnight. She was all smiles after I had pressed a few francs into her hand, assuring me that she and her husband were broad-minded people, and that it was quite in order for the young Monsieur to bring a *jeune fille* home with him. On the other hand she had that very morning had to administer a severe scolding to the Monsieur who occupied the room opposite for bringing a young man home with him three nights running. This was something which God-fearing people like herself and her husband would not tolerate.

It was almost exactly two years later, on coming down to breakfast in my parents' house in London, that I saw a picture of Vivvy on the front page of the *Daily Express*. Above it in large black type were the words 'English girl murdered in Monte Carlo'. The murder was described as a *crime passionnel*. 'May Vivian, aged 22, a dancer, has been shot dead by her lover as she was entering a car outside the Hôtel de Paris. A man has been arrested and charged with her murder.' That was all I ever knew about the death of this gay, warm-hearted girl, with whom I had shared a few short weeks of complete happiness.

The post-war elections resulted in the Coalition Government securing a huge majority over the Labour Party and Asquith's Liberals, but it was one of the worst governments this country has had the misfortune to suffer and it quickly lost prestige. The promised land which Lloyd George had predicted with such confidence did not materialise and almost immediately there was industrial unrest. Little more than six months after the signing of the Armistice there was a railway strike and within a few hours of the disruption of the train service the Second Battalion Grenadier Guards was ordered to proceed to the railway workshops at Stratford in the East End of London.

Our mission was to forestall any attempted acts of sabotage, and to protect the blacklegs from molestation. Every officer was issued with a revolver, with instructions to keep it loaded at all times and not to hesitate to use it 'if the bastards get tough'.

Of all the orders ever issued to officers in this country in peacetime, this must surely have been the most shocking. Men who had been promised the earth as a reward for defeating the Germans had already had a taste of what life would be like in the postwar years and, utterly disillusioned, they had come out on strike as a protest against the lies they had been told and in the hope of inducing the Prime Minister to fulfil the promises he had made them when the country was at war. But we, as officers in His Majesty's First Regiment of Footguards, were instructed to shoot them down if in their endeavour to secure better living conditions for themselves and their families they became slightly out of hand.

For many years now I have had a deep affection for Wimbledon Common where I walk with my beloved dachshunds every morning, but in the winter of 1919–20 I hated the place. As a military station it had all the disadvantages of both London and the country, and none of their advantages. Guard mounting, from this wooden-hutted camp, was a laborious affair rather than the pleasant duty it had been from Chelsea.

We paraded in pitch darkness at 6 a.m., marched to Wimbledon station, with the Colour shrouded in a macintosh cape, and took the Underground to St James's Park. We then marched to Wellington Barracks to breakfast and clean our equipment before mounting guard.

When it was their turn to do sentry duty some of the men had had little sleep for twenty-four hours, so it was not surprising that several sentries were found asleep at their post, a serious offence for which they were court-martialled. I always prayed that I would not find one of my sentries asleep, and did my best to prevent this by being seized with an uncontrollable fit of coughing as I approached each sentry-box.

I am thankful to say that all my sentries were awake when I interrogated them as to what action they should take in the event of something untoward occurring. Had I been alone I would have called a sleeping sentry every name I could think of and done nothing more about it, but in the company of a sergeant and my escort I would have had no alternative to putting him on a charge.

I went racing nearly every Saturday and I saw my first Derby. The race was won by Spion Kop carrying the blue and yellow colours of Major Giles Loder. Although Spion Kop was not one of the favourites his success was tremendously popular in the Brigade of Guards, as Giles Loder was second-in-command of the Battalion of Scots Guards, whose lines were next to ours, and I think I was the only member of the Brigade who didn't back him.

From the time I joined the Grenadiers I had been ordered to hunt, though no one had made a suggestion as to where I should find the money to buy a horse, pay for its keep, and pay the subscription. In the autumn, however, I met Eric Midwood who asked me to stay and hunt immediately after Christmas 1919. His father had a large house near Tarporley, and he later became the Master of the Cheshire. The Cheshire has been called the funker's paradise, as there are innumerable small fences to be jumped which put no test on one's nerve, but as a member of a field of two hundred I found it anything but a paradise.

There had been a hold-up on account of frost, and my mount, a magnificent chestnut, used to carrying sixteen stone, was mad fresh. As I hunted at less than ten stone he thought he had a postage stamp on his back, and I couldn't hold one side of him. We soon found a fox, and I lost control as we galloped towards a fair-sized open ditch, about a length behind a big man in a pink coat, mounted on a blood horse. My horse stood back and sailed over it, giving the blood horse a bump before landing in front of him. 'Pink coat' drew level with me, and the invective he poured on my defenceless head made the abuse of a typical Company Sergeant-Major seem like terms of endearment. In such a big field it was bad luck that my runaway mount should have chosen to take on the Duke of Westminster.

A couple of months before my application to leave the Army was granted, my military career took a turn for the better, as my friend Teddy Simmons became my Company Commander with 'Hatter' Dalkeith (subsequently Duke of Buccleuch) as his second-in-command. Although I had bitterly resented being treated like a juvenile delinquent, I had always taken an interest in the men under me and was indignant at the way in which they were bullied by the Company Sergeant-Major.

What I disliked most about the Army was that everything had to be done by the book, and it was a sin to treat soldiers like human beings. What chance has a man of defending himself against some charge when he is made to stand rigidly to attention and even has to ask for leave to speak?

I had a couple of rather awkward customers in my Platoon, and as I was soon leaving the Army I broke every rule in the book by having a man-to-man chat with them in the barrack room. The result exceeded my wildest expectations, and after I had left I received a much treasured letter from my Company Commander thanking me for what I had done in the Company since he had been in command.

My twenty-first birthday was spent in Wormwood Scrubs prison, where a number of Sinn Fein prisoners were incarcerated. Rumours had reached London District that an attempt would be made to free them, so a detachment of Foot Guards was installed in the prison with enough arms and ammunition to repel a full-scale invasion, and orders to shoot at the first sign of trouble.

The Irish prisoners, for whom I had considerable sympathy, seldom appeared, and my chief memory of this awful place was the eerie silence. No sound from the outside world penetrated the walls of this citadel of despair, and wherever one went in the grounds there was the imprint of arrows from the prisoners' shoes in the dust. At night, when they were locked in their cells, I seemed to feel the misery all around me. I am not suggesting that every prisoner did not deserve his sentence, but these were the reactions of a young man who had never before been face to face with the seamier side of life.

I have never been so pleased to leave a place as I was when our spell of duty ended at Wormwood Scrubs, but I think it had a salutary effect on me, as although I had never committed an offence which would have entailed a prison sentence, I realised for the first time that had I not been born with a silver spoon in my mouth I might well have done so. I place self-righteousness very high in my list of unpleasant traits, as there can be no virtue in refraining from doing something one has no inclination to do.

I was forbidden to talk to the prisoners, but as there were no warders about, and it was my twenty-first birthday, I got into conversation with an intelligent-looking young man who was tending a flower-bed. He told me he was in for bigamy, and with a self-deprecatory smile explained that he had loved too many women too much at the same time, and got himself into a jam. In a panic, and not knowing which way to turn, he had married one of his girl friends, a self-willed young woman of whom he was in considerable awe. As the years have rolled by, I have often thought of that young man bending over a flower-bed, and said to myself, 'There, but for the grace of God, go I.'

My father was pleased to have a son in the Brigade of Guards, and we had recently been on better terms than at any time since I was a child, when he had spent so many hours at my bedside reading to me. The rifts between us, for which my foolish behaviour had been wholly responsible, had healed, and I am glad to say that we remained on good terms for the rest of his life.

He had very much enjoyed dining with me on guard at St James's Palace, where he had been a great success. Civilian guests wore tail coats and white ties, and I had not seen him so clad since he and my mother attended Hunt Balls in my childhood. He was always at his best in the company of men, and after drinking more champagne and brandy than I had ever seen him consume, he kept the Guard and his fellow guests entertained with a fund of anecdotes. It was the only occasion on which I heard him tell, in public, the story of the shooting episode in which he deputised for King Edward VII, which I have already related.

I mean it as no reflection on my mother when I say that he would have been less awe-inspiring had he been married to someone less puritanical. A typical Victorian, my mother lived up to the high principles she had set herself, but although he adored her I think there were times when he longed for her to unbend. I once heard my mother laugh heartily at a story about someone getting locked in the loo, but if someone told a story even remotely connected with sex, she would gaze unblinkingly into the distance. It was therefore a revelation to me to see my father laughing till the tears came into his eyes at some very bawdy stories.

I had feared that our friendly relationship might be disrupted by my suggestion that I should become a civilian, and I broached the subject with some trepidation. But after I had pointed out to my father that as an officer I would be most unlikely ever to earn more than £600 a year, and that when I left the Army in seventeen years' time I should be virtually unemployable, he saw my point.

'What about joining the Bank?' he asked me, which meant Barclays, of which he was a director. I did not think that I would enjoy the life of a bank clerk, but remembering Gertrude Lawrence's advice about sitting on my ass in Chelsea Barracks, I replied that that would suit me fine.

Although a very small step, it was a step in the right direction, and once I was out of the Army who knows what might come along?

# 7 *Banker in Paris*

One week after I had taken off my uniform for the last time I entered Barclays Foreign Branch in Fenchurch Street as the most junior of several thousand clerks employed by that gigantic organisation. I had previously met the Chairman and several members of the Board, and they had received me with the geniality fitting for an officer in the Foot Guards, but now the gulf separating us was even wider than that which separates a Commanding Officer from an Ensign.

I was back to square one again, and I felt as insignificant as on my first day at my private school. I was given the job of sending out advices to customers, and in those days these were written in longhand – which was fortunate as I could not type. Neither, however, could I write, at any rate not in the copperplate hand expected from bank clerks. I have always been suspicious of men who wear rings on their middle fingers, and Mr James, the head of my department, was so adorned. I didn't take to him from the word go, and from the way he looked me over I gained the impression that the antipathy was mutual; he did not address a word to me till I brought my day's work to him for signature around four-thirty.

By reason of the fact that banks closed at 3 p.m. and at midday on Saturdays, many people believed that bank clerks worked short hours. Far from the truth; for a large proportion of the staff, the hardest work of the day does not start till the bank is closed.

I had hardly placed my labours in front of Mr James when he gave vent to a curious noise in which digust and jubilation each seemed to play its part: disgust that any clerk in his department could be responsible for such an unsightly scrawl, and jubilation that his opinion of me had been vindicated. I can still see the flash of that ring on the middle finger of his right hand as he tore my work across and instructed me, with a contempt in his voice that any adjutant would have envied, to go back to my desk and produce something which would not make the Foreign Branch of Barclays Bank a laughing-stock in the eyes of its clients.

My fellow clerks, of both sexes, had witnessed my disgrace, and I dared not look them in the face, but I felt friendly hands on my shoulder and heard friendly voices exclaiming, 'Never mind, we'll give you a hand and we'll have it done in no time.'

I have met a great number of people in many walks of life, in various parts of the world, but I have never worked with more warm-hearted and efficient people than in the four years I spent as a bank clerk. Nearly fifty years later they are still not particularly well paid, they work long hours, and they considered themselves fortunate if they got away by 1 p.m. on Saturday, and for that reason I made a point of never going to my bank on a Saturday, and I am delighted banks now close on that day.

Nora Swinburne was busily employed making a success of her career, and there was still no trace of Vivvy. I began to see a lot of a chorus girl at the Vaudeville though she referred to herself as a 'small part lady' on account of the one line she had been given for long service.

It got around that we were engaged and the rumour reached my father's ears with the result that he requested for me to be transferred to the Paris Branch. Foolish though I was, I had no wish to be married at the age of twenty-one to a girl two years my senior, who after five years in the chorus had advanced no farther than a one-line part. But when I told her my father would not hear of my marrying her, she got very high hat, and informed me that her mother would be horrified at the idea of her marrying into trade. So we were all square, and I was on my way to the rue de Bassano off the Champs-Elysées, where I was to live *en pension* for thirty francs a day.

My father had chosen well in selecting Paris as a city in which his son might forget his sentimental attachments in London, and I enjoyed my two years there, though from time to time I became homesick for London, a nostalgia which has remained with me all my life. No matter how much fun I have had in other parts of the world, I have always revelled in the sight and smell of London. Although I was born thirty miles from London I am a Londoner, and it is there I belong.

In the years 1921–2 the franc fluctuated very little, and at approximately fifty to the pound Paris was a wonderfully cheap place for an Englishman. In those days it was still the carefree, raffish, slightly down-at-heel Paris of Toulouse-Lautrec, with its cobbled stones and brothels, a Paris in which Parisians still went to Montmartre, and though they no longer danced the can-can, they danced all night to the music of Gershwin, Irving Berlin and Jerome Kern. I do not know where the Parisians go on a night out in this tough, neon-lit Paris of *Paris Match*, Danny Cohn Bendit, the Crazy Horse, and student protest, but they certainly do not go to Montmartre or Montparnasse, which are now strictly for the Americans, with a sprinkling of industrialists from Belgium and Germany.

The Paris of Toulouse-Lautrec was a good place to live in when one was young and in love with life. For a pound you could have a splendid dinner for two, and you could buy an excellent bottle of champagne for 10*s.* 6*d.* Even at the plush places like the Ritz, Ciro's, Frolics and the Café de Paris, prices were little more than half what they were in London, and a large dry martini cost 1*s.* 6*d.*

I arrived in Paris two years after the Armistice, and the Renault taxis which had transported the scrapings from the barrel of the French reserves to repel the Germans at the gates of Paris were still operating. Old scarlet boxes on decrepit wheels, they were incredibly uncomfortable and slower than the hansom cabs they had supplanted, but their elderly drivers, with their walrus moustaches, had wonderful tales to tell of how in 1914, when the battle was at its height, a call went out for every able-bodied man in Paris to proceed to the front line, and the taxis were the only available means of transport.

Despite the fact that there was hardly a family in France which had not suffered a bereavement, Paris was a far gayer city than it was after its liberation from the German occupation at the end of the Second World War. After the first war, Parisians were tremendously proud that their city had withstood the German advance, but in 1945 there was little but recrimination.

I love France and I will always be a Francophile, but I derive little pleasure from my visits to Paris these days. It seems to me that spontaneous enjoyment died in 1940 and that ruinously expensive restaurants and night spots cater only for the foreign mugs. In the early 'twenties the Champs-Elysées was an avenue of gracious living, fine houses and sumptuous apartments, with no neon lights, and though the Place Pigalle was not so brightly lit as it is today, it was the gayest spot in Europe.

On my first morning in Paris I took the métro from the George V to the Place de l'Opéra, something I was to do many hundreds of times before I returned to live in England. The métro is a great place for love-making, and I used to see the same couples, day after day, locked in each other's arms, swaying with the movement of the train.

As the son of a director, I was cordially received by the manager, one of the half-dozen or so Englishmen of a staff of over a hundred, and I realised that short of my committing some ghastly misdemeanour I was pretty safe. Managers don't like complaining about the sons of directors, and I regret to say that I took full advantage of this.

I was directed to the Comptabilité (accounts department), and on reporting there I was shown into a small room under the roof, where a middle-aged Englishman called Tattem, a very old Frenchman called M. Lievin, and a dark-skinned young man, whose nationality I never discovered and whose name I have forgotten, were engaged in a heated argument. The young man talked very fair English, and was the only linguist in the party, as Mr Tattem's French was worse than mine, and the old Frenchman did not speak a word of English.

I immediately took to Mr Tattem, a most genial man who muttered, 'Dirty old bastard, filthy old sod', as he listed the cheques and credit slips. These imprecations were directed at the old Frenchman, whose habits were a trifle anti-social at close quarters, and in that little room we were at very close quarters indeed.

M. Lievin rolled his own cigarettes from the strongest black French tobacco, and he was the wettest smoker I have ever come across. Pieces of wet tobacco, and even wetter paper, would drop from his lips, not only on to his own work, but on to ours as well. He would clear his throat with a most unpleasing sound before spitting on the floor, after which he would grin, exposing a solitary discoloured tooth, and exclaim: 'Ça va mieux.'

But his most irritating trait was his terror of fresh air. There were no windows, and light and air were admitted in small quantities through a skylight, and if this was opened by so much as a crack he would shout: '*Courant d'air, courant d'air.*' If Tattem, as the senior member, reopened it he would take his chair to the corner of the room, farthest from the skylight, and decline to do any work till it was shut again. The summer of 1921 was the hottest for many years, and this charade was performed half a dozen times a day.

The extremes of climate are far greater in Paris than in London, and cooped up in that little room under the roof in the rue du Quatre Septembre, it was stifling. I sighed for the sight of white figures against a green background, the music of bat against ball, and long evenings on the river.

Although Barclays already owned these French branches they still went under the name of Cox and Co. (France), and judging by the size of the turnover each day this branch must have been a profitable concern. I was, however, uninterested in all that went on, and only looked forward to the moment when Mr Tattem joyfully exclaimed 'D'accord', which signalled the end of our labours for another day. The French employees liked the two-hour luncheon break as it enabled them to go home for the mid-day meal, but I hated it as it meant staying in the bank till 6.0 p.m.

The bank closed at 4 p.m., but even if you had finished your work the doors remained locked till six. When Mr Tattem told me on my first day, after we had balanced the books at about 5 p.m., that we had to remain in the bank for another hour, I could not believe it. This seemed to me to be not only an insult but an assumption that we could not be trusted to do a day's work unless we were locked up. I discovered that this was the work of the Chef du Personnel, a big fierce-looking Frenchman with a moustache like Lord Kitchener's, and that it had nothing to do with the English manager or the Board of Directors.

Staff affairs were left to this martinet, and the French employees were all scared to death of him. I was amazed at the deference, amounting almost to servility, shown by the French clerks to their superiors, in particular to the Chef du Personnel, and my suggestion that they should band together in protest against this monstrous slur on their integrity, and should also demand higher wages, was received in shocked silence. There was going to be no storming of the Bastille as far as they were concerned, and their response to my loudly expressed view that nowhere in the world was there less liberty and equality than in the rue du Quatre Septembre was that it was all very well for an Englishman to stir up a revolt, but it was they who would suffer the penalty.

I knew nothing of French politics at the time but it seemed ironical that the citizens of a repubic should be so spineless as to suffer injustices without a murmur of protest. Their reluctance, however, to air their justifiable grievances was understandable. They had no union to support them, and with the purchasing power of the franc reduced to less than fifty centimes they lived a hand-to-mouth existence and dared not risk incurring the displeasure of their employers. In the years to come, measures were taken to bolster up the economy, and by the time the franc had cascaded to a thousand to the pound Paris was a cheaper place for the Parisians than it was for the English.

I could have moved to another department at the end of a week or two, as I was supposed to be learning the whole banking system in order eventually to take high office, but that hot smelly little room was a haven, and if one is fortunate enough to discover a haven, either as a soldier or a bank clerk, one is very foolish to leave it voluntarily. The job required no skill or knowledge of banking routine, the sole qualifications being the ability to inscribe, and subsequently add up, long columns of figures quickly and accurately. Saturday mornings were crucial: if hundreds of cheques and columns of figures had to be searched for a few missing centimes, I might miss the bus to St Cloud or Le Tremblay or wherever racing was taking place that day.

I have never worked with a more genial companion than Tattem, who was always grinning, even when he was calling M. Lieven the rudest names. One day he amazed me by telling me that he was an organist. 'And what do you think I am doing in Paris besides adding up bloody columns of francs?' he said. 'Playing the organ in Notre Dame,' I suggested. 'Not bloody likely, I'm sitting on my ass waiting for a divorce.' I never discovered whether it was he or his girl friend who was still tied up, but I hope they lived happily ever after.

Ruth and Ronnie Bodley, who had an apartment on the Left Bank, and John Beck, who subsequently led a Walker Cup team to victory and captained the Royal and Ancient, became my closest friends. Ruth was one of the loveliest people in Paris and was as nice as she was lovely. She and Ronnie weren't hitting it off too well and soon after I returned to England they separated. But we had tremendous fun together and when Elsa Maxwell came to live in Paris there were innumerable parties.

Elsa, who was on the threshold of her career as a party-giver on other people's money, was a remarkable woman. Devoid of physical attraction, she was short and dumpy, and to my juvenile eyes she already looked middle-aged, but she had a genius for finding people with lots of money who wanted to entertain 'the right people'. Elsa knew 'the right people'; if there was anyone in Paris whom she didn't know and thought she ought to know, you could bet your life he or she would be one of her closest friends inside twenty-four hours. Elsa Maxwell had more 'best friends' than anyone in France, and she never forgot a face or a name worth remembering. She did not bother with people whom she did not consider worth while, and the humblest of her coterie of 'best friends' had his or her part to play. Even someone as insignificant as myself was of use. I had been in the Brigade of Guards and I was a spare man, and a spare man might come to the rescue when someone more important dropped out.

I shall never forget the party she gave for Charles Wacker at the Vignon in the boulevard Madeleine. Wacker was a young American with a packet of money, and Elsa bought him premises in the rue Caumartin. She transformed it into a night-club and called it the So Different, though I don't think it was so different from any other night-club. Elsa had engaged the International Five, a coloured orchestra, with two members from the Versatile Four, and Florence sang with the band.

Apart from a bunch of Elsa Maxwell's 'best friends', only about a dozen people turned up on the opening night, and for several nights it looked like proving an expensive flop; but all of a sudden and for no apparent reason, it caught on, and you couldn't get a table for love or money. Elsa's greatest triumph was when Lord Birkenhead arrived with a party. The Lord Chancellor of England had dined well, and he bull-dozed his way around the crowded floor. Woe betide those who got in his path, but to Elsa's shining eyes his dancing had the skill and grace of Nijinsky.

Elsa had ordained that all the guests at the Vignon party should come dressed as children; the idea caught on afterwards at any number of parties, but as far as Paris was concerned, it was a novelty. Society gossip played little part in the French press, but the idea of grown-up people appearing as children was regarded as news, as Elsa hoped, and it provided valuable publicity for the So Different. In addition to her flair for attracting the 'right people', Elsa Maxwell was a shrewd business woman.

Ruth Bodley decided I should wear a matelot (a child's sailor suit). I was instructed to shave my legs, and having washed the oil out of my hair, she curled it and made up my face. The result was a replica of 'Bubbles' by Millais, which had been bought as an advertisement for Pears Soap. I had always regarded my juvenile appearance as a disadvantage, but dressed in a sailor suit with my face painted, my self esteem received a boost at the number of women I would not have dared approach, had I not consumed a lot of champagne, who seemed to enjoy my company.

I need hardly say that all the 'right people' were present, and around 1 a.m. Mistinguett arrived. She was accompanied by a most attractive young man with a wonderful smile, whose name I discovered was Maurice Chevalier. They were the only people not in fancy dress. I had never enjoyed a party so much and I spent the last two hours in the company of a married woman whose husband I hated, which made her readiness to spend so much time with me all the more enjoyable. I was wearing more make-up than she was, and she thought it a great joke when she saw that her face was covered with my lipstick.

It was after 5.30 when I got home and when I was called at 7.30 I leapt out of bed for fear I should go to sleep again, splashed some cold water on my face and left for the bank, thankful that it was a Saturday. Much against my will, I had been moved by this time to the Cashier's Department, and therefore worked in full view of the customers, and at about 9.30 M. Beigneux, the head of my department, sent for me. He fixed me with a look of horror, and for some time was speechless; but when he did find his tongue the words gushed out in a torrent of abuse.

I could not understand more than half he said, but I understood enough to appreciate that in his view I was one of the lowest things on earth, and that if he had his way I should not only be thrown out of the bank, but out of France as well. I was short of sleep, I had a man-size hangover, and as I gazed at him uncomprehendingly, my mouth fell open. This was responsible for another torrent of abuse, which I interpreted as meaning I was to get out of his sight, and, even more important, out of the customers' sight.

On reaching the lavatory I came face to face with an apparition: blonde curls, and heavily rouged cheeks; but it was the lips which were the biggest give-away, as my embraces of a few hours earlier had spread my lipstick so that there were traces of it from my nose to the point of my chin. Oh my God, so that was it! M. Beigneux had taken me for one of those! A full stage make-up takes some shifting with cold water, liquid soap and paper towels, but after half an hour's scrubbing I looked fairly presentable. On seeing me approach again, M. Beigneux made it clear that he would not be among those competing for my charms. I found it difficult to word my excuses as I did not know the French for 'queer', and 'je ne suis pas malade' did not seem to fill the bill; I decided to confine my apology to my appearance without referring to my morals. 'M. Beigneux, je vous prie vous m'excusez, mais j'étais au bal masqué hier soir, et j'ai oublié laver ma figure' – not perhaps all that grammatical, but it did the trick. M. Beigneux was 'desolé', but he smiled, we shook hands several times, and the matter was closed.

Round about this time I was a party to another misunderstanding, and on this occasion I was suspected of murder. John Beck and I had had a night out, ending up at around 4.30 a.m. with a sing-song in the company of some French people whom we'd picked up during the course of the evening at the Moulin Rouge. John couldn't get a taxi to take him to his lodgings at Auteuil, so he returned with me to the rue Châteaubriand.

On reaching my small room John thought we should get less in each other's way a few hours later if he shaved before he turned in. His hand cannot havc been all that steady, as although it was a safety razor he managed to cut himself quite badly. He insisted, however, that it was nothing and made himself as comfortable as possible on the floor. Right in the centre of my garconnière was a bidet, and unless he lay with his head in it or with his body curled round it, his legs came in contact with the door, but he was very tired and was soon asleep.

I was awakened by screams of terror and shouts of 'À l'assassin', and a few minutes later the ashen face of Madame Boulenger appeared at the door, followed by that of her husband, accompanied by a gendarme. It appeared that when Madame Boulenger came to call me she found a heavy weight against the door, but exerting all her strength she effected an entry to discover a bloodstained corpse.

It was too big for M. Gilbey, and looking across at the bed she had seen that I was asleep, so she could only assume that I was the murderer, though possibly I had killed in self-defence.

John was by this time sitting up and rubbing his eyes. No he did not wish to bring a charge against me, as the wound was self-inflicted. Oh, so the Monsieur had attempted suicide, which is a serious offence in France, his name and address, please, and his *carte d'identité*. 'When I decide to end my life it won't be by means of a safety razor, and I shall make a better job of it', John told the gendarme, displaying a wound of little more than half an inch on his chin. The matter passed off amicably with the gendarme complimenting John on being so full-blooded, and telling us that recently he had found a man whose head had been almost severed, but he had not bled to the extent that John had done.

I thought, however, that Madame Boulenger looked a bit sour, and I remembered how shocked she and her husband had been when the gentleman opposite had brought home a member of his own sex.

Had I possessed a grain of sense I should have formed an alliance with one of a number of attractive girls who worked in the bank. Apart from the advantage of having a 'steady', I should have learnt to speak fluent French from someone who would have been content to eat and drink in cafés, bistros and bars, where the nourishment was about a fifth of the price it was at the plushy joints I frequented with friends from England and showgirls, mostly English, who were currently appearing at the numerous night spots.

I have said that Paris, in the early 'twenties, was cheap, and so it was for the British who received fifty francs to the pound; but the franc was still a franc to the French, though it had lost more than half its purchasing power. Life must therefore have been a hard struggle for those in the lower income groups. 'Le smoking' was a status symbol among the bank clerks, not for evening wear but for weddings, especially for the bridegroom. My refusal, therefore, to lend mine to one of my colleagues for his wedding showed how selfish I was in those days. I should probably have had to have the *vin rouge* stains removed from it after the festivities, but even had it entailed my missing a party, the pleasure it would have given my colleague and his bride would have outweighed any disappointment I might have suffered. With what pride would they have shown the wedding photograph to their children, with Papa in 'le smoking'!

I dislike generalisations, but I think that the French are more money-conscious than we are, and the depreciation in the value of the franc was a bitter blow, following on the privations they had suffered when their country was overrun by the Germans, even though Paris, by a miracle, had remained intact.

Understandably, they had regarded themselves as the senior partner in the Entente Cordiale, in that the war was fought on their soil and, ghastly as our casualties had been, theirs had been even heavier. It therefore seemed grossly unfair that the British should be twice as well off as they were at the end of it.

It would have been an appropriate gesture if the Board of Barclays Bank had raised the salaries of the French employees so that they were on an equal footing with the handful of British employees, who were paid in sterling.

# 8 *'Gay Paree'*

With an allowance from my father and my salary, small though it was, paid in sterling, I was quite comfortably off, and it was entirely my own fault that I was always hard up. This constant state of insolvency was solely the result of my preference for such places as Ciro's, Frolics, the Ritz and the Café de Paris. I did not lose much money racing; I spent a long time studying form before making my bets, and of course I didn't win a fortune. As all my bets were ready money bets they were seldom more than 100 francs. What was important to me was that I was learning all the time; although I could not see my way to becoming a racing journalist in the near future, I had no doubt that I should achieve my ambition, and that I should make a success of it.

I never missed a Saturday or Sunday meeting when racing took place in the Paris district, and for the first few years after World War I, our horses were as far in front of the French horses as their horses were in front of ours at the end of World War II, and have continued to be ever since.

Three years running, an English horse won the Grand Prix de Paris, at that time France's greatest race, but one has never won it since. We also won the Prix du Président de la République, as the Grand Prix de St Cloud was then called, with Pomme de Terre, who, despite his French name, was bred by his owner Lord Zetland, and was trained by his son Lord George Dundas at Newmarket.

Many years later, when I was staying at Wentworth Woodhouse with Lord and Lady Fitzwilliam, parents of my great friend Peter Milton, Lady Fitzwilliam told me that she had been so elated at the victory of her father's horse that she had danced on the table at the celebration dinner party at the Prè Catalan that evening.

Although France had some good steeplechase jockeys, the American and English jockeys were so superior to the home products on the flat that the leading French owners employed them almost exclusively.

The American rider, Frank O'Neill, had been leading jockey for some years, and his services were also in great demand in England for the classic races. I saw him win our Derby on Spion Kop and our Oaks on Straitlace, and although my judgement was immature at that time, I have little doubt that he was one of the great riders of all time. When he retired, he opened a bar next door to the Chatham Hotel in Paris, which had always been a fashionable rendezvous for racing men.

Before the days of air transport the journey to and from Paris was a long-drawn-out and uncomfortable affair, especially if it was rough, but Joe Childs, Frank Bullock and Steve Donoghue went over to ride in most of the big races, which all take place on Sundays.

Racing was the only thing which I took seriously. I had long forgotten about my girl friend at the Vaudeville, and for once in a way I was not in love. Ruth Bodley was lovely and unhappy, but though it would have been easy to fall in love with her I did not think it would be reciprocated. I regarded the bank as a joke, and I knew it held no future for me, but I could not tell my father so right away. I was still very young, and life in Paris was enjoyable, the only snag being that I had not sufficient money to become a successful playboy, which seemed to me the only pursuit, other than racing, for which I was cut out.

Dicky Compton, an old friend of mine from Sandhurst and the Brigade, came to Paris at this time. My funds were at a low ebb and I was living in a *pension* for 20 francs (approx 7*s.* 6*d.*) a day. I changed my address frequently but no matter how broke I was, I never resided more than a mile from the Place de la Concorde.

Dicky and I lunched together every day and I used to meet him at the Ritz bar after I had finished my day's work, and we raced on Saturdays and Sundays. At the end of a week Dicky was down to his last mille (£20), which wouldn't cover his hotel bill. I offered to cash him another cheque but he declined, fearing it might bounce, so I had another bright idea. A week or two earlier I had seen a horse called Harold run well in a race at St Cloud and I thought he was sure to win the first race at Longchamp the following Sunday. I therefore suggested that Dicky should have his last mille on him. All too rarely in racing do things work out as you hope they will, but Harold won at 3/1 and Dicky won £60, and I won six.

To celebrate, we dined at Voisin in the rue St Honoré, once one of Paris's most famous restaurants but, alas, no more. The patron M. Braquesac was ninety years old, and owned a couple of race horses, one of which had won that day at 55/1. Of course we hadn't backed it, but we offered the old gentleman our felicitations and he told us that he only had a louis on it himself. He was a charming old-world character, with the flowing white moustache worn by the Frenchmen of his time. He had been born sixteen years after the battle of Waterloo and six years before Queen Victoria came to the throne. He told us stories of the Franco-Prussian War, and how he and his family had been reduced to eating rats, adding with a twinkle in his eye, 'They needed very careful cooking to make them edible.' We had a superb meal and a bottle of Château Yquem, at ninety francs a bottle, the most expensive wine on the list.

After dinner Dicky exclaimed: 'And now for the Avenue MacMahon, and the party's on me.' I pretended to be shocked, as although it was in order for one to accept a friend's hospitality in a restaurant, it was another matter to allow him to satisfy your sexual appetites in the Avenue MacMahon, and there was a very ugly name for men who did so.

The establishment in question, a few yards from the Place de l'Étoile, was conducted in a most seemly manner, and Madame la Patronne had beautiful manners, as had her protégées. My cousin Derek Blyth, who delighted in telling stories at my expense, said that I had introduced so many friends to the establishment – including himself, I may add – that every now and then Madame invited me to have one on the house, an allegation which was without foundation.

At the end of World War II, a busybody named Marthe Richard

was responsible for the closing down of all these establishments, and in so doing rendered a grave disservice to the community. Before I went to live in France I imagined that the women in such places had been shanghaied as young girls and kept under lock and key by their cruel proprietors. Nothing could have been further from the truth. No more than half the girls in the Avenue MacMahon were on the regular staff, and the others used to pop in when they were short of cash, though one and all had to undergo a medical examination once a week. I never met a girl who was in any way ashamed of what she was doing, or in the least depressed; on the contrary they seemed happy and contented with their lot. In contrast to England, venereal disease was non-existent in Paris in the early 'twenties, but I have it on the authority of a French doctor that since sex has been forced underground, it is now prevalent.

Toulouse-Lautrec, so Pierre La Mure tells us in his delightful book *Moulin Rouge*, used to spend a week or so at his favourite bordel when he felt depressed. The food was good, and he found the company most congenial. I particularly like the story in which the *patron* told him proudly that he was a self-made man, having started in a very small way with only his wife and her sister, and that he owed everything to their hard work and unswerving loyalty when the business was in its infancy, adding, with tears in his eyes: 'There's nothing so precious as the love of a good woman.'

Shortly after Dicky left Paris I was introduced by Elsa Maxwell to a very affluent couple who entertained extensively but whose friends were unknown to me. I had met most of my new acquaintances through Elsa, but I knew very little about them except that they were rich – and to Elsa that was all that mattered.

This was a good-looking couple, both blond and, at a guess, in their late twenties or early thirties. He was English, and she was half Russian. Although I had been around quite a bit by this time I was still not all that sophisticated, and although they were pleasant enough I never felt at ease in their company, and so I felt sure I appeared pretty dumb to them.

I was therefore astonished when I received a note from them, left at the Ritz bar, asking me to dinner at their apartment. We were a party of six: a French couple, who made no impression on me, and a very attractive Frenchwoman in her middle twenties with a boyish figure, brown close-cut curls and a flawless skin. I still regard her as the most exciting person I have ever met. The apartment was sumptuous and the dinner excellent, but, as I expected, the conversation was carried on exclusively in French, and no one paid much attention to me.

I was bored to tears and was about to make my farewell, when my hostess asked me if I had been to the Perroquet, the night club then in vogue. I said that I had and that I liked it very much. 'That's fine, because that's where we are going, and I hope you like dancing as you'll be Renée's partner', she told me. I took this remark as a belated attempt to bring me into the conversation, but we had hardly sat down in the night club when Renée announced, in the peremptory tone I was to know so well: 'We'll dance.' This seemed a sensible idea as there was still room on the floor while in half an hour's time it would be packed tight with human bodies, unable to move more than an inch or two at a time.

She danced well, and I was delighted to find that her English was superior to my French, which was no great accomplishment. I could hardly believe my ears when she told me that she had decided to meet me after seeing me at the party at the Vignon, adding, '. . . where you and Mme G.F.G. were devouring one another, and you were behaving in a very grown-up manner for a little sailor boy.' We returned to the table, drank some champagne, and again she announced: 'We'll dance.' As we danced she gave me to understand that I would suit her needs, with no more emotion in her voice than if she had been telling a *vendeuse* that she had decided on a certain garment and would take it home with her. Andt his is exactly what she did. About 1.30, early by French night-club standards, she told our host and hostess that she was leaving and that 'le petit' would see her home.

As we left the table knowing glances passed between my host and hostess, and the latter whispered in my ear: 'Bonne chance', and something about a grand success.

I was still walking on air as I entered her apartment near the Place St Michel, though I have forgotten the name of the street.

My first impression of the apartment was that it was singularly un-French with its big armchairs and spacious sofa. She lit a cigarette and said: 'Now we can talk', but it was she who talked while I listened with open mouth, nodding my head from time to time as she laid down the terms of our relationship.

I suppose there is a strain of masochism in all of us though it may remain dormant in those who never meet someone like Renée, and when I left her in the not-so-early hours, and walked the two miles back to the Place St Philippe du Roule – no sign of a taxi – there was a song in my heart. The evening which had begun so inauspiciously had ended with my becoming the lover of this marvellous woman who was so different from any woman I had met before. A whole vista of new and wonderful experiences stretched out before me, and I was to see her again that evening when we were to dine either at her apartment or at a bistro in the 'Boul' Miche'.

A few days later an American attached to the bank said to me: 'You were at the Perroquet with a fine bunch of queers the other evening.' Highly indignant, I told him that though I knew nothing about the morals of the rest of the party I was sure that Renée was a hundred per cent normal. 'I should hate to disillusion you, but I think you're the irregular verb, the exception which proves every rule. I advise you to make hay while the sun shines,' he told me.

For nearly two months I belonged to Renée body and soul, the only time I asserted myself being on Saturdays and Sundays when I insisted on going racing. In every facet of our relationship she was the dominant partner, and I was perfectly happy for her to be so. She was incredibly selfish, without a spark of tenderness or sentiment, and how long I should have been content with such a relationship I cannot say, as it was she who terminated it as abruptly as it had begun.

I invariably met her at her apartment at the appointed time, and we never dined anywhere except on the Left Bank. Montparnasse had not yet come to rival Montmartre, and one seldom ran into members of the international set except in the few well-known restaurants in her quartier, which we avoided. I found her madly attractive and I think that her hardness was an additional attraction. She was so unlike anyone I had met before and it was a new and exciting experience.

I invariably went by bus to the races, but one day someone gave me a lift home, with the result that I arrived at Renée's apartment earlier than arranged, and as I was about to ring the bell the door opened and out came a very young and very pretty girl with ash blonde hair.

I walked through the open door into Renée's bedroom where she was standing in front of the looking glass making up her face. She had not heard me come in, and was only aware of my presence when she saw my reflection in the glass.

'Darling, who was that lovely girl?' were my first words. They could not have been worse chosen. Turning round to face me, she broke into French and there was a look of fury on her face I had never seen before as she shouted: 'Mêlez-vous de vos affaires' ('Mind your own business'). I apologised humbly and admitted that it was no business of mine, but my curiosity was aroused, and I wondered why my meeting a friend of hers on her doorstep should have produced such an outburst.

Although our affair was now in its seventh week, I knew nothing about her except that she either owned or managed a dress shop in one of the numerous streets adjacent to the Rond Point des Champs-Elysées, and all she knew about me was that I worked in a bank and wanted to be a journalist.

I did not know the address of her place of business, but a week or so later, while she was having a bath, I found several bills on her desk, made out in her handwriting, bearing an address in the Avenue Matignon. On the following day I left the bank at midday and made my way to the Avenue Matignon. The shop was small, but everything about the establishment looked expensive as I had imagined it would. Plucking up courage, I advanced till I could see the brightly lit interior, where I saw an unmistakable ash blonde head. Its owner was wearing a low cut evening dress of great splendour, and a middle-aged woman was prodding her, as middle-aged women seem to consider necessary before they make up their minds to buy a creation which they know in their hearts is twenty years too young for them. Ash blonde was certainly a knock-out, and for the first time since I had met Renée I felt the desire for something young and something new.

I could not drag myself away so long as ash blonde remained in view, and that dress was certainly revealing. So the girl I had seen on Renée's doorstep was a mannequin, as a model was called in the days when, apart from the biggest fashion houses, her social status and salary were on a par with that of a waitress.

What could be more natural than that one of Renée's employees should call on her to receive some instructions in connection with the business? Quite so, but why had Renée flown into such a temper? As I returned to the bank, however, I was more concerned as to whether it might be possible to make a date with ash blonde on one of my evenings off.

From Renée's expression, when she opened the door to me that evening, it was evident that I was for it. There were no histrionics this time, and having lit a cigarette with the deliberation of a judge about to pass sentence of death by the guillotine, she calmly informed me that I was finished. I had come spying on her, and from the look on my stupid face as I gazed open-mouthed through the shop window it was obvious I had a thing about Lucille. Raising her voice for the first time, she warned me not to try any funny business in that direction, and the look on her face left me in no doubt that I should ignore this warning at my peril. Lowering her voice, and in the same tone she used when telling me to put another log on the fire or perform some other chore, she said: 'Get out.' I had never disobeyed her, and as this did not seem a very propitious moment to start asserting myself, I got out, and stayed out.

In his book *Indiscretions of a Young Man*, published in 1931, Ronnie Bodley wrote: 'I further discovered two other Etonians who were studying to become bankers – Quinny Gilbey, a Grenadier, and . . . Gilbey has now left the bank and I believe follows in his brother's footsteps as a sporting journalist, for which he is much better suited than a banker, for of all the wild, scatter-brained, pleasure-loving young men I have met he had no equal.

We used to spend all our leisure together, and I know of no one who had such an instinct for getting the greatest possible fun out of life.'

Could this really be me, the man who in the years to come worked six, and sometimes seven, days a week, in the course of which he often turned out as many as twenty thousand words? Yes, I must admit that it was a fair assessment of my immature character, though, strangely enough, my only action during those years of which I am ashamed was committed at the instigation of Bodley.

He was far more conscious of being an Old Etonian than I was, and he was very incensed when a member of the French staff took to wearing an Old Etonian tie, and suggested that he, another Old Etonian and I, should request the young man to remove it, and if he refused we should do so forcibly. It so happened that the perpetrator of this enormity was an odious young man, and this fact, rather than any indignation at his wearing a black tie with a pale blue stripe, was responsible for my co-operation in what I have always regarded as an unforgivable act of arrogance.

We could not have been so naive as to regard that unattractive building in the rue du Quatre Septembre as 'a corner of some foreign field which is for ever England', and I think that our action was that of a particularly unpleasant type of Englishman, who for no apparent reason considers himself superior to any damn' foreigner, and can't understand why the damn' foreigners don't like him. When ordered by Bodley to remove his tie, the young man quite rightly replied that although in England a tie of this particular pattern might be the sole prerogative of Old Etonians, this was France, where it had no significance. So the tie was forcibly removed, and in the process it got torn. Forty-seven years later I regard this as one of the most reprehensible acts of my career. There is, and always has been, far too much regimentation as to what a man should and should not wear, and I remember as a small boy one of my brothers telling me that some man must be an outsider as he wore the wrong kind of breeches out hunting. I am not enamoured of the clothes worn by many young men today, but I heartily approve of the determination they have shown in refusing to be dictated to as to what they should wear and when they should wear it.

Although I would not dream of wearing an Old Etonian, Guards, or an M.C.C. tie, I would not attempt to dissuade anyone from wearing all three at the same time if he were so minded. If I have achieved one virtue in the course of my life it is that of doing what Renée told me to do, minding my own business.

There was one excellent piece of advice which my brother Ronald gave me, but for which I might have fallen a prey to the crooks who abounded in Paris in the early 'twenties.

Before the Ritz bar opened, Claridge's bar in the Champs-Elysées was the popular rendezvous between 6 and 8 p.m. It was there that smart women met their lovers, and less smart women hoped to pick one up. Showgirls dropped in on their way to work, and mannequins on their way back home. Business men and play-boys, a jockey or two, and young men like myself – and the crooks.

The three I have in mind were a big burly Australian whom we will call O, a well-turned-out young man, who said he was half French, whom we will call R, and a small middle-aged Australian, whom we will call W. I had three friends we will call A, B, and C, and I had noticed that they were frequently in conversation with O, R, and W. They were together when I entered the bar one Friday evening, and after O, R, and W had departed my three friends told me they were on to three certainties at Longchamp on the following Sunday, and would I like to be on them too. 'Of course, what are their names?' I replied. I was told that they did not know the names of the horses, but that O, R, and W were going to back them for them. A, who was a year or two older than the rest of us, had handed over two mille (£40), and the other two a mille each. If I wanted to come in, they would telephone their benefactors.

I was speechless at their gullibility, but all I could do about it was decline their offer as there was no way of getting their £80 back; not that they would have entertained the idea, so convinced were they of the integrity of O, R, and W, and their ability to win them a large sum of money.

I cannot remember what story the crooks had concocted, but I have an idea that they claimed to have fixed the jockeys. Any story, however, no matter how far-fetched, would have been enough to induce these three young mugs to hand over their money.

After the fourth race at Longchamp, they rushed up to me, incoherent with excitement. A had won £400, and the other two £200. 'Poor old Quinny, you were a prize mug to turn down such a chance.' We arranged to meet at Claridge's bar after racing, and they would stand me dinner. They were sitting at the bar when I arrived, and three more dejected young men I never hope to see. They had been the victims of the most diabolical luck, in that O, R, and W had heard of a cast-iron certainty in the last race and invested not only all their winnings, but their original stakes as well, and the horse had been beaten by a short head.

I think that in the course of dinner, which was on me, I managed to convince B and C that they had been the victims of one of the oldest confidence tricks in the world, but A, to his cost, still believed that only bad luck had stood between him and a small fortune.

A worked for one of the best-known fashion houses. He was a charming person, but he was a homosexual, and like so many of his kind, appallingly indiscreet. He had fallen in love with a very young *chasseur* at Frolics, and called for him every evening. At that time Frolics was the most fashionable restaurant in Paris, with good food, a first-rate band and cabaret, very much on the lines of the Savoy in London.

That famous Parisian character, Frank, was the barman, and when Frolics was about to close, he told me that he had been approached to open a bar at the Ritz. This was an innovation for this somewhat pompous establishment, and Frank told me that he was not optimistic about it. But at the end of six months it had become the best-known bar in the world, and has remained so ever since. One of my few claims to fame is that I had a drink on the house on the evening it opened.

A would arrive at Frolics, an hour before it closed, and sit drinking in the bar, making no secret of the fact that the good-looking young *chasseur* was the reason for his presence. His father was a wealthy art dealer in London, and A had in his possession a valuable *objet d'art* belonging to the firm. I cannot recall what it was, or why A had it with him in Paris, but he had told O, R, and W about it and they had said that they knew of a collector who would almost certainly buy it. Accordingly, A handed it over to them.

I knew nothing of this until A rang me up at the bank saying that he was in desperate trouble and that he wanted my advice, something he had hitherto ignored. On leaving the bank that evening, I called at his apartment; he certainly had not exaggerated the seriousness of the situation. At the end of a week he had asked the crooks whether the collector had made up his mind, and was told to come round to O's apartment. O and R were there, but not W, and he was informed that they had had him followed every evening and knew exactly where he took the *chasseur* and that they had looked through the window and knew what went on. If he made any attempt to recover the *objet d'art* they would go to the police and place all the evidence concerning A and the *chasseur* before them. They also hinted that O, who had the appearance and physique of a gangster's bodyguard, might feel compelled to give him a 'going over'. My advice was to catch the next boat to England and go straight to his solicitor and tell him the whole truth.

I never saw A again, and I have no idea what the outcome was of this sordid affair, but a year or so later I read that O and R were on trial for fraud on a vastly larger scale than the one they perpetrated on my friends. Both men were found guilty and received long sentences. W came to live in England, where he became a professional backer, and so far as I know, conducted his affairs with scrupulous honesty.

My brother Ronald's advice never to trust a stranger, or hand over money without having first received the goods, has stood me in good stead, but in rendering him an insignificant service, I laid myself open to a heavy fine, if not imprisonment.

A few days before I was due to come to England for Ascot – I always spent part of my annual holiday at the Royal Meeting – I received a letter from him enclosing a five-pound note with a request to bring him back some 'rude books'. I knew nothing about pornography or where to procure it, but Frank, who was a great friend of mine and remained one till he died shortly after the Second World War, could produce anything from a dirty book to a *wagon lit* on the Blue Train for which there was a waiting list a mile long, and he directed me to a shop in the rue Vivienne behind the Paris Bourse. For five pounds I purchased six books in English, every paragraph of which concerned sex in one of its many aspects.

In order to get a preview of this literature before I handed it over to Ronald, I put the books into a dispatch case instead of packing them in my suitcase.

At Dover, the Customs Officer opened my suitcase, and as he chalked it, asked me what was in the dispatch case. 'Just books', I answered, and after a moment's hesitation he chalked that as well. A few weeks later I read that a man had been fined £75 for trying to smuggle pornography through the Customs, and that the magistrate had told him that he should consider himself lucky not to be sent to prison. One of the greatest mysteries to me, and one which my legal friends have never been able to explain, is that in the eyes of the law cruelty is a very trivial offence, while those in which money or morals are concerned are heinous crimes. I had just written the above when I read that a man who had inflicted the most excruciating agony on a hundred and twenty-five cows by cutting off their tails without an anaesthetic, had been fined five pounds.

I cannot believe that anyone has ever been corrupted by reading a dirty book, and the worst that can be said about it is that it may encourage solitary pleasures. I do not include literature dealing with sadism in this category. The publication, distribution and even possession of such literature should be regarded as a criminal offence. After I had left Paris, and was again living with my parents, Ronald arrived with a parcel containing the 'rude books'. They were dog-eared and some of the pages were loose, which testified to Ronald having got his fiver's worth. As I had already read as much of them as I could take, I stuffed them into my bookcase behind my Ruff's Guides and other racing books, and forgot all about them till several months later my father told me that he heard I had some dirty books in my room.

It appeared that a tearful housemaid had informed my parents that she was pregnant, adding: 'It's Mr Quintin's fault.' 'What!' exclaimed my horrified parents in unison, my father adding piously: 'Good God.' The poor girl went on to explain that it wasn't Mr Quintin what had done it, but it was his books what had put the idea into their heads. My father sent for the young man and as a result of the interview he made an honest woman of her, and as far as I know they lived happily ever after, while had it not been for the dirty books they might never have got married at all.

Early in 1923 I received a letter from my mother saying that she and my father would be staying the night in Paris on their way to Biarritz, and if my father could arrange it they would like me to accompany them. I wrote back that there was nothing I should enjoy more. In nearly two years the farthest I had travelled from Paris was Chantilly, and the idea of spending a week on the Atlantic coast filled me with delight, especially as I was on very good terms with my parents, having only seen them for a few days at a time since I had come to live in Paris.

I lunched with my mother, and she told me that we should be in a party which included Lord and Lady Newton, of whom she appeared to be somewhat in awe. I was warned to be on my very best behaviour.

At dinner in the Hotel Regina, on our first evening in Biarritz, a man who had been with me at Eton stopped at our table, but I had forgotten his name and couldn't introduce him, explaining after he had moved on that we had always called him Po-face. There was a deathly silence and my mother assumed her far-away look. 'What did he say?' asked Lady Newton, who was very deaf. 'He said they called him Po-face at Eton,' roared Lord Newton, his voice echoing round the restaurant. 'Po-face,' echoed Lady Newton, clapping her hands. 'What a lovely name! If I meet the young man again I shall call him Po-face.' In the space of a few seconds my status had changed from that of the reprobate son to the blue-eyed boy.

In the afternoons my mother and I went for drives through the mountains by way of Ascain to St Jean-Pied-de-Port and other delightful towns and villages. I fell under the spell of the Pyrenees and it has remained with me ever since.

If King Edward VII had gone to bed with all the women he was alleged to have done he would have made Aly Khan look like a selling-plater, but Mrs Hope Vere, the First Lady of Biarritz, was undoubtedly one of his lady loves, and it was on her account that he spent so much time there. Born Marie Elisabeth Guillemin, she was a member of a distinguished French family, and her grandfather, the Duc de Montebello, was one of Napoleon's generals. She was an old friend of the Newtons, and although, since she was 'one of those women good Queen Alexandra had to put up with', she was by no means my mother's cup of tea, my father was fascinated by her, and after a superb dinner in her house he agreed to take her to San Sebastian for the day. She was very superstitious and thought the Biarritz casino was unlucky for her, so whenever she could get someone to accompany her she would cross the Spanish frontier, and my father had no idea what he was letting himself in for. He enjoyed the drive over, but that was all he did enjoy, and when he arrived home at 11.30 that evening he was on the verge of a nervous breakdown.

On arriving at San Sebastian, Mrs Hope Vere said that she couldn't have luncheon till she had found her hunchback. This mystified my father, but he followed her around the less salubrious quarters of the town till the hunchback was run to earth, sitting on the pavement outside a fish shop, eating shrimps. Having rubbed his hump with a circular movement of her hand, to the accompaniment of some incantation, and tapped him three times on the head, the King's lady informed my father that she was ready for lunch, and that the portents were now favourable for their session at the tables.

My father had never been inside a casino, but he followed her in, and with a sinking heart watched her purchase her chips and sit down at a table. When the shoe came round to her she asked him if he would like to share her bank; but he could not have been more horrified if she had asked him to share her bed. He always dined punctually at eight, but nine o'clock struck and she was still hard at it. When she at last rose from the table, my father declined to give her dinner and ordered the chauffeur to drive back to Biarritz as fast as possible – an order he had never given before, as he hated going more than thirty miles an hour.

The restaurant was closed when he tottered into the Regina, so my mother had to make him some bread and milk in their bedroom, secretly delighted, of course, that the day had proved such a fiasco. This would teach him to go off for the day with a King's mistress.

I got on very well with Mrs Hope Vere, and she gave what she called 'a young things' dinner party' in my honour. Her chef, who had been in her service when the King was a frequent visitor, was world famous, and the food and wine were fabulous. I sat next to an American girl called Mary Forbes, whom I fell in love with at first sight. I never saw her again, and forty-five years later I still remember what she looked like.

Little did I think that evening, when I said goodnight to my hostess, that the Hope Vere family would play such an important part in my life, and that the next time I met her she would cut me dead. My week at Biarritz was a very happy one, and I got on very well with my father's friends. One of them took me to the casino and taught me to play *chemin de fer*, by far the best of all the gambling games, and one I was to play a great deal in the years to come.

I had missed the 1921 and 1922 Derbies, won by Humorist and Captain Cuttle respectively, both ridden by Steve Donoghue, and I think it was Lord Newton's good offices which were responsible for my father arranging for me to get forty-eight hours' leave from the bank to see the 1923 Derby. The previous year I had induced the manager to allow me to organise a Derby Sweep amongst the staff. Although they knew all about State Lotteries, a sweepstake on a horse race was an innovation, and my French colleagues were deeply suspicious of it. When, however, it was explained to them that the manager would draw the horses, in full view of the staff, it caught on. The first prize was 1,000 francs, the second prize 500 francs and the third prize 250 francs.

I bought twenty tickets, but if ever there was a sweepstake I did not want to win this was it, and I had visions of what joy a prize of 1,000 francs would bring to the family of one of the underpaid French clerks. It might mean a holiday by the sea with his wife and family, or enable a young couple to get married earlier than they had thought possible, a thousand francs being, at that time, two months' wages for a junior clerk.

But the first horse out of the hat was Captain Cuttle, and the lucky drawer was Quintin Gilbey. Captain Cuttle duly won the race and all I could say was that I was sorry, while all those who had failed to draw a horse muttered '*Perfide Albion*' as they pored over their ledgers, or counted up other people's money.

On the evening before the 1923 Derby I was sitting with my parents when I was summoned to the telephone and, to my surprise, it was Lord Newton. He had had a red hot tip for Papyrus, but as he had not got an account with a bookmaker, would I put a fiver on each way for him. 'Who was that?' my father asked. 'Only Lord Newton,' I replied, as if this elder statesman was in the habit of ringing me up every evening. 'Lord Newton!' he exclaimed; 'what on earth did he want to talk to you about?' 'Nothing very important, he only wanted me to put a fiver each way on Papyrus for him.' 'Did he, by Jove, did he,' my father chuckled, delighted that his old friend had chosen his son to execute his commission, though he himself never had a bet. Sir Shadforth Watts had kindly invited me to watch the race from his box, and I nearly deafened his party with my 'Come on Steve', as the champion jockey brought Papyrus with a beautifully timed run to win by a length. I had put two pounds each way on for myself as well as the five pounds each way for Lord Newton and we won £37 10*s*. and £15 respectively.

I had a disastrous Ascot and when the last race came along I was losing £110. In order to reduce my losses to a level hundred I laid thirty pounds to ten on a horse which could not possibly get beaten, but he achieved the impossible and I left the Royal Heath poorer by £140. If one is foolish enough to land oneself in the sort of jam I was in, the honourable course of action is to call and see one's bookmaker and put one's cards on the table. On the Monday morning I called at Ladbroke's office and asked to see one of the directors, my proposition being to pay £25 down and the remainder in instalments.

My experience of bookmakers is that they are remarkably patient people provided their clients play the game by them, and the chairman, Arthur Bendir, knew I would meet my commitments or die in the attempt. The question which now exercised my mind was what I was going to use for money when I arrived back in Paris the next morning.

I travelled back to Paris via Newhaven–Dieppe, and as I walked to my second-class carriage at 3 a.m., feeling pretty miserable after a rough crossing, my collar felt so tight that I undid it as I lay down on the hard seat to get some sleep; I had to be at the bank in six hours' time. As we ran into Paris I went to tidy myself up and the apparition I was faced with was as horrifying as the one at the bank following the fancy dress party. The lower part of my face and neck were so swollen that my collar was almost invisible.

I had bade farewell to the broad-minded Boulengers, and had booked a room at Claridge's while I was looking around for new digs. I had been confident I was going to win at Ascot, having lost there on the two previous years, but here was I with only seven pounds in my pocket and the certainty that any cheque I might cash would bounce, checking in at one of Paris's most expensive hotels. I turned up my coat collar to hide my grotesque appearance and asked the receptionist to request the hotel doctor to visit me. The doctor diagnosed an impacted tooth, and obligingly gave me a certificate on which he stated that I should return to London for treatment by my own dentist. Having paid the hotel bill for one night and a third class fare to London, I had exactly five francs left. I have often wondered what would have happened to me if my wisdom tooth had not become impacted. Truly, an ill wind . . .

# 9 *Back to London*

Back home at Upper Berkeley Street I lived free, and my parents paid for the operation on my jaw. A week before I was due to return to Paris, my parents told me they thought that I had been long enough in Paris and that my father was arranging for me to enter a London branch. I was appointed to a recently formed branch, No. 32 Strand, at which the staff numbered only seven: the manager, chief clerk, two cashiers, the waste-book clerk and two dog's-bodies, of which I was one.

All the world loves a smiling face, but my experience is that one should beware of a face which smiles all the time as did that of the manager, Mr P. No one in his right mind finds something to smile about every moment of the day, so the smiling face can be a façade behind which lies a scheming mind.

I have discoursed at some length on how I managed to steer clear of the crooks in Paris, but before I had been home a month I was had for a mug, and of all places in the bank in which I was employed.

I was listing the cheques presented for clearing one morning, when the manager popped his head out of his office and asked me to come in and have a word with him. The smile on his large face was even more genial than usual, as he asked me if I would like the afternoon off. This would have been surprising in any circumstances, but particularly so on a Friday, always a busy day. 'You deserve an afternoon off,' he added, and as this was palpably untrue it should have put me on my guard, but who was I to contradict the manager! I thanked him profusely and was about to leave when he said: 'There's just one other thing, will you be going to Kempton Park?' 'You bet I will,' I answered, at which the smile enveloped his entire countenance as he went on to say that he thought that he and I ought to go into business together and make ten pounds a day each by backing favourites, to which I agreed.

When I called for Ronald and told him of my new business venture he told me that I must be out of my mind, and when I repeated that my partner was my bank manager he said that he didn't mind if he was the Archbishop of bloody Canterbury, adding: 'Your bank manager's a crook, and not only a crook but a bloody fool into the bargain.' How right he was, but I couldn't believe that the genial Mr P would ever let me down.

The object was to win ten pounds and then stop, and as the first favourite was an even money chance I put him ten pounds on it, and down it went. I therefore had to win him twenty pounds on the next favourite, a 2/1 chance, so I again put him ten pounds on. This was also beaten, so in the third race I had to win him thirty pounds, and as it was an even money chance thirty pounds went on it. When it, too, was beaten P was owing me fifty pounds, and as the fourth favourite was a 6/5 chance I should have had to put him fifty pounds on it to win back his losses plus ten pounds. It was here that Ronald stepped in and insisted on my sending P a telegram saying that he had lost fifty pounds and that I could do no more business for him that day. As luck would have it the fourth favourite won, but Ronald had been absolutely right.

It soon came to light that P was head over ears in debt, and that most of his creditors were customers of his branch. A fortnight later he got the sack, and that was the last I saw of him and my fifty pounds. I am sure he regretted knocking one of his clerks for fifty pounds, but when a man is being pressed on all sides for money he will snatch at any straw, and the experience I gained that afternoon at Kempton was worth all of fifty pounds. I was never had for a mug again.

The new manager did not pay me any compliments nor suggest I might like an afternoon off. On the contrary, he insisted on my clocking in at five minutes to nine, but it was a pleasant atmosphere in this small branch, and I was on friendly terms with a number of the customers.

In his determination to increase the number of customers at his branch, P had encouraged all and sundry to open accounts, most of them being recruited from the Strand Palace Bar. Promptly at midday, he would inform his chief clerk, Mr Jones, that he had to go out on business, and he would return an hour or so later, often arm in arm with a new customer, whom he would introduce to the members of his staff as if he was Rockefeller.

I cannot believe that in the history of banking one small branch ever possessed so many insolvent customers, and at the end of business each day there was a pile of cheques marked R.D. P never stopped asking me to get new accounts, but most solvent people are satisfied to remain where they are, and most of P's new accounts belonged to people who were already overdrawn, and would therefore not be able to draw against any cheques they might pay in.

I introduced only one new customer, the son of a very wealthy jeweller, and as he was always in the right places with very expensive-looking women, I assumed that he had no financial worries. When, therefore, he asked me to open an account with a cheque for two hundred and seventy-five pounds, 'just to be going on with', P was delighted, and allowed him to draw against it before it was cleared. Imagine my horror when it was returned 'Payment Stopped'. It turned out that the cheque was from a bookmaker, and in between its issue and presentation the jeweller's son had lost two hundred and fifty pounds. Although it subsequently transpired that he was on the verge of bankruptcy, I managed to get the money out of him, after which I closed his account. From that day on I left the recruiting of clients to the manager.

Drama was constantly being enacted in that little branch, quite a number of our accounts belonging to ladies of easy virtue. In forty-odd years on the Turf I have heard people call one another some original names, but for sheer vituperation I have never heard the equal of a lady who has been given a bouncer by her bedfellow. Some of these ladies were unknown to us and were presenting the customers' cheques over the counter.

I acted as cashier on occasions, and I was once party to as close a finish as can ever have been decided in a bank. I had just cashed a cheque for a lady when its drawer rushed in, and on seeing his companion of the previous evening inserting ten one-pound notes into her handbag, he uttered a howl of frustration. He endeavoured to snatch the bag, but I am glad to say she was too quick for him, and with a feint worthy of a rugby football player, she sold him a dummy and was halfway to Trafalgar Square before he could reach the door.

On another occasion a cheque for £50 was presented, drawn on a Pall Mall bank by a Mrs C whose husband was giving a big party that evening in Park Lane to which I had been invited. I had always regarded the 'C's as fabulously wealthy, and I remonstrated with Mr Jones when he forbade me to let one of our more insolvent customers draw against it but suggested that I should pop across to Pall Mall and obtain a special clearance. To my amazement the cashier marked it R.D. without even referring to the ledger.

The party was one of the most sumptuous I have ever attended, with two bands, a cabaret and enough champagne to float the *Queen Mary*. I enjoyed it enormously, but I could not help wondering how my hostess had come to give a bouncer that morning; judging by the cashier's manner, she had been in the habit of giving bouncers for some time past.

I knew most of my fellow guests by sight, but there were half a dozen men in dinner jackets whose presence mystified me, as they appeared out of place and kept entirely to themselves. Luigi of the Embassy, who had supplied the food, drink and all the trappings, subsequently told me that they were the broker's men, but that at that time he had no more idea than I had that the 'C's were insolvent. The party cost over a thousand pounds and he never got a penny of it. C was arrested shortly after, and received a long sentence for fraud. His wife, who subsequently ran a number of clubs, also did time, though for nothing more serious than offences against the licensing laws.

There were some strange people around London in the gay 'twenties, and I can recall several men, reputed to be of great wealth, who ended up behind bars. As the third decade of the twentieth century progressed, the search for pleasure increased among the young, and I must admit to being typical of my generation. Many parents excused their children's behaviour as an aftermath of the war, but while this may have been true in 1919 and 1920, a man of twenty in 1925 had been only thirteen years old when the war ended.

Although I think we made more noise than the youth of today, our behaviour, during the era of the charleston and the black bottom, was no better and no worse than that of the 'swinging London' of which we now hear so much. Young people were less promiscuous than they are today, when neither party would dream of entering into matrimony without having a previous sex relationship, but on the other hand we were completely indifferent to the lot of the have-nots, while the boys and girls today evince genuine concern at social injustice. Any young man or woman who advocated any kind of social reform suggesting that he was a fraction left of centre, would have been labelled a Bolshie, the worst thing one could say of anyone in the 'twenties.

Against a background of political strife, strikes and rising unemployment, the West End of London was still enjoying a boom. The stock market was still buoyant and speculators continued to make fortunes overnight. The restaurants and night clubs had never had it so good. Luxury trades, such as tailors, hosiers, dress-makers and jewellers, were doing a roaring business.

The Embassy Club in Bond Street, under the guidance of Luigi Naintré, London's most distinguished restaurateur, was the place to go, and its list of members was compiled almost exclusively from *Burke's Peerage* and *Debrett*. Luigi had made a great success of Ciro's during the war, but came up against the licensing laws, and the club was closed down and Luigi heavily fined for selling drinks out of hours, which brings me to the subject of D.O.R.A., the mere mention of which caused those on leave from the trenches to explode with rage. 'We live for months on end in stinking trenches, knee deep in mud, and scared stiff, twenty-four hours a day, and when we get a week's leave the bastards in Whitehall treat us as if we were a bunch of juvenile delinquents', Noel Abbey, my fag master at Eton, told me on his last leave before he was killed.

While there may have been some reason for imposing licensing laws in time of war, there was no excuse for their retention after peace was declared. But some of the restrictions imposed on us over fifty years ago are still in force today, though admittedly in a modified form.

The knowledge that one's bottles and glasses will be removed at a certain hour has defeated its own object, and has been responsible for far more drunkenness than there would have been had we been allowed to drink at our leisure. I have always been a slow swallower, and the attempt to drink half a bottle of champagne, with the waiter standing over me, invariably meant my doing the nose trick.

Slightly built, with a very erect carriage, grey hair and moustache, Luigi's appearance was far removed from the accepted idea of an Italian waiter, and although he had perfect manners he was never obsequious, rather the reverse. If there wasn't a table vacant, there wasn't a table vacant, and no matter who it was, he declined to put in an extra table, thereby inconveniencing those who had booked ahead. He was a connoisseur of food and drink, and though he appeared to be taking little notice of what was going on as he sauntered round his restaurant, exchanging a word here and there with his customers, nothing escaped his eagle eye.

Cocktails of all sorts were very much in vogue, and a delicious cocktail made of absinthe, grenadine and lemon juice was named after Luigi, while I think he was also the originator of the sidecar, of which brandy, Cointreau and lemon juice were the ingredients. Barmen from the more *recherché* establishments wrote books on the subject of cocktails, all of which were guaranteed to put you on top of your form if imbibed in the right quantity, and under the table if taken too liberally. Today, all the cocktails, except the dry martini, have disappeared, and when recently, feeling a trifle nostalgic, I asked the waiter for a sidecar he looked at me in blank astonishment. I think the disappearance of the cocktail dates from the second war, when it was impossible to obtain the requisite ingredients.

Vodka, in pre-war days only drunk after eating caviar in order to clean one's palate, is now all the rage and is taking the place of gin as an apéritif. The improvement in our relations with Russia is not responsible for the popularity of their national beverage, the reason being that if you have consumed three martinis, made with gin, it is painfully apparent before you close the front door, but you can drink five dry martinis, made with vodka, and fall flat on the floor, without your breath giving you away.

The Prince of Wales and the Duke of Kent patronised the Embassy Club whenever they were in London, and the Duke of Gloucester, whom I knew from our Eton and Sandhurst days, occasionally dined there. The majority of the members were also members of either White's, Boodle's, the Turf, Buck's or the leading Service clubs, and everyone knew everyone else, something which will never happen again, now that money is so widely distributed.

It was at the Embassy that I was introduced to the Prince of Wales. I was dining with Joan Pickering, a girl friend of mine, who was as nice as she was lovely. She couldn't do an unkind thing if she tried. We had finished dinner when the Prince, who had been to a boxing match, came in with 'Burghy' Westmorland* and 'Fruity' Metcalf, both of whom I knew well. After they had finished supper 'Burghy' came over to my table and, after I had introduced him to Joan, he asked me if I would mind if the 'little man' had a dance with her. I, of course, agreed, they were introduced, and off they went to the music of Ambrose and his orchestra, his Royal Highness having assured me, with one of his captivating smiles, that he'd take good care of her. A man looks a bit of a mug sitting alone at his table while another man dances with his girl friend, though when the other man is the Heir Apparent to the Throne the loneliness is easier to bear.

In 1925 Rolie Cubitt (Lord Ashcombe) put me up for Buck's and I am still a member. At that time all four Royal Princes were members, but though we had many friends in common I had not the wherewithal to hunt in the Shires and I was at no time a member of the Prince of Wales's set.

He loved hunting and was completely fearless, with the result that he had a number of heavy falls, after every one of which the press reported that he had fallen off. The law of gravity being what it is, a rider cannot remain in the saddle when his mount falls. The Prince also rode in numerous point-to-points, and I recall his finishing third in a flat race at Sandown on a horse trained for him by 'Burghy' Westmorland.

* The Earl of Westmorland.

A few years later I was playing in a foursome on the Chiberta links at Biarritz with Smut (Lady D'Erlanger) against Donny Player and his wife Leila (subsequently Lady Manton). We were all incredibly bad, but after half a dozen shots I managed to place our ball securely – or so I thought – on the green, only for Smut to putt it off again, at which I remarked: 'Well tried, darling! Why didn't you take your driver?'

Smut thereupon threw her putter at me, narrowly missing my head and also that of the Prince of Wales, who was on his way to the next tee in company with Archie Compston. He picked it up, and with his most charming smile handed it to Smut with the words: 'I have an idea this belongs to you.'

I first met June at the Embassy, where, partnered by Frankie Levison, she did an exhibition dance. She also sang an entrancing song, and it was there that Charles Cochran saw her potentialities, and she subsequently starred in a number of his shows. She left the stage when she married Lord Inverclyde. In the early 'twenties Babe Barnato, the wealthy racing motorist, was her constant companion.

Another prominent figure at that time was Doris Delavigne, whom I first met at Maidenhead with the night-club operator Gordon Halsey, a genial young man who will be remembered with gratitude by those who were exasperated by the ridiculous licensing hours.

Mrs Kate Meyrick, owner of the notorious 43 Club, and other establishments, went to prison at regular intervals for permitting drink to be consumed out of hours on her premises. She presumably considered the game was worth the candle, as no sooner had the gates of Holloway slammed behind her than she was back again at the receipt of custom, raking in the shekels. Ma Meyrick was one of the few people responsible for our entertainment at that time whom I never met, but I always admired her for her courage, and for the fact that she kept her business life separate from her private life, and married her daughters into the peerage.

Having been associated with several establishments which had been closed down, Gordon Halsey hit on the bright idea of the bottle party. Although it was a punishable offence to sell drink after hours, there was nothing in D.O.R.A. to prevent the customers from drinking their own drink, so Gordon opened a wine shop opposite his night club from which customers bought a bottle which was therefore their own property.

Doris Delavigne told me at Murray's Club, Maidenhead, on the occasion of our meeting, that her ambition was to become a courtesan in the best traditions of that profession, and she certainly succeeded. She left Gordon Halsey in order to better herself, and for a couple of years was known as the Goldsmiths and Silversmiths girl, as she was seen at the Embassy or Ciro's on alternate evenings with Walter Mappin of Mappin and Webb, and Norman Stewart Dawson of the firm of jewellers of that name. They too were given the go-by when Sir Mike Edgar came along. Mike Edgar was a Canadian financier who had made a fortune in a variety of business ventures. One of his financial killings was when he made a corner in pepper. He was a lavish spender, and his previous girl friend, lovely Elsie Scott, who had thrown him over, was always beautifully dressed and bejewelled. When Doris Delavigne from Maidenhead caught his eye, as she had had every intention of doing, nothing was too good for her. She was certainly a sight for sore eyes as she swept into the restaurant, and when she swept out again into her Rolls-Royce. The little girl from Maidenhead had certainly made good. Mike Edgar, who was a most genial host, as well as a most generous protector of the opposite sex, also owned a string of race horses, several of which, including Silvo, the best steeplechaser of his time though he never won the Grand National, were owned in partnership with Walter Midwood, father of my fellow cyclist Eric.

Doris had two other fabulously wealthy men dancing attendance on her in Arthur Bendir, chairman of Ladbroke's, and the young American, Laddie Sandford, who won the Grand National with Sergeant Murphy. With the possible exception of the Dolly sisters, I have never known a woman who had so many rich men at her beck and call at one and the same time, with the capacity for keeping them all happy.

Diners at the Embassy and other places frequented by Café society had the surprise of their lives when she married Valentine Castlerosse, as a more ill-assorted couple it would be hard to imagine. I knew them both quite well but not well enough to enquire what on earth induced them to form this alliance. Valentine's employer, Lord Beaverbrook, who knew him better than anyone, and of whom he was in considerable awe, could only answer 'God knows', when I asked him this question years later in Jamaica.

Although Valentine had very little money except what he earned from Lord Beaverbrook, to whom he was permanently in debt, he would be unlikely to have married Doris for her money, and no one has yet suggested that she married the grossly fat viscount for love. She was too materialistic to be dazzled by his title, and my own explanation for this extraordinary action on the part of these two worldly individuals is that Valentine found Doris's physical attractions so devastating that he offered marriage and that she accepted him knowing how much it would infuriate Lord Beaverbrook and others who might have looked down their noses at her, either because they disapproved of her, or because they were jealous. The marriage was of short duration; Valentine subsequently married Enid, previously married to Lord Furness, but Doris never married again. She remained in America throughout the war and took her own life shortly after her return to this country. Despite her faults, she was very kind-hearted and excellent company, and for a number of years I doubt whether she would have changed places with anyone in the world.

It was while I was working at Barclays in the Strand that I bought my first car, and what a horrible little car it was. For many years now the name Citroën has stood for elegance, speed, stamina and all the other qualifications which go to make up a magnificent motor car, but my hideous little yellow affair, with a pointed backside, was the most unsatisfactory car that can ever have reached our shores from France. Soon after I had given someone a fiver to take it away, I saw M. Citroën playing *chemin de fer* at Monte Carlo in the company of the Dolly Sisters; and it was no consolation to realise that I had subscribed towards the entertainment of these two very expensive glamour girls.

I had bought my first car on the never-never, on the proceeds of two good wins, and it was a bitter blow when it turned out to be a dud. My parents had opposed my purchasing the Citroën, but they demonstrated their sympathy in the most tangible way possible by making the down payment on a Morris Cowley to replace it. My snub-nosed Morris Cowley proved as reliable as the Citroën had been unreliable, and though as the result of my driving it full out it developed a rattle, which suggested it was about to fall to pieces, I cannot recall that it ever let me down.

I had little knowledge of the stock market in those days, but from what I have learnt subsequently there can have been few periods when there was such large-scale speculation and manipulation. Men made fortunes overnight in worthless shares, and in most cases lost them as quickly. These speculators were a greater enemy of capitalism than were the Left-wing politicians who clamoured for the nationalisation of all industries. The miners were being asked to accept reductions in wages to well below what they were earning in 1914, while every week they read of someone in the City of London having made a killing of hundreds of thousands of pounds.

Mike Edgar was a business associate of Jimmy White, the best known of all the wartime and postwar speculators, and between them, at one time, they were worth several millions, but they fell out and both died penniless with the Public Prosecutor taking rather more than a passing interest in their affairs. White, who hailed from Rochdale, never lost his Lancashire accent. Bluff and outspoken, he made no attempt to ingratiate himself with the Jockey Club, though at one time he owned more horses than any man in the country. With disaster staring him in the face, he committed suicide.

As the result of nine months at 32 Strand, I learned a lot about human nature though little about banking, except how unwise it could be to cash a cheque for anyone in the West End without first consulting his bank manager. When it was considered that I had learnt all there was to be learnt at a small branch, I was transferred to the Stock Exchange branch in Angel Court.

My job at the Stock Exchange branch consisted of buying and selling shares for the bank's clients. At the close of business I would dictate letters to a rather good-looking shorthand typist. I have always fancied myself sitting behind a large desk dictating letters to a good-looking girl in a short skirt, and taking her out to dinner at the end of a day on which I had outsmarted my business rivals. As a racing journalist, however, I have never needed a secretary, and I have never even had an office of my own. Four-fifths of the very considerable wordage I have been responsible for has been telephoned, and when I was not racing I have found it more convenient to do my work in the news room, where I had access to the agency reports.

In my year in the City I lunched most days at the City Athenaeum Club which ran its own private tote. Many of my school friends were working in the City and we had great fun. My closest friend, however, was Francis Egerton, though he was twice my age. Francis and Wilfred Egerton were brothers of Lord Ellesmere, and Francis, who was a jobber, thought of little else other than racing, on which the basis of our friendship was formed. By the time I was twenty-five the majority of my associates were considerably older than I was, the reason, in most instances, being that my knowledge of racing was far greater than that of most young men of my age. This was not surprising as it had monopolised my thoughts from the time I went to Eton. The discipline was far laxer in the Stock Exchange branch, and I usually took over an hour for lunch, and in the course of the afternoon paid several calls to the starting price offices of Leo Harwood in Warnford Court, with whom I had an account.

On Saturdays Francis and I often went racing together, and when racing was held in mid-week at Newmarket, Epsom and Ascot, his jobbing had to take care of itself. I received the greatest kindness from Francis Egerton and spent more of my time in White's, of which I was not a member, than in the Guards' Club and Buck's, to both of which I belonged.

Gubby Allen was keen on racing, one of his close friends being the famous trainer Jack Jarvis, who was very keen on cricket. They first met at Fenners when Gubby was playing for Cambridge. 'I suppose you're going to Ally Pally on Saturday, and I think I'll have a winner for you', Gubby told me as we left the City one evening, and when I met him on the course he told me that the good thing was trained by Jack Jarvis and ridden by his star apprentice Charlie Elliott. The horse won and Gubby, who had had a good win, asked me to meet him at the Junior Carlton wherehe would introduce me to Jack Jarvis. The only famous trainer I had met was Atty Persse, when I was still a boy, and it was a great thrill to meet Jack Jarvis who had no superior in his profession.

Since that evening forty-five years have elapsed, in the course of which I have written thousands of articles in which Jack Jarvis has figured, but I am proud to say that he never took exception to anything I wrote. As we said goodnight, he said, 'I want you to meet my brother-in-law, "Jack" Leader; he's a grand fellow and you're just one another's cup of tea.' I paid my first visit to Newmarket two weeks later and Jack Jarvis introduced me to the man I still regard as the best sportsman I have ever met and a splendid trainer, who was to a large degree responsible for whatever knowledge I may possess concerning the sport which was my profession for over forty years.

George Carter Campbell, a friend of mine at Eton and in the Brigade, had a few horses in training with Jack Leader, and in consequence I paid several visits to his stable at Exning near Newmarket, and Jack was obviously impressed with my enthusiasm, for he took me under his wing.

After I had left the bank I often stayed with him, and rode out before breakfast with his string on Newmarket Heath. In due course he made me very proud by entrusting me with a portion of the stable commissions. Jack's owners were not gamblers, but most of them liked to have a fair-sized bet on anything they fancied, as indeed he did himself.

A memorable day in my life was the one on which my father informed me that he did not think there was much future for me in the bank. I thought that the worst must have happened and that all the managers under whom I had worked had got into a huddle and sent in an adverse report to head office. But my fears were groundless, and it turned out that he had fallen out with the Chairman, Mr Goodenough, on a matter of policy, and that he feared this might adversely prejudice my chances of promotion. He had therefore asked the editor of the *Morning Post* to take me on in a business capacity.

# 10 *Journalist*

A few months earlier Lady Bathurst had sold her controlling interest in the extreme right-wing *Morning Post* to the drink trade, whose representatives had buried their differences in their desire to acquire a highly respected journal in which to voice policies favourable to the wine and spirit trade. My father had been largely responsible for the acquisition of what had been, for as long as I could remember, his favourite newspaper. Its policy coincided with his own views, and it had all along been hostile to Lloyd George, a hostility which was carried on during the war when it sided with Lord Northcliffe and the Generals against the Prime Minister.

My appointment was therefore nepotism on a grand scale. H. A. Gwynne, the editor, was a charming person and was respected by his friends and foes alike, but it was fortunate for him that he was not connected with racing as throughout his career in Fleet Street he had an uncanny knack of backing the wrong horse. On the day I entered his office for the first time I was not concerned with the paper's policy. Right, left or centre, it was all the same to a young man who was grateful for his rescue from life as a bank clerk, and was determined by hook or by crook to force his way on to the editorial side as soon as possible. Gwynne welcomed me warmly and explained that I was to act as a liaison officer between the editorial and the circulation departments. He thought that I was just the man for the job, though on what he based this assumption I still have no idea.

I was introduced to the News Editor and the Circulation Manager, whose offices were at opposite ends of the building, and told to report back for work at 7 p.m. the following day.

This was splendid news as it would enable me to go racing every day so long as my funds permitted.

On my reporting for work, the News Editor informed me that he and the Circulation Manager had not spoken to one another for five years, and without looking up from the proof he was studying he handed me half a dozen galley proofs, and motioned, with a nod of his head, to a chair in the farthest corner of the room. The Circulation Manager was slightly more genial, but he was sorry he could not stop for a chat and left me to my own devices.

I therefore returned to the news room, where I was handed some more proofs, and shown into an empty office. I only set eyes on the Circulation Manager at rare intervals, and the above procedure was repeated every day, except Saturdays, for the next month; nobody spoke to me except the boy who brought me the proofs and once asked me if I would like a cup of tea. And then one day I realised that I was reading the proof of an article that had appeared a couple of days earlier. I had been thinking for some time that I might create a good impression if I informed the Editor that I felt I was not pulling my weight, and this seemed to be the right moment.

With the proof in my hand I knocked on his door and, having apologised for my intrusion, I explained that the article had already appeared. In the space of seconds, Fleet Street's forgotten man was a hero. I had saved the paper, my perspicacity boded well for my future in Fleet Street, and would I like to accompany him round the building and see the paper put to bed. My eyes lit up with enthusiasm, and I told him I wanted to learn everything there was to learn about the birth, each evening, of a great newspaper. This went down very well, though, truth to tell, after forty years I still have only the haziest idea what happened to my copy after I had handed it to the Chief Sub-Editor.

That proof, however, was a great bit of luck, and Gwynne told my father, when he met him at lunch in the Carlton Club the next day, how I had saved the paper from ridicule and what a smart young chap I was.

Another factor in my favour was that I played cricket, and Gwynne was very keen that we should win the Newspaper Cup, which we eventually did. I was fortunate in making 40 not out in a low-scoring match against the *Daily Telegraph*, and this assured me a place in the Editor's good books, come what might, for at least another six months.

Our big match was against the Lords and Commons. We were at a considerable advantage in having 'Plum' Warner as our cricket correspondent, and he and my father and I drove together to the *Morning Post* ground at Morden. I had bought a new bat for the occasion, and 'Plum', having admired it, asked me where I had bought it. 'Selfridges', I replied. 'Selfridges?' he echoed in horror. 'Do you realise, Alfred, that Quinny bought his bat at Selfridges?' In vain I pointed out that as the bat was one of the well-known brands there was no reason why it should not drive as well as one purchased from the makers.

Despite the presence in our side of the ex-Captain of England, we were beaten, and my father and Gwynne were disgusted when I was bowled for a duck by Gwilym Lloyd George, the son of 'that rascally little Welshman'. 'Plum' said, 'What could you expect with a bat from Selfridges,' As I had failed to make contact, this seemed rather unfair on Selfridges.

I have read every word 'Plum' has written, and I still maintain that his books, *How We Recovered the Ashes* and *England v. Australia*, are the most thrilling books ever published on the subject of cricket. 'Plum' loved talking cricket and he found me a most receptive listener. It pleased him when I recited passages from his books, and on one occasion, when he and Gubby Allen were lunching with me at Buck's, he told Gubby he'd be a better Captain if he 'knew as much cricket history as Quinny'.

So long as my working day extended from 7 p.m. to 11.30 p.m., and nobody cared whether I arrived late or left early, I went racing on an average of four days a week. Such was my enthusiasm that I went as far afield as Leicester, Nottingham and Wolverhampton. I took to wearing a dinner jacket to the office, going on afterwards to a night club or a private party.

Of all the parties I have attended, the one with the most regrettable, though at the same time hilarious, repercussions was the bachelor party given by George Carter Campbell at Claridge's before his marriage to Diana Kirkwood, sister of my friend Bobby (Sir Robert).

We were all friends, and the party went with a swing until our host made a surprising error for a man of his sophistication; before we had finished the savoury, he had the champagne whisked away and replaced by liqueurs. So long as your guests go on drinking champagne they won't come to much harm; they will probably get a bit tight, but they won't get stinking as they will certainly do if they drink liqueurs for an hour and a half as we did that evening.

I gave the Cointreau a bashing, and when it was suggested that we should go on to the Cabaret Club, I realised that I had had it, and I prayed that I wouldn't disturb my parents on my way to bed.

The next thing I remember is the persistent ringing of a bell. Still only semi-conscious, I lifted the receiver and heard the unmistakable voice of Jack Leader: 'Sorry to trouble you, old boy, but we ran into a spot of bother last night after you left us. Poor old Victor [Lord Suffield] was run in for being drunk and disorderly, and half a dozen of us have been charged with insulting behaviour and trying to obstruct the police in the course of their duty. Would you mind coming along to Marlborough Street and see that none of this gets in the papers.'

During my long friendship with Jack he has, from time to time, paid me a compliment, but never one comparable with his touching faith that I as a cub reporter could quash the story of a Peer of the Realm being charged with being drunk and disorderly, and of half a dozen well-known men being on the mat for insulting behaviour and obstructing the police.

Feeling like death, I dressed hurriedly and on arrival at Marlborough Street found the reporters from every paper from *The Times* to the parish magazine milling round Victor and the other delinquents, trying to get a story. All the defendants, except Jack, whose pink cheeks were wreathed in smiles, looked green as most men do with a hangover, and far removed from the gay throng I had left at Claridge's eleven hours earlier.

It appeared that Victor had been refused admittance to the Cabaret Club, and that half a dozen of his companions had protested. A scuffle had ensued and a policeman arriving on the scene, as policemen always do when you least want them, arrested Victor and marched him off to Marlborough Street, followed by his fellow revellers, all protesting that he was being victimised.

The case would inevitably make the headlines in the evening papers, unless someone had been raped or murdered in the meantime, but evening paper circulation is a local one, and the next day's mornings would have given it no more than a couple of paragraphs if only they had pleaded guilty; in which case Victor would have been fined a few pounds, and the others let off with a caution, and that would have been the end of it.

But Victor, supported by his solicitor, was determined to fight the case. He was just about to become a director of Cunard's, of which his father-in-law, Lord Kylsant, was Chairman, and a conviction would create a very unfavourable impression with the rest of the board. The case was therefore adjourned for a month, and I went to Switzerland for winter sports with Mollie and Geoffrey and their children.

While I was there I received a letter from Victor's solicitors telling me the date of the hearing, and asking me to be sure to be present as I was a key witness. It meant curtailing my holiday, but in the circumstances I had no alternative, and when I arrived at Marlborough Street I found I was not merely a key witness; I was the only witness for the defence.

I had to say, on oath, that when I left the party at Claridge's they were all sober, and the soberest was Lord Suffield. Had I not been the worst for wear of all of them, I would doubtless have been in the party outside the Cabaret Club, but I said my piece, and if it was perjury it was the only occasion on which I have committed that offence. We are told in the Prayer Book not to bear false witness against our neighbour, but if I had borne false witness it was in favour of my neighbour, certainly not against him.

One of the party, 'Boy' Wilson, was asked why he arrived at the Cabaret Club on the roof of a taxi, to which he replied: 'Because there was no room inside'; a fair answer, but not much help to us in our effort to establish Victor's sobriety.

In his summing up, the magistrate said that on the one hand he had the evidence of Mr Gilbey, who maintained that Lord Suffield was sober when he said goodnight to him at Claridge's, and on the other hand he had the evidence of the police who said that Lord Suffield was drunk when he arrived at the Cabaret Club a few minutes later. As Mr Gilbey had spent the evening as the guest of his friend Mr Carter Campbell, and the police had spent it in the execution of their duties, he preferred to accept the evidence of the police. Victor was found guilty, while the rest got off with a caution.

Victor's conviction had no adverse effect on his business career, but a few years later Lord Kylsant, the fear of whom had deterred him from pleading guilty, was convicted of a much more serious offence.

I was an usher at George's and Diana's wedding, and saw them off on their honeymoon to Monte Carlo, from which George returned alone at the end of a week, followed several weeks later by Diana. A number of my friends have failed to stay the matrimonial course, but George and Diana's marriage was the briefest of any of them. He was killed in a bobsleigh accident at St Moritz a few years later, and Diana never married again, though certainly not for want of offers.

It was at a party given by 'Stewey' (Brigadier) Forster in a private room at Ciro's that I again met Noël Coward. He obviously had not starved. Charles Cochran had recognised him as a budding genius, and he had already written the words and lyrics for two shows, and was shortly to play the lead with Gertie Lawrence in another Cochran production.

After dinner, Noël played and sang to us. All his songs were tuneful and many of them are still played today, but it was his lyrics which made the greatest impression on me. Hitherto, anyone who could rhyme 'June' with 'moon' and 'tune' was considered to be a librettist, but Noël's lyrics were the product of a first-class brain allied to a marvellous sense of humour.

'Stewey' was a lavish party-giver, and the one I remember best was the one he gave for Diana Carter Campbell's twenty-first birthday. Diana had been having a wonderful time since the failure of her marriage; when a beautiful girl of twenty parts from her husband during the honeymoon it is she who gets all the sympathy. George sold his race horses, and spent much of his time abroad, but Diana seemed radiantly happy and was constantly being told how lovely she looked and that marriage obviously suited her; the joke was in poor taste, but it made her chuckle, as most women will at any remark complimentary to their appearance.

I was changing for dinner on the night of her party when Diana rang up: 'Darling, be an angel and pick Vera Bailey up, she's expecting you', and before I could say 'No, I won't', she had rung off. I thought VB would probably be middle-aged, or some ghastly relative, as women seldom ask a boy friend, even if he is only one of a dozen, to call for anyone except a dud.

I rang the bell, and the loveliest child I have ever seen opened the door. She was wearing a full red dress, which was very fashionable at the time, and in a tiny voice she said: 'So you're Mr Gilbey, how kind of you to call for me.' It seemed that she couldn't be more than fourteen at the very most. We chatted away about nothing in particular, but before the taxi drew up at Kettner's I asked her why she wore that absurd ring on her third finger. She fixed me with blue eyes which couldn't possibly belong to a grown-up person, and answered somewhat haughtily: 'Because I am married and, what's more, I have got a son of nearly two.' I had been placed next to this child mother and it was a most enjoyable meal. She was a marvellous dancer and after dancing together exclusively till the party broke up, we went on to the glass-floored Quadrant Club and danced some more.

'If you think I look young, you should see my sister Clare', Vera told me. I met Clare a week or two later, and she too looked as if she was well below the age of consent. They had been born in India and their mother had married them off, each at the age of seventeen, to two men, Mr Bailey and Mr Shakespeare, who were old enough to be their fathers. I was broken-hearted when Mr Bailey appeared on the scene a few weeks later and warned me off. That was the end of our romance, as a year or so later a friend of mine, Sydney Emanuel, declined to be warned off by

Mr Bailey and married Vera; they have lived happily ever since.

They are great friends of mine; dining with them recently, I sat between the two sisters, neither of whom looked a day over thirty-five. Clare had subsequently hit the jackpot by marrying the Duke of Sutherland, who like her first husband was considerably older than herself.

The best way to mend a broken heart is to offer the pieces to another woman, and the chances are she will mend it so skilfully that it will be as good as new; though there is no guarantee that she won't throw it on the floor and stamp on it at the approach of someone she considers more worthy of her favours.

On this occasion, I offered it to two women. They both accepted! One was an ex-debutante aged twenty, and the other was twenty-three, married with a small son, but separated from her husband. Strangely enough, my friend Rupert Higgins was responsible for my meeting both of them. Rupert was always broke, though his family had owned a large part of the Ritz, which, deplorably in his view, they had not passed on to him.

Rupert had asked a friend, who had a lovely daughter, to dinner at Ciro's and asked me to make up a party of four. I got on very well with the daughter, whom I will call R, and though girls of twenty in those days did not enjoy anything like the freedom that they do today, R and I managed to see one another after that nearly every day. I was by no means her first boy friend, and she had already become a champion fixer with her parents. If she wanted to do something they disapproved of, she always got her way by some devious means or other. Her father was immensely rich and had a large house in London and another near Brighton, at which I was asked to stay for Goodwood. R was very keen on riding and we used to ride before breakfast high up on the Downs near Findon, where Ryan Price now trains. This was the first time I had been to Goodwood, and as I won money on three of the four days it was a memorable meeting.

I was having supper with Rupert Higgins at Ciro's after doing my stint at the *Morning Post*, when I saw a lovely girl with a stout man more than twice her age. I pointed her out to Rupert, who answered: 'It couldn't be easier, old boy, she's with an old friend of mine.' So he went over, and a couple of minutes later beckoned me to join them. The two men began talking business and I asked the girl to dance. I was no longer shy and tongue-tied with a pretty girl, and I told her that she was the most exciting person I had ever met. This seemed to please her, and before we sat down we had it all fixed up.

Her companion didn't like late nights and would be taking her home quite soon. I was to wait ten minutes before picking her up at her house. All went according to plan and we went on to a night club where Layton and Johnson were singing. We lunched together the next day and had supper together that night and the following night.

My new friend, whom I will call B, was not only exciting and beautifully dressed, but was a most entertaining companion. There was plenty of competition for her favours, a member of the Royal Household being one of her most ardent admirers. Once, she refused to speak to me for a week. She accused me of striking her savagely at the Café de Paris, but she wasn't in the least hurt, and I suspect she had other fish to fry that week. I was admittedly two-timing her, but from what I learned later I have little doubt that she was three- and perhaps four-timing me. The year in which R and B each had a bit of my heart was one of the happiest of my life, and I would have been very hard to please had it not been. Of course it was too good to last. R's parents spent every winter in their villa at Beaulieu, while R stayed with friends in England as she wanted to hunt. She managed to get up to London to see me once a week and asked me how I would like to go with her to Beaulieu when she joined her parents in the spring.

I had enjoyed Biarritz immensely, and I thought that I should enjoy the South of France, with a girl friend, even more. I have met few girls more capable of taking care of themselves than R, but she wrote to her parents that she dreaded the long journey alone. Her parents wrote back, as she knew they would, telling her she might bring a friend with her. I think they had meant a girl friend, but they welcomed me cordially when we arrived by the Blue Train, and we had a glorious week together.

When I said I was going away for a week B's suspicions were

aroused. 'Yes, I know, you're going to the South of France with that bitch. Let me tell you this, if you do go I shan't be around when you come back', and she wasn't. Some years later she married a relative of mine and made him very happy.

A charming young man called Russell, who had replaced the original News Editor, told me he thought it would be a good idea if I joined his editorial staff. This was a big day in my life, but an even bigger day was the one on which he told me I was to be appointed as assistant racing correspondent to the highly respected elder statesman of the journalistic world, Arthur Coaten, who wrote under the *nom de plume* of Watchman.

I cannot pretend I enjoyed being a cub reporter, except on the rare occasions when a story of mine made the final edition and appeared on the breakfast table at Upper Berkeley Street. I would arrive about 10.30 a.m. and as likely as not would sit around for three or four hours, chain smoking and reading all the newspapers from cover to cover in search of a story on which there might be a 'follow up'.

Sooner or later, as the result of a telephone call or a News Agency report, one would be sent to the scene of the crime. The 'crime' might be anything from a Mothers' Union meeting to a murder, and it was always long odds against its getting into the first edition, much less the last.

By and large, a young reporter's job is a heart-breaking affair and I often arrived home in a great state of excitement about some story which had pleased the night editor, only to search in vain for it the next morning.

R stayed in Paris on her way home from the South of France and wired me to meet her there for a party. Like so many entertainments in the more aristocratic circles in France, the party was very dull, and we made a getaway before midnight, and went to a night club where Josephine Baker was performing. She was very attractive, but as coloured girls were not as popular as they are today, some people were very shocked at the liberties she took with the male members of the clientele.

I had promised to be back at the *Morning Post* office by midday, so I had to fly home. Although many of my friends had fought the Germans in crates tied together with string and propelled by engines which sounded like motor bicycles, I had never been in an aeroplane, and was scared stiff at the prospect. I was not frightened so much by the thought that we might crash, as by my terror of heights, not realising that vertigo disappears immediately one leaves the ground. I can't remember what the machine was called, but it was a biplane, painted dark blue. The cruising speed was 80 m.p.h., and the flight to Croydon took approximately two-and-a-half hours.

I again stayed with R's parents for Goodwood and we thought the time had come for us to legalise our affair, which had been going on for eighteen months. On the last evening of the Goodwood meeting R broached the subject to her parents, while I made myself scarce with a large whisky and soda.

After about a quarter of an hour a white-faced manservant informed one of my fellow guests, who was a doctor, that he was urgently needed upstairs; R's Mum had been so horrified at her daughter's choice that she had had hysterics. The doctor administered a sedative, but she continued to repeat: 'The wicked ungrateful girl; we gave her a most expensive education, and a coming-out ball which cost hundreds of pounds, and she repays us by saying she wants to marry the youngest son of a wine merchant.' I left early the next morning and never saw her outraged parents again.

I cannot believe that a newspaper reporter ever forgets his first big story. Russell called me over one morning and told me he thought there was a story at Wimbledon on bad decisions and the players' reactions to them. It was the day of the Ladies Singles Finals and Suzanne Lenglen was playing; her opponent served underhand and won the first two games of the first set. They were the only two games she did win. I was not required to describe the tennis, but I managed to get a number of interviews with leading players and officials and was able to serve up a story with plenty of quotes. The sub-editors did not alter a single word and it went through every edition.

If I had not become a racing correspondent I should like to have written about cricket, and I was very excited and proud when I was told I was to deputise for 'Plum' Warner at Lord's and describe the Middlesex *v.* Kent match. Kent had fallen from grace, and though Frank Woolley was still the greatest left-hander in the world, they were a mere shadow of the side which had won the championship four times in eight years. I managed to write three impartial articles on the match, and they were well received. Had Watchman not struck one of those lean spells which come to all racing journalists, I might have become a cricket writer.

'Quinny, I want to have a serious chat with you', Russell shouted at me across the newsroom, far too early in the day for any story short of a murder or an earthquake to require immediate attention. He asked me what I thought of Watchman's tipping. I replied that he was out of luck, but that he was a splendid journalist, which he was. 'Nobody doubts that,' he said, 'but our readers are beginning to get fed up with nothing but losers. Do you think you could do any better?'

I couldn't believe it. It had happened at last. I was going to write an article on racing. God had indeed been kind to me. I naturally said that I was sure I could, and he told me that my *nom de plume* would be Bellman and that I was to write 250–300 words every day, giving my selection for each race and the horse who was a danger to it.

Racing on the following day was at York, and off I went. My selection won the first race at 6/4, with the danger second at 4/1, so I had got off on the right leg. Enjoying novice's luck, I selected a flock of winners in the course of the first few weeks, several of them at good prices. Although this luck could not last I did well enough to attract the attention of Mr Harry Heywood of Allied Newspapers, who offered me the job of Carlton on the *Daily Despatch* and Galliard on the *Sunday Chronicle*. Allied Newspapers, late Hulton Newspapers, had carried on the Hulton tradition of getting the maximum out of their reporters for the minimum wage. I was, it is true, being paid more than on the *Morning Post*, where I had done practically nothing, but it was a very small wage for a six- and often seven-day week.

Geoffrey, to whom I owed so much, had made a success in

journalism in a style completely his own. He had never been a reporter, seldom troubled to secure an interview, and did not know the meaning of quotes. News was of secondary consideration to his own opinion, and on occasion he would go off at a tangent and write about something in no way connected with racing. The public lapped it up, however – all credit to him – and he was a great success.

As Bellman in the *Morning Post,* I had little opportunity to show if I had the makings of a racing journalist, my sole function being to tip winners. But when I joined Allied Newspapers at the beginning of the next season, I was given plenty of space and I made a proper hash of it.

I was still very inexperienced, and as my brother had made a success of his own style of journalism I decided to model myself on him. The experiment was doomed to failure, and I blame Geoffrey and my other colleagues for not kicking my backside and impressing on me what a silly young ass I was to try to copy him.

I doubt whether Geoffrey would have lasted long with Allied Newspapers, who were concerned with facts, news and the odd interview, and were not in the least concerned with their correspondent's opinions except, of course, his opinion of their selections.

# 11 *No longer a bachelor*

As I had wanted to be a racing journalist from the moment the war ended one would have imagined I would have worked my fingers to the bone in order to please my Editors. But when at the end of a month they made it abundantly clear that they thought little or nothing of my efforts I took umbrage, and they became as much my enemies as those in authority at Sandhurst, the Brigade, and the bank. Looking back over the years, I find it incredible that after my prayers had been answered far sooner than I dared hope for, I should have thought that I knew better what the public wanted than did my chiefs.

So once again I began cocking snooks at authority, oblivious to the fact that opportunity seldom knocks twice. It was utterly insane of me. The Editor is always right, and if he tells you to write your article upside down in Arabic you will, if you have any sense, write your article upside down in Arabic.

The chief aim of every journalist should be to be as professional as possible. Amateurs have been paid handsomely for playing tennis, but not for writing articles; at any rate, not in daily newspapers. Money may not be everything, but it is the sole reason why anyone in his senses goes to work. If you are receiving an adequate reward each month for your services, and your Editor is not querying your expenses, you are twice blessed, and you should keep your fingers crossed.

Never threaten to resign unless you have a better job lined up for the following week. It is always possible that you aren't as smart as you think you are, and that your Editor has been waiting for just this opportunity to be shot of you. Any Editor will slap you on the back, when you nap a long-priced winner, but you should be prepared to lay down your life for the man who does not allude to the fact that you have tipped thirty consecutive losers. The Editor who blames the journalist for tipping losers is on a par with the cricket captain who curses a fielder for dropping a catch. These things are not done on purpose.

In 1924 I met a delightful young American and his charming sister. They had taken London by storm in a musical comedy called *Stop Flirting;* their names were Fred and Adele Astaire. It did not surprise me to hear that it was Noël Coward who had advised them to come to London, but it was Sir Alfred Butt who produced *Stop Flirting* at the Shaftesbury Theatre. Sir Alfred, who became a close friend of mine in his later years, had started life as a call-boy. He had many irons in the fire, but his first love was the theatre. He owned a large string of racehorses, and this constituted a bond with Fred, who was mad on racing.

Strangely enough it was Adele who made the greater impact with English audiences on their débuts in London, but it was not until her retirement in 1931, on marrying Lord Charles Cavendish, that Fred became the legendary figure whose fame spread to the farthest corners of the world.

Although Fred and Adele were 100 per cent professionals from the moment they entered the theatre, they were so modest when one met them socially that they seemed like a pair of kids from next door. Fred bought a couple of race horses called Mabel and Topsy-Turvey, and as they were trained by my friend Felix Leach jun, with whom I often stayed for Newmarket meetings, we saw a lot of one another.

All the women were crazy about Fred, but he appeared unaware of their existence. I suppose he had been on the stage so long that he had had a surfeit of female admirers, but I often said to him 'Oh Fred, what a waste'; at which he would smile that smile which women found so devastating, and change the subject to racing.

One day, when I visited him in his dressing room, during the run of *Gay Divorce* in London, he told me that he had had an offer to make a film. Talkies had obviously come to stay, and were getting better with every film, but nobody had as yet attempted to film a long dance routine, and 'Moaning Minnie', as Adele always called him, feared it might be a flop. He was, however, going to have a shot at it. The picture was called *Dancing Lady*, and the stars were Clark Gable and Joan Crawford, but though Fred had a comparatively small part it was big enough to prove conclusively that his dancing went over as well on the screen as on the stage.

Fred soon became very popular in the racing world, but from time to time his trainer got very angry with him. Fred's fellow owners liked to bet, and they began to grumble at the short prices at which their horses were starting. The leakage was traced to Fred, who out of the kindness of his heart would pass on stable information to members of the cast. Information of this kind spreads like a bush fire, and down comes the price.

In the early spring of 1926 my mother was taken ill; it was found later that she had been suffering great pain for several weeks before she consulted our doctor, Ted Gordon. Ted was not only an excellent doctor but a charming man, and I shall always be grateful to him for his sympathetic care of my parents.

My mother's reserve and her reluctance to discuss her health was such that even my father had no knowledge of her illness till Ted told him that she must be X-rayed. This revealed an internal growth, necessitating an operation. She went into hospital on the opening day of the flat racing season, but she would not hear of my remaining in London as it would entail my missing Lincoln and Liverpool, my first assignment for Allied Newspapers.

Mother's inability to communicate the affection she felt, and evoke the affection she needed, had meant that never once had I managed to say the things which come naturally to most children when talking to their mothers, and when I went to say good-bye to her the words still wouldn't come, and I burst into tears. I was ashamed of my weakness, though at least it told her that I cared, something I had been unable to put into words.

When I arrived home from Liverpool I found my father red-eyed and exhausted, sitting before the fire in his smoking room with one of the dachshunds on his knee. The operation had been more serious than had been expected, and her life was in the balance.

Since my mother's illness I had been living at the Guards' Club, and when I called round to see my father the following morning he had just heard that he could see her for a minute or two that afternoon. 'Come along with me, dear boy, I'll need a bit of support.'

In the dim light I could see only her eyes which gave a flicker of recognition as my father took her hand. She tried to speak, but she was too weak, and all my father could say was, 'Beatrice, we'll come again tomorrow when you'll be stronger.' The tears were running down his cheeks as we left her room, and he said, 'I hope your mother didn't notice', words he had often used when he and I had done something we shouldn't have done, or left undone something we should have done.

But this frail little woman did not die, though in the months that lay ahead my father was often to say, 'If only she had never come round from the anaesthetic.' She was allowed home at the end of a fortnight, after which her recovery appeared so rapid that we went to the theatre together several times. As we drove home from the last of these outings, which gave her so much pleasure, she said to me, 'It's wonderful to feel well again', but the next morning she complained of slight pain and decided to stay in her bed. She was never to leave it again.

The dreaded word 'cancer' had never been mentioned, and it was still unspoken. But from that day my mother's condition deteriorated rapidly. Nevertheless, the flickering flame refused to be extinguished, till one day she asked for me. She was lying propped up on pillows as she had been for weeks past, but her voice was stronger than for several days as she asked me to place my arm around her. I did so and she said she was going to die very soon and she wanted me to know how much she had loved us all.

All her life my mother had been a very timid person. As a young girl she had learnt to ride a bicycle, but could never bring herself to ride it on the road, and although my father gave her the quietest horse he could find, she seldom had the courage to ride him. The motor car brought fresh terrors. Her most unreasoning fear, however, was of cows, and she would not venture into 'the Park' at Wooburn, where our cows were grazing, unaccompanied. Yet this woman, who was so fearful of the hazards of everyday life, was meeting death with far less trepidation than she would have felt at making a new acquaintance.

Ted arrived a few minutes after I had left her, and when he joined us he told my father that she was sleeping peacefully. 'Pray God she never wakes again', my father said, and there was the look of a pleading child in his eyes as he took Ted's hand. She was still sleeping peacefully the next morning, and she died in her sleep that day.

My mother had not long returned home after her operation when the miners went on strike rather than accept lower wages. On 1 May 1926 the General Council of the T.U.C. called out the workers in all other industries in sympathy, and the country was paralysed by the General Strike.

Although I was on the side of the strikers, and especially the miners, I signed on as a railway worker at Finsbury Park station in company with two friends who were also living at the Guards' Club. Our job was to load and unload milk cans. From this distance of time I cannot determine my exact reaction to the strike, but while those nearest me were blackguarding the strikers and their leaders, I was certain that this united action would not have been decided on without good cause. In the circumstances I now feel that I should have been much better employed devoting my time and energy to helping alleviate the distress among the strikers' families, and the miners' families in particular.

On the second evening of the strike my parents were entertaining for the first time since my mother's return, and, filthy dirty and smelling strongly of sour milk, I arrived home just as they were going in to dinner, to be given as rapturous a reception as if I had performed some feat of courage. Shaming remarks were bandied about, such as 'Your boy's answered the call of duty', and 'Not much wrong with the country when Old Etonians are not too proud to turn their hand to a bit of manual labour', but this commendation only increased my feeling that my behaviour was far from honourable.

It was a year earlier that I had visited a coal mine. My friend

Anthony Jackson, who had been in the Grenadiers with me, had asked me to stay for a Nottingham race meeting, and before racing on the second day, took me down the pit at which he was employed, learning the business.

The coal mines have improved since those days, but I cannot think of a more ghastly form of employment than that of hewing coal in that awful place forty-five years ago. On our arrival at the pithead Anthony was informed that there had been a subsidence during the night, and he said he must inspect it at once.

'I'm afraid it's a bit of a walk to the coal face', Anthony shouted as the cage descended at such a rate that I got the impression that my stomach had been left behind. He had neglected to say that the seam became progressively narrower till one was virtually on all fours, and that at one point we had to crawl through a narrow hole from one level to another. We eventually arrived at the scene of the subsidence, and found the corridor was blocked by large pieces of rock and smashed pit props. 'Is there likely to be another subsidence?' I asked timidly, but Anthony considered it unlikely, adding it was the result of the miners neglecting to erect sufficient props.

I was not a member of the NUJ at that time, and in consequence I was paid by Allied Newspapers during the strike, but I joined soon afterwards, and have been a member ever since.

The General Strike collapsed as the result of disagreement among the various unions, but the miners remained locked out until the middle of November.

Casting my mind back over the years I am left with the inescapable conclusion that I have always been backward. I do not mean that I was mentally retarded, but that things seemed to happen to me later than they did to most people. My prospects of survival seemed so remote that I was baptised on the nursery table at the end of a week, and as a result of this insurance policy in respect of my immortal soul, I was not christened in church, in the presence of my godparents, till I was over a year old.

I had golden curls, which fell in ringlets over my shoulders till after my fifth birthday, when my portrait was completed and hung in the Royal Academy. As a result of my illness I was nearly twelve when I went to Twyford, and at fifteen I was the oldest boy in living memory to enter Eton.

For all my fine talk I was nineteen before I lost my virginity, and three years older before I was at my ease when alone with a pretty girl. I was twenty-five before I became a journalist, and thirty-five before I made a success of it. In the Second World War I was one of the oldest lieutenants in the Army, and in my middle fifties I was cited as co-respondent, though admittedly for the second time.

In most cases, circumstances beyond my control were responsible for my being so far behind the clock, but I can put forward no excuse for my failure to develop a social conscience before my twenty-seventh birthday.

In the autumn of '26 I stayed with a friend near Dunfermline for the Scottish Circuit, and in the course of my journeys I came face to face with poverty such as I could never have believed possible, had I bothered to think of anyone but myself.

The miners stood idle and sullen at the street corners, their faces lined with the hopelessness of their cause, while their womenfolk, old before their time, their shawls tightly knotted to hide their pinched faces, hurried from shop to shop in their quest for the inadequate food they could afford on their strike pay. Children, sharp-faced with hunger, stood with their noses pressed to the windows of shops in which cakes and sweets were arrayed, unable to remember the time when they had tasted such luxuries.

My reaction to this unnecessary suffering was a desire to stamp my foot and shout obscenities, just as I had done in my childhood on seeing a horse being ill-treated. How dare faceless men, whose only concern was their profits, reduce women and children to near starvation, and why the hell didn't the Government do something about it? Most young men become concerned about social injustice between the ages of eighteen and twenty, but I was nearly twenty-seven before my eyes were opened.

I can put forward no excuse for my indifference; it showed a strange lack of feeling that I should never have been incensed at the treatment of the have-nots by the haves till I witnessed at close quarters the heart-breaking results of a six months' lock-out. The lock-out still had two months to run when I left the coalfields, and I shudder to think what conditions must have been like by the middle of November.

In the end the miners were defeated by the hunger of their families and had to go back to the pits and work longer hours for lower wages. Their working hours became the longest for miners anywhere in the world, and their wages were lower, in proportion to 1914 rates, than those of the German miners of the Ruhr. Had the miners resorted to force that autumn of '26 I like to think that I should have joined them, but I know I would not have had the courage.

By this time I had got to know a large number of Turf professionals and every evening, either at White's or at the Embassy Club, Francis Egerton and I would pool the fruits of our hours of study of the form book, and any information we might have gleaned from the various sources available to us. Francis raced intelligently and had a retentive memory, but he was also a shameless tout, and had no hesitation in asking an owner, a trainer or a jockey whether he fancied his horse for a certain race. He had such charm that he received fewer snubs than most people would have done. Racing is a business, and Francis was very definitely at fault in prying into affairs which were no concern of his.

Wilfred Egerton knew little about racing except what he was told, though as the youngest brother of the Senior Steward of the Jockey Club (Lord Ellesmere) he had raced since boyhood. The Egerton brothers were devoted to one another and Francis was overjoyed at Wilfred's return from America after three months' absence, early in 1927. He was in cracking form and told me he had made some money bootlegging from Nassau to the States, and that on the homeward journey on the *Majestic* he had met the most beautiful girl he had ever seen, and that he was going to bring her along to the Embassy to meet us.

Her beauty had been the talk of the ship and Freddie Guest (Chief Liberal Whip) and Admiral Lord Beatty, two highly respected connoisseurs of feminine beauty, had been knocked head over heels by her. She was introduced to us as Miss Betty Ball from Chicago, and she certainly was an eyeful. Although she had a 'rock' the size of Gibraltar on the third finger of her left hand, she told me she would not be eighteen for another three months.

Betty and I hit it off from the word go, and I was soon spending much of my spare time at the Connaught Hotel where she and her mother were staying. I was lazy, until the breaks came my way, and having got the sack from Allied Newspapers, I was in no hurry to get another job on a daily paper so long as the legacy from my mother lasted.

The weather, that February, was particularly unpleasant, but when I pointed out to mother Ball that there was plenty of sunshine and mimosa to be had only a few hundred miles away, she looked at me as if I had suggested that she walk barefoot from Cairo to the Cape, carrying her daughter on her back. Having ascertained that they would like to go to the South of France, I arrived at the Connaught the following evening with three *wagon lit* tickets for the Blue Train for the forthcoming Wednesday, and reservations at the Hôtel Bristol, Beaulieu. They could not have been more impressed had I arrived with a magic carpet, and that evening my stock soared high.

The trip was a great success, and by the time we arrived home Betty was no longer wearing the 'rock' on her third finger. A month later I replaced it with a star sapphire, only a fourteenth its value.

My father liked Betty very much, and approved of our getting married. He had taken to his bed soon after my mother's death, and he never left his room again. Several times every hour he was seized with paroxysms of coughing which left him so exhausted that it seemed that he could not survive another attack, but the weeks passed, and though each attack left him a little more tired, he would rally in the evenings when Lord Ernest Hamilton and other friends, mostly members of the Carlton Club, visited him. Once again the dreaded word 'cancer' was not mentioned, though it would not have troubled him. His brain remained absolutely clear to the end, but his body was worn out even before the growth on his lung became apparent.

I had been best man to my brother Oliver when he married

Tinker Burroughs, one of England's leading horsewomen, soon after my mother's death, and my father said 'I'd like you to marry this beautiful American girl before I go.' So we arranged to be married at St Peter's, Eaton Square, on 14 September, and Mollie's mother, Lady Watts, kindly lent us her house for the reception.

So obsessed was I with racing that I was not ready for marriage to any girl who had not been brought up in a racing stable. The fact that I had come unstuck over my first opportunity as a racing journalist had whetted my appetite for betting. I was now writing only as a freelance, and it was essential that I should cover my expenses. This not only required a constant study of current form, but my attendance at race meetings five days a week.

By this time one or two stables were entrusting me with small commissions, taking the view, no doubt, that the bookmakers might lay longer odds to someone they regarded as a young mug than they would to a professional.

In the week before my marriage, Geoffrey and I broadcast the St Leger, the first occasion on which this race was described over the air. It was an easy race to broadcast, the light being good, while all the colours were familiar to us. The race was won by the favourite, Booklaw, in the colours of Lord Astor. Geoffrey had made me promise not to have a bet on the race, so as to ensure my impartiality, but I could not resist having £14 to £8 about Booklaw, who I thought was a certainty.

Apart from the Egerton brothers, who were old enough to be Betty's grandfathers, and Derek Blyth, who was abroad on business much of the time, my closest friends were trainers and jockeys, not the ideal companions for an 18-year-old girl who had never set foot on a race course till she arrived in this country.

My sex life had been, I think, typical of a middle-class young man of my generation, but Betty was the product of the puritanical Middle West. The wedding invitations were already out when I had my first inkling of what we were up against. I was engrossed in the form book, with, as usual, a cigarette stuck in the corner of my mouth, when Betty asked me how many affairs I had had. Without looking up, or removing the cigarette, I answered, 'I've no idea, but fewer than most men.' It was not till several minutes later that I heard some sniffs and I realised that my reply had upset her.

As Wilfred Egerton had introduced us, he insisted on being my best man, and he and I must have appeared an ill-matched couple as we stood side by side, waiting for Betty to walk up the aisle on her father's arm. Wilfred was not only twice my age, but he could give me seven inches in height, and the high white collars he affected made him look still taller.

As my father was so ill, we spent our honeymoon in England. At the end of our honeymoon, we stayed with friends for Nottingham races and, on arrival on the course, I received a telegram from Geoffrey saying that my father had died that morning.

Greyhound racing, introduced from America in the previous year, had caught on in a big way, and the highlight of our honeymoon had been the news that my dog Mickey Free VIII had won a race at the White City. I had paid £30 for him, which appeared reasonable, but when I visited the kennels my trainer wasn't all that enthusiastic and hoped I hadn't paid too much. 'Only thirty quid', I told him, to which he replied, 'Quite enough, he's no flying machine, and he's not getting any younger.' I knew nothing about greyhounds, and Mickey, who was snow white, to me looked beautiful. He ran several times for me without distinction, but had qualified for the semi-final of an important race by finishing second. Unlike horses, greyhounds are tried by the clock, and short of something untoward happening, can be relied to run true to form.

Mickey didn't appear to have a cat in hell's chance in this semi-final as all his opponents had run the 525 yards in two seconds' faster time than he had done, and he accordingly started at 20/1. I had not, of course, had a penny on him, and when I returned to London my trainer told me that Mickey's victory was the most astonishing turn-up in the history of greyhound racing. He had only run true to form according to the clock, so his opponents must have taken over two seconds longer than they should have done.

We were staying at the Connaught Hotel, and the day after our return to London the hall porter announced that a person wanted to see me on business. He looked far from affluent, and I thought to myself, 'There's a touch coming'; but to my surprise he produced a large wad of soiled notes from his pocket and said he wanted to buy Mickey. Hiding my astonishment, I replied, 'So do al ot of people; he's a very high-class dog and I'm very fond of him', neither of which was true.

My reluctance to part with my white dog resulted in my new-found friend asking me what I would take for him. '£100', I replied, this being the first figure which came into my head. He considered it a bit steep, and that £75, which he had brought with him, was nearer the mark. I told him he must be joking, but that as he'd taken a fancy to Mickey, and I knew how disappointed his family would be if I refused to sell, I would split the difference and let him have Mickey for £90. I added that I did not know what my wife would say at my selling our most cherished possession, but I quickly pocketed the £75, and a couple of days later received a cheque for £15, which ended my career as an owner of greyhounds.

We spent Christmas at Sils Maria in the Engadine with Mollie and Geoffrey and their children, and the first time Betty put on skis she broke her ankle. We therefore cut short our Swiss holiday, where the shortage of snow had been our misfortune, and went on to Monte Carlo, where there was too much of it. Although Betty's ankle was still in plaster, we were entertained lavishly, entirely on her account. I have been married to two very beautiful women, and I have never had any illusions as to why I was so popular during my married life.

One party stands out in my mind: a luncheon at which Augustus John was present. He spoke very little, but never took his eyes off Betty during our three hours' repast, and afterwards insisted on sitting next to her on the drive to Monte Carlo, in the course of which he encased her leg, just above the knee, with his hand. This was not at all to the liking of my Middle-Western bride. Unfortunately she made it quite clear; otherwise I might have a priceless masterpiece hanging over my desk today.

On our return from Monte Carlo we sailed by the White Star liner *Doric* from Liverpool to America.

The ship started to pitch in an ominous manner as soon as we left the Mersey. No one was allowed on deck for five days – not that anyone in his right mind would have contemplated leaving his cabin. From our port hole the huge waves looked black and terrifying; at one period we were covering only 120 miles in twenty-four hours, and we were two-and-a-half days late.

As Betty was still lame, her mother was allowed to take her straight to the Plaza Hotel, while father Ball and I battled with the Customs. I have never met an American woman who travelled light; the more beautiful she is, the more she carries around. Betty had twelve pieces of luggage, including two innovation trunks which stood over 4 ft high, and weighed a ton. Every piece of luggage was locked, and I had been handed twelve keys.

The Customs officer, whose soft Irish brogue was a snare and delusion, asked me if I happened to have a bottle of whisky anywhere around, and I was subsequently informed that if I had said 'Yes' and made him a present of it, I should have been on my way, instead of waiting for well over an hour while he searched in every nook and crannie of Betty's twelve, and my two, pieces of luggage.

On our first evening in New York, a reception was given by my in-laws 'to meet Betty's British husband'. They were nice friendly people, and every man took me aside and handed me a card bearing the name and address of a bootlegger or a speakeasy. Drink and how to get it, what to avoid, how much you should pay, and, most important of all, the password to the various joints, monopolised the conversation, while an elderly lady produced a bottle of whisky from her voluminous under-garments, and presented it to me with a flourish.

My happiest memory of those few days in New York, before we travelled on to Chicago, was meeting Fred and Adele Astaire again. Fred had heard we were coming, and on checking in at the Plaza I found two front-row stalls awaiting me, with a message from Fred to come round after the show. I think the show was *Funny Face*, and I know we both enjoyed it, and I shall never forget the moment of triumph outside the stage door. There must have been a crowd of fifty clamouring to see the stars, or to obtain their autographs, but the stage-door keeper ignored them and asked if there was a Mr Gilbey amongst them. When I said 'Yes' he told me that Mr Astaire wanted to see me, but he was sorry he could not see anyone else that evening. The disappointed fans regarded us with awe, obviously wondering who these V.I.P.s could be. In his dressing room we talked racing, and I told Fred I had seen a two-year-old of his which showed much promise. He and I went to a speakeasy, but Betty, who was pregnant, was still feeling the effects of the voyage, and she and Adele went to the Plaza, where I found them later, still gossiping.

My father-in-law was a typical product of the Middle West, a kindly man, devoted to his daughter and, at that time, tolerant of his son-in-law. He was always 'figuring things out'; he couldn't figure out how I had managed to lose my way in the loop (Chicago's downtown centre); he figured out that if his wife went up to change for dinner at six she should be downstairs when the guests arrived at eight, and he figured out that if I bought some stock in a company of which he knew the President, I would make a thousand dollars in the space of two weeks. He had figured this out correctly, and I was most grateful to him.

# 12 America and beyond

The Depression was still a year away, and all shares, irrespective of their yield and prospects, continued to soar. It was a crazy world with everyone getting richer and richer, and confident that the boom would continue indefinitely. My knowledge of economics was extremely limited, but it seemed to me that a mentally retarded child of nine could foresee that with stocks standing at such inflated values, and still climbing, there must, sooner or later, be a day of reckoning. When I expressed this view at a luncheon with my father-in-law's business associates, I was told that although such a thing might happen in Britain, I must remember that I was now in the United States.

My chief recollections of Chicago are the piercing cold outdoors, and the sweltering heat indoors, a combination which resulted in my catching two streaming colds and a bad go of flu during my two-and-a-half-months' stay. My father-in-law's house was old but comfortable, though the central heating made a noise like an army of old men suffering from dyspepsia. Neither my father-in-law nor the plumber could 'figure out' how to stop it. Peter, Betty's 14-year-old brother, and I had become good friends when his father brought him over for the wedding; he was the youngest member of the family, but easily the most sophisticated.

I found it hard to believe that Lake Michigan, the world's largest lake, was not the open sea. It was often very rough, and presented an astonishing sight when the large waves froze solid. I have never known such extremes of temperature; the thermometer once fell 50 degrees in one hour.

For weeks on end I did not meet an Englishman, and it was a great joy when Sydney Emanuel arrived on a business trip. There was always plenty to do, with first-rate theatres and movies, but

I longed for London and racing, and at the end of a month I was homesick. Al Capone was the most powerful man in Chicago; both the Mayor, 'Big Bill' Thompson, and a large proportion of the police were in his pay. 'Big Bill' hated Britain, and had announced that he would like to punch King George on the nose.

Most of the killings were the result of gang warfare, and the only citizens who were bumped off were those who got in the way when a fight was in progress. Some sinister-looking types were pointed out to me in a night club as Capone's men, but they kept to themselves and the nearest I got to a fight was hearing a volley of shots several blocks away, when we were dining in my father-in-law's house.

I paid a visit to the stockyards, and was nauseated by the smell, and horrified by what I saw and heard. For several weeks I could not eat meat without recalling the terror of those unfortunate animals at the stench of blood, as they were being driven towards their executioners.

As a doctor, my father-in-law received a regular supply of Bourbon, which I came to like better than Scotch. I was never poisoned, although I drank in some strange places. I took the view that if the stuff didn't smell too bad it was O.K., and my sense of smell came to my rescue on one occasion. We met some of Betty's ex-boy friends at an ice hockey game, and one of them offered me a drink; its smell was appalling and I said 'No thanks'. He was partaking of it freely, with the result that he went blind that night. He recovered his sight, but there were numerous cases of people being blinded for life.

Back in England, mother Ball and Betty went house-hunting, and acquired a huge house in Hyde Park Square. Father Ball paid one half of the purchase price and I the other. Betty was very keen to have her baby at home, but the house was not ready. No young couple have ever been so overhoused, but I was too dumb to realise that my mother-in-law was making sure that there would always be a spare room. Although Betty and I were getting along reasonably well I had a feeling that we should not be occupying that large house for very long.

I have always laughed at people who fuss about the supernatural, but if ever there was a strange house it was the one in Hyde Park Square. I am not giving its number as it might upset the present tenants. Long before Betty and I parted I hated the house, and I subsequently learned that several of its former tenants had also had good reason for disliking it. When we were at Liverpool for the Grand National our 18-year-old housemaid was burnt to death. The poor girl was leaning over the fireplace, with her elbows on the mantelpiece, when her dress caught fire. On another occasion I heard screams and discovered the butler chasing his wife, who was the cook, around the kitchen, brandishing a knife. He was very drunk, and his nimble better half was in no serious danger. When I asked him for the knife he handed it over most politely.

I was invariably one of Francis Egerton's guests at the dinners given by the H. B. Club, prior to the big races. The food and drink were excellent, but the star event was the Selling Sweepstake. Tickets were £1 each, and after the draw the horses were sold by auction. You could buy the horse you had drawn for half price.

I always bought five tickets, but had never drawn a horse till the 1928 Derby, when I had a wonderful bit of luck in drawing a horse belonging to Mr Solly Joel, who was the auctioneer, and the outsider Felstead. As Mr Joel's horse fetched £130 I received £65, but Felstead, who had no form, was knocked down to my friend Price Harrison for only £30.

The dinner took place ten days before the Derby, and meanwhile Felstead won a good race at Hurst Park. Had that race taken place before the dinner Felstead would have fetched at least £200, so Price had picked up a wonderful bargain. He had not thought highly of Felstead's chance and had I had the pluck to bid £35 the ticket would have been mine for a paltry £17 10*s*. Ten days later Felstead, ridden by Harry Wragg, won the Derby, and Price collected approximately £2,200. What made it even worse was that I had had a big bet on Flamingo, who finished second. This was by far the most galling experience of my racing career, and I had no one to blame but myself.

Although my journalistic career was making little progress I was making money betting, and three years running showed a handsome profit. By that time Betty had left me for Gerald Wellesley, who was twelve years older than I was, and twenty-two years older than Betty.

In the summer of 1929 Geoffrey received a letter from the Western India Turf Club in Bombay, asking him if he knew a man with an extensive knowledge of racing to act as a stipendiary steward, and Geoffrey recommended me, as he always did when there was a job going.

We left our small son Robin in good hands, and having managed to let our vast house, we sailed from Marseilles on the *Viceroy of India* early in November. I still looked young for my age, and the Turf Club officials raised their eyebrows when they met us on the quay at Bombay. I proved equal to the job, however, and was asked to sign a five-year contract; but my roots were in England, and I knew that I should become acutely homesick after a few months.

There had been scores of people of our age on the crowded ship, either going out to take up jobs or to join their parents, and we had the whale of a time. But an incident stands out in my memory as the second biggest crime of my life, one of which I am still bitterly ashamed.

There was a large number of Indians on board, and a very friendly Parsee, having asked what Betty was going to wear at the Fancy Dress Ball, offered to lend her one of his wife's lovely saris. We thanked him profusely, and that was that, at least we thought it was. A couple of days later, over pre-lunch drinks, the subject of the Fancy Dress Ball came up, and I said that Betty had been lent a sari, at which a liverish-looking middle-aged man, who I think was a District Commissioner, exploded with rage. 'D'you mean to tell me, young feller m'lad, that you're going to dress up that lovely little wife of yours in a bloody wog's dress? Let me tell you that if you do you'll be blackballed from all the Clubs in Bombay and no decent white man will speak to you.' Instead of telling him to jump in the sea I gave in, and made the excuse that when I had accepted the offer of the sari I had not realised the strength of the colour bar. My Parsee friends were obviously deeply hurt when I made my lame excuse for not accepting their offer. I wonder if they realised that pressure had been brought to bear on me, and that as I was going to India for the first time I was in a difficult position.

We all bought sola topees at Port Said, as until well into the 'thirties exposure of the head to the tropical sun was believed to be fatal. Of the women, only Betty retained a semblance of attractiveness in this monstrous headgear, but she looked pretty in anything. The heat in that part of Bombay known as the Fort was terrific, but a wonderful piece of luck came our way when the Secretary of the Turf Club, 'Bunny' Hughes, fell ill and returned home. He and his wife shared a lovely bungalow on Malabar Hill with a couple called Hamilton, who invited us to take their place. Hamilton was a leading gynaecologist, and they had dozens of well-trained servants, who waited on us hand and foot, and we lived in the lap of luxury, high on the hill with a superb view over the bay.

The Towers of Silence (the Parsee funeral towers) were just along the road, and the vultures sat all day long, waiting for a corpse. They were alleged to take less than a minute to transform a corpse into a skeleton, but I never visited them at feeding time.

My days started as 6 a.m., when I drove to the racecourse in my second-hand car to supervise the early morning gallops. There was little for us to do, but it was good fun riding on the dew-covered course before the sun was high in the heavens. Except at holiday times, racing took place only on Saturdays, when there were usually nine or ten races. These were watched by the stipendiary stewards from crows' nests situated at strategic points.

Every morning after breakfast, we conducted a sort of orderly room at which defaulters were interviewed and dealt with, and complaints were heard. Three or four races each day were confined to Arab horses, the majority of which had travelled across the Arabian Sea in dhows. Their owners slept with their horses, and were usually penniless when they arrived in India.

They helped one another as far as they could, but when the money was not available they borrowed from the Club. They were honourable people and always paid their debts as soon as they had a winner. I found the work on race days well within my capabilities, and as nearly all the jockeys were either English or Australian there was no language difficulty; but when conversing with the Arabs I sometimes had to employ two interpreters, one to translate Arabic into Hindustani, and the other to translate Hindustani into English.

It was a good life, with first-rate bathing, four clubs, sailing, tennis, and any amount of parties. The racecourse, with modern stands, and its paddock ablaze with flowers, was more glamorous than any course at home.

Between Malabar Hill and the racecourse, however, lay one of the worst slums in Bombay, a city which has always been notorious for its squalor. The stench was appalling, and no one with the glimmer of a social conscience could remain unaffected by the misery all around one in this great sprawling city. Even in the more salubrious neighbourhoods there were beggars at every corner, and thousands without even a hovel in which to shelter slept on the pavements.

The British Raj had failed in its duty to provide for the subjects of the King-Emperor, and the pomp and ceremony, without which the Viceroy and the various Governors seemed unable to attend to their everyday functions, contrasted strangely with the hideous poverty through which they drove in their state coaches, preceded by a bodyguard of black-bearded, scarlet-clad Sikhs, mounted on horses as magnificent as themselves.

Of the Bombay clubs only the Willingdon opened its doors to Indians. The ruling Princes entertained the British aristocracy in lavish style, and the British returned this hospitality by barring them from their clubs.

The most lavish party I attended was that given in his Bombay house by the Maharajah of Rajpipla, at which we ate off gold plate. The Governor of Bombay, Sir Frederick Sykes, arrived, preceded by his bodyguard, and was treated exactly as if he were the King.

Nearly all the guests were celebrities in their own line of business, and I am quite certain that I was invited only because I had a pretty wife. We all drank an immense amount of champagne, and our host made a memorable speech. In the years to come 'Pip' and I became close friends and I dined with him at the Savoy on the evening after his Windsor Lad had won the Derby at Epsom. His son, who is also known as 'Pip', is now one of our most respected and enthusiastic owners, and makes a habit of winning the jackpot.

Civil disobedience was making life difficult for motorists as, in response to Gandhi's appeal, Hindus, wearing white Gandhi caps, were lying down in all the main thoroughfares, hoping the police would come along and arrest them before someone ran over them. I found it impossible to get a clear idea of what it was all about at the time, as the British became incoherent with rage at the mention of Gandhi's name, and the Indians whom I knew were content with the *status quo*, and in consequence were often more British than the British.

Although I did not proclaim the fact in the Yacht Club, and other Empire strongholds, I was on the side of the Indians, taking the view that if the British had done their job even reasonably well, millions of unfortunate Indians would not be living under unspeakable conditions, and dying of starvation.

The Indian Princes accepted the white sahibs' snubs in barring them from their clubs, in the knowledge that, if India was given self-government, they would be stripped of their power and some of their fabulous wealth. For generations, the Princes had been scratching the backs of the Viceroy and his Governors, and vice versa, while India starved.

Tony Ashley (Lord Ashley), ex-husband of Sylvia, and my friend from private-school days, was A.D.C. to the Governor and in consequence we spent a lot of time at Government House. I enjoyed race days immensely, though of course I was not allowed to bet, and I took my responsible job very seriously. It was the first job of which I had made a real success. The longer, however, I stayed in India, the stronger was my realisation that a year was all I could take of this unhappy country, and I began counting the days until the end of the racing season, when I could go home on leave.

Betty's beauty had created a stir in London; in Bombay, where the standard was not so high, she was a sensation, but our marriage was disintegrating.

We travelled home on the *Ranpura* in late March 1930. All our friends were either returning home on leave, or had come to see us off, and we had a big party on board. Visitors were ordered ashore at midday, but we did not sail till evening. The heat was suffocating in Bombay docks, and I spent the afternoon stripped naked, gasping for air and reading Evelyn Waugh's *Vile Bodies*, which seemed appropriate.

We disembarked at Suez before dawn, and drove across the desert to Cairo, where we spent the day, catching the ship again at Port Said. After the heat of the Red Sea the morning desert air seemed piercingly cold, so much so that we all began to fidget. Our dragoman, noticing our discomfort, halted the cavalcade of cars, and we all disembarked. On this wide expanse of desert, any form of concealment was out of the question, but our tactful dragoman informed us that the ladies would find the view magnificent on the right of the cars, while the gentlemen would find a similar view on the left side.

In our enthusiasm for the Tutankhamen museum, the Mosque of Mohamed Ali, the Pyramids, the Sphinx and Shepheard's Hotel, Betty's and my differences were temporarily forgotten, and we spent a wonderful day. On our return we found our small son in the best of health, but the rift between us was too wide for any chance of reconciliation. I began to spend all my days on the racecourse, and Betty, I assume, spent her time with Wellesley.

# *13 Racing between the wars*

Racing is undoubtedly the most esoteric of all the sports which provide enjoyment for those who are willing to pay to watch people competing for something more tangible than honour and glory. Although no high degree of scholarship is required to master the principles of horse racing it is a fact that while laymen can, and often do, write entertainingly on football, boxing, cricket and tennis, they almost invariably err over some technicality early in their articles on racing.

Racing is the only sport known to me in which you can follow all the rules and yet arrive at the wrong conclusion. A man can design a motor car which he knows will do 150 miles per hour. Someone, of course, may design a car that will do 160 miles per hour, but he can be sure that, provided those responsible for its construction have carried out their work according to his specifications, he will own a very fast motor car. Those responsible for the mechanics of racing are the breeders; and they have no such assurance. They may mate the Derby winner with the winner of the Oaks and the result may be a dud, while those who allow others, with a greater knowledge of breeding than themselves, to buy them a yearling for 20,000 guineas, may see no return for their money. The same uncertainty applies to betting. I have seen every member of the field, in every Derby, in its previous races, and spent hours weighing up the value of their respective performances against one another. I have made a careful study of the pedigrees and have determined which horses are likely to be seen at their best over 1½ miles, and which are likely to find the distance too short and which too long. I have been in constant touch with the jockeys and trainers, and may have watched some of the home gallops. But with all this data, I cannot guarantee that my selection will defeat the horse your wife has picked with a pin, nor would I dream of attempting to deter her from backing it. Having attempted to forecast the winner of thousands of races, big and small, on behalf of my readers, I am thankful to say that people soon forgive one for tipping them a loser, but that no sin is comparable with that of dissuading someone from backing a winner for which he or she had expressed a fancy; and the longer the price, the bigger the sin.

The serious side of racing concerns the breeding of horses, the object being, of course, to produce a horse which will run faster or stay better – preferably both – than his opponents. The process of deduction which I and my fellow journalists have employed in order to find the winner of the Derby is mere guesswork compared with the study of pedigrees, blood lines, past performances, confirmation, stamina indexes, fertility records, just to mention a few of the problems which face a breeder in the search for a suitable husband for one of his mares.

A knowledgeable breeder once told me that after several lean years he bred a top-notcher as the result of one of his stallions jumping over a high fence into a paddock where some of his mares were grazing. Although your wife's pin and your stallion's choice may hit the jackpot from time to time, a slapdash approach to racing problems must inevitably lead to disaster. No rules are infallible, but it is only by faithful observance of them that the best results can be achieved.

Racing was once referred to in a court of law as 'a common highway whereon brilliant nobodies travel to association with the nobility, and sometimes even with Royalty'. It cannot be denied that people have become owners for social advancement, but the vast majority of men and women take up racing, either as owners or merely as spectators, because they find that they derive a greater thrill from it than from any other sport. All the way down the social scale, however, racing is regarded as a status symbol. The man with recently acquired riches derives much satisfaction from rubbing shoulders with members of the peerage, while the patrons of the silver ring are referred to by their colleagues in the office or factory as racing men, which carries more prestige, unfairly in my opinion, than that of football fans.

Ownership is the most expensive method of obtaining social recognition, and now that money is so widely distributed there is no guarantee that the possession of a classic winner will ensure an introduction to those whose names figure in *Burke's Peerage* and *Debrett*, and of whom many are now so impoverished that their colours are rarely seen in public.

As I have already stated, my own enthusiasm for racing was born of my father's belief that the road to ruin began at Newmarket and ended up at Doncaster via Epsom and Ascot, and was nurtured by my elder brothers, who in my eyes could do no wrong. Having been educated at a school at which titles were two a penny, and where the son of the reigning monarch's only claim to fame was that he had an unusually small head and had to have a top hat specially made for him, social advancement was certainly not one of the reasons for the lure of the turf as far as I was concerned, though snobbishmess did enter into it. I had always been a hero-worshipper and a hero-worshipper easily becomes a celebrity snob, an idolater who longs to be identified with his idols. Jockeys are possessed of glamour in inverse ratio to their size, while they enjoy considerable success with the opposite sex. I longed for the day when I would be in a position to call those mercurial little men by their Christian names, and exchange a word or two with a leading rider in full view of the denizens of the paddock, as he made his way from the weighing room to the parade ring.

The first jockey to become my friend was Jack Leach, who had ridden winners for Geoffrey, and through him I met his elder brother Felix, and his younger brother Chubb. Felix soon became too heavy for a jockey, but as a trainer he was an instantaneous success, and it was for his stable and Jack Leader's, for whom Jack Leach also rode, that I first executed commissions.

As I spent so much of my time in the company of jockeys, I was, I was told unofficially, suspected of betting for them; I was never interrogated on the subject and on a number of occasions I may have done so unwittingly. A trainer, and occasionally an owner, would ask me to put any sum from £10 to £500 on a horse, and a portion of this sum may well have been on behalf of the jockey, though this was no concern of mine. So far as I can recall, I only put money on a horse, on behalf of a jockey, on three occasions, and once I laid one.

Steve Donoghue was one of the greatest riders that ever lived, but off a horse he was a mug. He was champion jockey on ten consecutive occasions, and he won the Epsom Derby four years out of five and two wartime substitute Derbies at Newmarket; but he would take the advice of anyone who professed he knew a good thing, even if it was running in the same race in which he was riding a fancied horse. Time and again he would ride the winner of a race in which he had backed another horse.

We travelled down to Newmarket together towards the end of his career, Steve having caught the train, as he always did, by the skin of his teeth. We had both been to parties the night before, and Steve said, 'What about a hair of the dog?' It seemed an excellent idea, and over a bottle of champagne we discussed every aspect of racing till we were approaching Newmarket, when Steve asked me if I knew a winner, adding that he had only one ride and that it had no chance. 'Yes, Steve, I think I know three,' I replied, 'but they will be at very short prices.' I told him their names, and having glanced at the paper he said, 'I think you are right, I'll have a £10 treble with you.' I lost him in the crowd and leaping into a taxi with four others, did not see him again. They all won. On the following Monday at Birmingham I handed him a cheque for approximately £60. He looked astonished, and when I reminded him of his bet in the train, he gave me one of those smiles which had stood him in such good stead throughout his long career, and thanked me as he pocketed the cheque. That was the only financial transaction I ever had with Steve, though we were friends for many years, but those who had betted for him in the past told me that, had one of the three horses been beaten, it would have taken me quite a while to collect the £10. In his own eyes, Steve Donoghue could do no wrong, but if another jockey's conduct had matched up to his own he would have been horrified. I am referring in particular to his treatment of his employers and fellow jockeys. A contract was just a piece of paper as far as he was concerned, and, even though an owner had spent a large sum of money in order to retain his services for the season, he thought himself at liberty to ride any horse that took his fancy in the Derby. He also had no compunction in approaching the owner of a horse he wanted to ride, despite the fact that another jockey had been engaged, but such was his reputation at Epsom that he usually got away with it. Owners were surprisingly lenient with him, but I cannot imagine that a jockey today would be permitted to ride rough-shod over his employers and fellow jockeys in the way that Steve did forty years ago.

Jack Leach, a constant companion of mine when we were young, and one of the straightest jockeys that ever lived, rang me up one morning in 1929, and asked me to take £250 to £10 about Trigo for the Derby for him. 'I rode him in a gallop this morning,' he said, 'against good class opposition, and he won it like a great horse and I have been booked to ride him in the Classics. Stable jockey Michael Beary will have to ride the Aga Khan's horse Voleur, so it's a lucky ride for me.' Jack went on say that he would give a dinner if he won the Derby, and that the £250 – I put on Jack's £10 and a fiver for myself at 25/1 – would pay for it. There was no ante-post market before the Guineas in those days, but I had a good bet on Trigo, only to see him fade at the Bushes and finished unplaced. Jack was terribly disappointed and said he didn't stay a mile, so he had no chance in the Derby (1½ miles). It certainly looked like that, but I should have ridiculed the idea. He was bred to stay any distance, and the reason for his collapse was that he had been taken off his legs by two very fast horses in Mr Jinks and Cragadour in the early stages of the race. The best stayer in the world can be beaten at the end of five furlongs if he is ridden all out from flagfall.

Anyhow, Jack begged off Trigo, who had gone out in the betting to 40/1 for the Derby, in which he was ridden by Joe Marshall, one of Stanley Wootton's apprentices. He had gone well in a gallop over the full Derby distance, and came down to 33/1, but I had long since written off my bet, and so had Gerald Wellesley, who, on my information, had backed him to win £1,000. In the race Trigo was always going well amongst the leaders, and drew out some way from home to win very comfortably. Jack Leach was heartbroken and was never quite the same man again. He could not even raise a smile when I handed him my cheque for £250. The disasters for which one has only oneself to blame are always the hardest to bear.

The prize for stupidity, however, went to the man who on hearing I had had a fiver on the winner at 25/1 said what a pity I hadn't waited till after the Guineas, when I could have got 40/1.

Felix Leach jun. died at the early age of twenty-eight. He had been told that he had a grumbling appendix, and on the Monday following the final meeting of the season at Manchester, where we had a good touch on a grand old warrior, suitably named Tommy Atkins, who time and again came to our rescue when things were looking black, he drove himself to the local hospital at Newmarket and asked them to cut it out. What went wrong I never discovered, but I was racing at Kempton on the following Thursday when I heard of his death.

Chubb, who six years earlier had won the Chester Cup with 6 stone 4 in the saddle but had put on weight rapidly, took over the stable with Jack as first jockey. When Felix's two horses, an old selling-plater called Wearing A Crown and a two-year-old called No Argument came up for sale, Bill McGowan, Victor Malcolm and I bought them, and as my partners did not want their families to know that they had become owners, the horses ran in my name and colours, black, with pale blue sleeves, and black and pale blue hooped cap. The first occasion on which we fancied Wearing A Crown was in a selling race at Redcar, a very humble meeting before Major Leslie Petch took command and transformed it into one of the best appointed courses in the country. There was no photo-finish in those days, and I thought it was a dead heat, but Jack had ridden the race of his life to win by the shortest of heads. There are few thrills comparable with seeing your colours carried to victory for the first time, but as he had started at 13/8 and we had to buy him in, the profit, divided amongst the owners, was negligible. I nevertheless felt as proud as if I had won the Derby. He won again for us at Pontefract, but had little chance in two subsequent races, in which he was ridden by his owner, whose colours he carried.

I had ridden all my life, but there is a world of difference between riding out hunting and riding in a flat race on a small saddle with my stirrup leathers four or five holes shorter than I had ever ridden before. I was also very unfit, even as amateur riders go, and Wearing A Crown's pounding action at forty miles per hour resulted in my running out of breath with two furlongs of the five furlongs race still to be run. I finished third on him at Lewes, and when I weighed in I overheard a woman say to the man with her, 'Hark at that poor horse, he's broken-winded', to which he replied 'Don't be so daft, that's not the horse, it's the bloody jockey.' It was after I had ridden him a couple of times in public that my good friend Geoff Harbord wrote in the *Tatler*: 'I hear that since Wearing A Crown's owner has taken to riding him in races, the horse's name is to be changed to Carrying A Cross.'

Despite my failures, the late Fred Winter, father of the greatest steeplechase jockey of all time, and himself a splendid jockey in his day, asked me to ride a horse of his in a 1½-mile race at Lewes. In order to do so I had to motor the 500-mile drive from Biarritz in a single day, leaving my car in Paris and flying on to London. When I got to Lewes, Fred told me that my mount had been stopped in his work and he needed the race. Having been second as far as the straight, he took the lead. With a hundred yards to go, I thought a miracle was about to happen, but he tired close home, and we finished third. Fred was delighted and said he was sure to win next time out, which he did, but with a professional jockey on his back. Our other purchase, No Argument, was an expensive failure. I have never discovered why a horse which declines to exert itself should be called a dog; this is an insult to the most faithful animal in the world, who always aims to please. But No Argument was well named in that he always gave way to the other horses. On the home gallops he had co-operated so amiably with his jockey that Chubb thought that he was sure to win a humble race at Yarmouth. But No Argument did not put up even a token resistance and finished fifteenth of the seventeen runners, of which one was lame. I cannot remember exactly what happened to him, but I think someone gave us £20 for him, and we considered him well sold.

Several of us used to share a house near the course for the St Leger meeting at Doncaster, and in 1930 I had rooms with three trainers and three jockeys. One of the jockeys was riding what he thought was a certainty in the first race on the final day, but when I arrived on the course I saw him looking wild-eyed, still dressed in a lounge suit. He was almost incoherent with rage as he told me that the horse's trainer had informed him that he would not be needed as he had engaged Dick Perryman. 'I've dropped him out three times, and last time out I had to strangle him, and risk my bloody livelihood, and now the old bastard jocks me off.' (Which translated means that he had ridden the horse three times, and had not tried to win. On the final occasion it had required a feat of strength to prevent him winning, and by so doing he ran the risk of being warned off. To be 'jocked off' means to be replaced by another jockey.) 'Will you do me a favour,' he went on, 'and put £100 on for me and have a good bet yourself. Get in quick and pinch the old bastard's market', he instructed me. By accepting the price offered when the betting opened I should probably get better odds than the agent who was doing the stable commission. I got 3/1 to £175, the extra £75 being £25 each for two friends, for whom I often betted, and £25 for myself. The horse started at 13/8 and won easily. Those friendly rivals, Mr William Hill and Messrs Ladbroke, are millionaires, owning vast blocks of office buildings. They still live in great luxury, despite Mr Hill's comparison of himself to an orange from which the juice has been extracted, by means of the betting levy and the betting tax, though anyone who looks less like a squeezed orange than Mr Hill I have yet to meet. Mr Hill and Messrs Ladbroke do lose occasionally, but do not be too depressed on Mr Hill's account when he tells you that he lost £200,000 over the winner, as he may have omitted to tell you that he won £500,000 over the horses who failed to win and those who did not even start; you lose your money over a non-runner if you have accepted what appeared to be an absurdly generous price, when you saw the quotation in your morning paper. No matter whether the winner starts at 10/1 on or 100/1 against, the Tote gets its cut just the same. The principle is the same as in a casino, where the punters have only to play *chemin de fer* long enough for them all to go broke.

I gave up betting shortly after the war, on account of the fact that I was churning out at least a column and half daily for the *Sporting Chronicle*, and three articles a week, which were syndicated among the firm's provincial papers, and a Sunday article for the *Empire News*. Having used up a ball-point pen each week, I should have looked pretty stupid if I'd been out of pocket at the end of it. The only way in which one can hope to make money betting is by studying the market, which can only be achieved by hanging round the rails that separate Tattersall's ring from the Members' Enclosure, and if I had done that, I should have missed my deadline six days a week. Two tasks at the same time can be successfully discharged only by a genius, and I have never regarded myself in that light.

Today it seems to me that every bookmaker has his card so well marked that they are better informed about the horses than the owners themselves. I have worked dozens of commissions, but the whole structure of the market has changed to such an extent that I would have no idea how to go about working one today.

Having established, beyond all reasonable doubt, that the dice are loaded against the punter, no matter whether he bets with the bookmakers or the Tote, I must admit that my sole venture as a bookmaker was disastrous, though I knew the horse I laid wasn't trying, and even if he had been, would have had no chance. Fair Weather Jack, trained by Felix Leach jun and ridden by Chubb Leach, was running in the first race, a selling plate at Gatwick, and on the journey down I asked Chubb whether he was fancied. 'Be your age,' he replied. 'He hasn't got a cat in hell's chance of beating Linkman. He meets him at level weights today, and in a selling handicap at Pontefract next week he is set to receive 21 lbs. My instructions are to give him a nice easy race.' When betting opened Linkman was a 7/4 on chance as I had expected, while Fair Weather Jack, to my surprise, was at

3/1 against. Those odds were responsible for my having a brain wave, which I explained to Chubb as he made his way from the weighing room to mount his non-trier in the paddock. As Fair Weather Jack was at 3/1, most bookmakers would be pleased to back him with me, if I laid them 7/2. I therefore proposed to lay £70 to £20 against him if Chubb thought it was a good idea, which he did, adding, 'That's the easiest twenty quid we'll ever pick up.' All went according to plan as far as the bend into the straight, where two of Fair Weather Jack's seven opponents ran so wide that they were out of the race. There still seemed no cause for worry as the odds-on favourite was going easily in the lead, four or five lengths in front of Fair Weather Jack. But two furlongs from home it happened. The favourite faltered, and in the course of half a dozen strides he was transformed from a conquering hero into a hopeless cripple. There was only one thing for Chubb to do, and he did it with a flourish, giving Fair Weather Jack a kick in the belly with his heels to draw away and win by four lengths. My sad story does not end there. Immediately he had weighed in, a white-faced Chubb emerged from the weighing room and told me to buy him in if he went for less than 300 guineas. I went up to 320 guineas, but a local trainer, impressed by the way he had won, not realising that he had beaten nothing, was determined to buy him, and I had to give him best. Fair Weather Jack's owner, Mr Harvey, had only recently joined the stable, and on being told his horse had no chance had not been present. On reading in the evening paper that his horse had won, having started second favourite, he assumed that he had been put away, and without waiting for an explanation, moved all his horses to another trainer. Fair Weather Jack failed to win a race for his new owner, and of all the many thousand races I have witnessed I think that this race at Gatwick required the least winning.

It was also at Gatwick that I unwittingly became involved, for the only time in my life, with dope. On the first day of the two-day meeting Charlie Chapman asked me if I would do some business for him on the following day; to which I agreed, and arranged to meet him after the first race. Charlie was training for my brother Geoffrey, for whom he had been very successful, and was regarded as one of the up-and-coming trainers. He asked me to put him £450 on Fenimore Cooper, a horse he trained for the American owner, Mr Victor Emmanuel. This I agreed to do, but I pointed out that his horse would be favourite in a small field and that the market at Gatwick in August was very weak.

Few bookmakers, if any, would have accepted such a sum in one hand, so I gave £150 of the bet to a professional backer, and between us we averaged just over 6/4, with 11/10 the best price when we left the ring. The race was to be run over the straight mile and it was not possible to see from the stand exactly what was happening, but I saw Dick Perryman had dismounted from the favourite, who was being examined by a vet. The race started without him, and I learned with relief that he had not come under starter's orders, so we had not lost our money. Dick Perryman told me that, on approaching the start, Fenimore Cooper had become 'set fast' (unable to use his limbs), but no one at the time suspected that he had been doped. A motor horse box collected him from where he was standing in a semi-paralysed state, and that was the last I ever saw of him.

The following spring Don Pat, also trained by Charlie Chapman, was found to be doped after he had won a race, and Charlie Chapman was warned off. I have no doubt that Fenimore Cooper had also been doped, though whether by a sedative to make him lose, or by a stimulant to make him run faster than ever before, which had worked the wrong way, I have no idea. I have never wavered in my view that Charlie Chapman was innocent, and that he was the victim of his 'friends', a number of whom did not exactly inspire confidence.

Throughout my career it has been my experience that 'easy money' invariably proves to be a snare and a delusion. It is the ability of the unbeatable to achieve the impossible which constitutes the 'glorious uncertainty' of the turf.

The most confident tip I ever received, however, was in connection with the Boat Race. One evening in the West End, I met my cousin, Gully Nickalls, one of the greatest oarsmen of his own or any other time, and over a drink he asked the rhetorical question, 'Would you like to pick up a tenner?'

'You don't mean you'll know the result beforehand, Gully?' I asked him.

'Oh, yes, I know the result all right', he answered me, as if he was in the habit of backing winners after the 'All Right' flag had gone up. I am not easily shocked, but I had known Gully since we were at Cothill together as a man of the highest integrity, and I told him I would be no party to his ramp. 'You've got it all wrong, old boy', he answered. 'It's Oxford, I've been coaching them and they're a great crew. It simply won't be a race, but those crazy bookmakers are only asking for odds of 5/2. All you have to do is to lay £25 to £10 on Oxford and on Monday morning you'll receive a cheque for £10.' I took his advice.

On our way to Hurst Park, on Boat Race Day, Geoffrey and I took up a position on the towpath, about a mile from the start, and as they passed us, Cambridge were leading by four lengths, and were drawing farther ahead with a long effortless stroke, while the Oxford crew, already showing signs of distress, were shipping quite a lot of water. Geoffrey, who was a great one for looking on the bright side, said, 'Perhaps they'll do better when they settle down', at which a near-by spectator exclaimed 'God forbid: if the poor perishers settle any lower they'll drown.' On arrival at Hurst Park, I learned that Cambridge had won by ten lengths.

Day after day, year after year, my colleagues and I endeavoured to find the winners of races in which there might be anything up to fifty runners. A highly paid and extremely knowledgeable official, known as the handicapper, had spent many hours on these races in an endeavour to make the entire field run a dead heat. He has yet to accomplish this feat, but he invariably contrived to make our task as difficult as possible, and often half a dozen horses finished within a few inches of one another.

After one of these races, friends would sometimes ask me whether I had tipped the winner, knowing perfectly well that I hadn't, and when I confessed my failure, gave me the sort of look which parents give their children when they have failed their 'O' levels for the third time. Although Gully's inside information cost me £25, I think it was money well spent, in that the memory of it has brought consolation to me when my selections have been wide of the mark and disgruntled punters have written to the Editor suggesting I should be better employed tipping a four-letter fertiliser out of a cart.

Geoffrey and I, having broadcast the St Leger of 1927, were not again employed by the BBC until 1937, when we were signed up to broadcast the Derby, Oaks, Ascot Gold Cup, Eclipse Stakes, Cesarewitch, and Cambridgeshire. Racing broadcasts were still in their infancy, and the BBC tried out several applicants for the job before reverting to the Gilbeys, whose St Leger broadcast had received a verdict of 'Very accurate but very dull'. Compared with Peter O'Sullevan and Tony Cooke today, we were very amateurish, but we were novices at a far more nerve-racking job than many people think. Race reading today is even more difficult than it was in pre-war days. With the wider distribution of wealth there are twice as many owners, while there are not more than a dozen owners with a string of over ten. Even so, the Derby is one of the easiest races to read, as the commentator is familiar with most of the colours; on the other hand, how Peter and Tony manage to rattle off the names of twenty-five horses running in colours they are seeing for the first time in a handicap in the North, or in a hunter's chase anywhere, I shall never know. What I do know is that their fluency is only achieved by hours of work, committing the colours to memory.

On the first day of the Epsom meeting of 1937 the dress rehearsal for the Derby passed off without incident. Our box was at the top of the highest stand, and the colours were plainly visible throughout. I therefore went to bed that night in a happier frame of mind than for many days previously. I cannot pretend that I ever enjoyed broadcasting; immediately we were shut in that little box, I broke into a sweat at the thought of what would happen if I shouted out what I believe to be considered the rudest of the four-letter words. As an Ensign I had suffered from a similar attack of the horrors at the thought of what would happen to me if I dropped the Colour in Buckingham Palace Yard.

We took it in turns to describe the parade and the topography of the course, and Geoffrey described the start, handing over to me after approximately three furlongs. The light was perfect and

Renardo (Steve Donoghue), in the well-known colours of Sir Victor Sassoon, was leading, when all of a sudden they disappeared as effectively as if the earth had opened up and swallowed them. On the opening day, what few buses there were had been parked on the far side of the track, but on Derby Day they had been parked also along the inside rails, and for the best part of a furlong – it seemed like ten miles – the horses were obscured from view. What I should have done was to repeat the order of running, before they disappeared; but I panicked and for several seconds there was dead silence. There is a quality in broadcasting known as 'commentator's selective silence', but this was not an instance of it. Geoffrey took over in the straight, and his brilliant description of the closing stages of an exciting race more than atoned for my incompetence in the face of adversity.

The Derby is a race apart from all others, in that each yearly event bears its own stamp, unrelated to any preceding Derby in a race run for the first time in 1780. I have missed only three Derbies since 1920, and every race is clearly etched in my mind, though I derive much pleasure from refreshing my memory from Roger Mortimer's *History of the Derby* in which every detail of our greatest race, from its inception, is described.

The field for the 1937 event was slightly substandard, and the winner Midday Sun was bought by Mrs G. B. Miller for 2,000 guineas in partnership with her mother Mrs L. M. Talbot, who thus became the first women owners to win the Epsom Derby, though Lady James Douglas had won a wartime event at Newmarket with the immortal Gainsborough, paternal grandsire of Midday Sun. The winner was trained at Kingsclere by Fred Butters, brother of the Aga Khan's trainer Frank Butters, and was ridden by the voluble Irishman Michael Beary, of whom I shall have more to say in a later chapter. The most astonishing feature of this Derby was that, but for the intervention of Midday Sun, the race would have been won by the 100/1 chance Sandsprite, also owned by a lady, Mrs Nagle. I can still hear Geoffrey's 'Here comes the unconsidered Sandsprite' as this extraordinary horse came with a long run to take second place $1\frac{1}{2}$ lengths behind Midday Sun, but how he managed to finish in front of nineteen opponents will forever remain a mystery. He was never to win a race of any sort, despite the fact that he descended the social scale after his great effort at Epsom.

I have far more pleasant recollections of the Oaks, run two days later. Although Steve had monopolised the Derby in the 'twenties he had never won the Oaks, and he was retiring at the end of the season. His mount was Sir Victor Sassoon's Exhibitionnist, who had won the Thousand Guineas and appeared to possess an outstanding chance. Like Midday Sun, she was by Solario, and had run the Derby winner to three-quarters of a length, giving him 6 lbs in the Free Handicap. But a few days before the race she went sexually amiss and it was touch and go whether she would run. I was doing my diary for the *Evening Standard*, which necessitated my being on Epsom Downs by seven o'clock each morning to see the horses canter, and phone a story to catch the lunch edition.

On the morning of the Oaks I was lucky in running into Steve Donoghue on the Downs; he told me that his mount had fully recovered and would win, while Bobby Jones, a fine jockey and a great friend of mine, said 'Lord Astor's Flashpoint, in the Ebbisham Stakes, is a bigger certainty than Exhibitionnist.' Both fillies were trained at Manton by Joe Lawson, for whom Bobby Jones also rode. Geoffrey had caught a bad cold and could hardly speak, so it was up to me to prove that my Derby effort was too bad to be true. There were no buses in the way this time and the race was the answer to a broadcaster's prayer. Exhibitionnist took a clear lead early in the straight, and went right away to win by four lengths. I had had a good bet on her and doubled her with Flashpoint. Nobody could have thought my commentary of the closing stages of the race lacking in enthusiasm, but whether it was strictly impartial is open to doubt. Flashpoint had a very light weight, so the small apprentice Wally Wing, son of the Irish jockey, Morny Wing, was engaged to ride her. The steep hill down to Tattenham Corner has proved the undoing of many a good horse, and Flashpoint made the descent like a very old lady going downstairs; she became unbalanced and lost lengths. Her prospects appeared hopeless, but Wing, riding with the confidence of Steve himself, got her balanced again in the straight, with the result that she got up in the last stride to win by a head, with a short head separating second and third. Not till the 13-year-old Lester Piggott appeared on the scene after the war did I see an apprentice ride with the insolent confidence that young Wing displayed on this occasion. Eighteen months later, when riding in India, he caught pneumonia and died. Had he lived I am convinced he would have become a great jockey.

I had had a bad week, but I backed two more winners on Oaks Day and not only got out but showed a handsome profit on the meeting.

On the first day of the Royal Ascot meeting, I was the cause of the Ascot Authority finding itself in a dilemma from which it was rescued by the ingenuity of one of its junior officials, a mere stripling of around sixty, who kept his head in the face of what seemed an insoluble problem. John Lotbinière, head of outside broadcasting, had asked us to meet him at the Ascot office at 1 p.m. in order to collect the necessary passes and make arrangements for a rehearsal that afternoon. On our arrival we found a number of officials in a huddle, and I got a nasty feeling that they were talking about me, and that what they were saying was not 100 per cent in my favour. I could only hear snatches of their conversation, but I distinctly heard the word 'divorce'. By this time my marriage to Betty had broken up, and the outcome was that an elderly gentleman, whom I took to be the Clerk of the Course, announced 'I regret that we are unable to issue a voucher to Mr Quintin Gilbey, and I can only assume that you were unacquainted with the fact that he has not only been divorced but has subsequently been cited as co-respondent, or you would not have made this application.' It appeared that the commentator's box was in the Royal Enclosure, from which I had been debarred as the result of 'behaving like a gentleman' at the Grosvenor Hotel (a story which I tell later). As I had a contract with the BBC, which I had no intention of letting them break, and Geoffrey, loyal as ever, would not accept a replacement, we were at an impasse till the aforementioned underling suggested 'Why don't we issue him a footman's badge?' With a sigh of relief, sounding like an escape of air from a punctured tyre, they chanted in unison 'A footman's badge, that's the answer.'

Her Majesty's servants who guard the gates of the Royal Enclosure, clad in green velvet coats and breeches, with top hats decorated with gold braid, are well known to all race-goers, but never in my wildest dreams had I pictured myself masquerading as one of them. My disguise, however, only extended to their badge of office, a scarlet leather disc, several inches in diameter, engraved with gold letters. In the distance it resembled the ten-mille plaque I had once been handed in the Sporting Club at Monte Carlo, on one of the few occasions I had run a bank more than twice. As it reached from the point of my left shoulder half-way across my chest, it created as much comment as did some of the monstrous hats then in fashion.

My emergence from the Ascot office as a member of the noble order of footmen, was, however, by no means the end of our troubles. In order to reach the glorified rabbit-hutch from which we were to do our stuff, we had to cross a narrow passageway with a sheer drop of goodness knows how many feet on either side. I have referred to my terror of heights, but compared with Geoffrey I am a steeplejack. When we arrived at this hazard he declared that nothing would induce him to take it. Eventually, however, he was blindfolded, and with Lotbinière pulling, and another man pushing, we at last installed him in the hutch. Thirty years later, I saw a reluctant horse manœuvred into the starting stalls by precisely the same methods.

The favourite, Precipitation, won the Gold Cup very convincingly, and this was the easiest race of all to broadcast, though I doubt whether we succeeded in making a dull race sound very exciting.

Directly after the race I was shorn of my footman's badge in much the same way as an officer is deprived of his rank and medals after being convicted by court martial of some particularly shameful offence. The Eclipse Stakes winner Boswell was, like Precipitation, trained by Captain Cecil Boyd-Rochfort, but this was not one of our happiest efforts. For some reason they got us on the air six minutes early, and the race started six minutes late, so for twelve minutes we had to talk about the six runners, a task which would defy the combined efforts of Peter O'Sullevan, Clive Graham, Julian Wilson, Tony Cooke, and John Rickman, much less those of the brothers Gilbey. Boswell had gone down to post very short, and we decided that this would prove a good talking point. If we said once that a horse who was in such obvious discomfort could not possibly win we said it half a dozen times. At long last they were off, and it only remains for me to say that Boswell, ridden by Rufus Beasley, won easily.

We did not broadcast the St Leger, and perhaps it was just as well, as I had napped the winner Chulmleigh, who started at 18/1, having backed him at 28/1 before I knew that Gordon Richards would be available. His trainer Tommy Hogg, with whom I watched the race, said that I deafened him with my shouting when Chulmleigh took the lead close home to beat Lord Derby's Fair Copy by half a length, with Midday Sun three-quarters of a length away third. Midday Sun was most unlucky, Michael Beary told me, but when you stand to win a lot of money over a horse, as I did over Chulmleigh, you only have eyes for him, for which reason racing journalists should not bet.

I had only recently joined the *Daily Sketch*, and it was a wonderful piece of luck to give a long-priced winner of a big race so early in my career with the paper. The sports editor was L. V. Manning, father of Jim Manning, whose articles in the *Daily Mail* are now so widely read. Manning senior was regarded as a difficult man to please, but after the victory of Chulmleigh I could do no wrong, and even after the prestige of this success had worn off I invariably found him helpful and understanding of the problems entailed in writing a daily column.

The Hon. George Lambton, brother of Lord Durham, for whom he won the Oaks with Beam in 1926, was one of the most distinguished trainers of all time. He twice won the Derby for Lord Derby: with Sansovino in 1924 and Hyperion in 1933. He possessed such an uncanny knowledge of horses that those who knew him best declared that he could tell what a horse was thinking. He was also a polished writer, and his book *Men and Horses I have Known,* published shortly after the First World War, is regarded as a text book on the subject of racing, and was reprinted only six years ago.

I did not know him well, but on the few occasions when I interviewed him I found him most courteous and helpful. His widow still races regularly, and breeds many winners at her stud. Their son, Teddy, a friend of mine since his early years, has inherited much of his father's skill and understanding of horses. He has yet to train a classic winner though David Jack, trained by him, finished third to Sodium and Charlottown in the St Leger in 1966.

Fred Darling had few characteristics in common with George Lambton, except his skill as a trainer. Small of stature, he was a dynamic figure, darting around his stables at Beckhampton and the various racecourses like a ferret in search of a rabbit. Nothing missed his eagle eye, and he was a stern disciplinarian. He was quick-tempered, and was feared by those members of the press who asked him what he described as damn' fool questions.

I must have been fortunate in my choice of words when I interrogated him, for we became friends, and I was once able to render him a small service, which he promptly repaid. I was riding on Newmarket Heath before breakfast, watching the various strings going through their paces, when I met Fred, who was on foot. He was scarlet in the face with fury as he pointed out three of his horses getting smaller in the distance. The lads riding them were unfamiliar with that vast stretch of heath, and were heading for the wrong starting point. He told me where he had intended them to go, and I galloped up to them and explained where they had gone wrong. A few days later I found myself next to Fred on the members' stand at Gatwick. I made a point of never addressing a trainer before a race in which he had a horse running, but in response to my nod he thanked me for helping him out on Newmarket Heath, adding: 'I think I'll win this race, you'd better pop down and have a few quid on him.' I did, and the horse won at 3/1.

In the course of an exceptionally severe winter, when no racing had taken place for weeks, and I was at my wits' end for something to write about, my Editor suggested that I should travel down to

Beckhampton, easily the most powerful stable at that time, and obtain an exclusive story from Fred Darling on the stable's prospects for the forthcoming season. I rang him up, and with some trepidation asked him if I could pay him a visit. 'Certainly, Quinny', he answered most genially, adding after a pause: 'if you can get here; but there's several feet of snow and the horses haven't been out of their boxes for over a week.'

Another pause, and then: 'I've got a much better idea, if you'll wait a minute while I get my note-book.' He then proceeded to tell me all I wanted to know about his leading contenders for the next season's Classics and other big races; as a result, I was able to write a two-column article full of local colour, which delighted not only my Editor but Fred as well. The fact that I had given a detailed description of his horses and of the deep snow on the Beckhampton gallops, without going within ninety miles of the place, appealed to his sense of humour, and he often referred to what he described as 'the best article you have ever written'.

Fred won five Epsom Derbies with Captain Cuttle, Manna, Coronach, Cameronian and Bois Roussel, and wartime substitute Derbies with Owen Tudor and his own horse Pont l'Eveque. On the day that Pont l'Eveque won in 1940, I was on sick leave after a serious motor accident, and I met Fred as the horses left the paddock. He asked me if he could watch the race with me from the press stand, and of course I agreed. As the horses were at the start, he told me that the substitute Derbies were not at all like the real thing, and he couldn't get worked up about them. Even as Pont l'Eveque passed the post, a winner by three lengths, he appeared quite unmoved.

Fred died in 1953, three days after Pinza, a horse he had bred and sold for 1,500 guineas to Sir Victor Sassoon, had won the Derby, ridden by Sir Gordon Richards. A suitable epitaph would have been 'He did not suffer fools gladly'. After all, why should he, and, come to think of it, why should any trainer or jockey? The highest tribute to this remarkable little man was paid by Sir Gordon Richards, his jockey for over twenty years, who described him as 'the greatest Guv'nor a jockey ever rode for'.

That truth can indeed be stranger than fiction was the moral of the 1932 Derby. Had a novelist, before the success of April the Fifth, made his hero start life as a policeman, combine the professions of actor and trainer of racehorses, and win the Derby with a colt, bought as a yearling for two hundred guineas, his book would have been thrown into the wastepaper basket as being utterly preposterous. April the Fifth proved the contrary. He was by a disappointing sire, out of a mare who was useless on the racecourse, and came from an undistinguished family. He was called April the Fifth because he was born on that day, which was also the birthday of Mr Sidney McGregor, who owned him in half shares with his trainer Tom Walls, though he ran in the latter's name and colours. He was a leggy, backward colt when I first saw him, but he impressed me when winning a small race at Gatwick, on the strength of which I had a nice win over him when he won the first-ever race for the Lingfield Derby Trial Stakes, having also backed him at 28/1 for the Derby. Orwell, the mount of Bobby Jones, was a hot favourite at 5/4 for the Derby on the strength of his victories in the Greenham Stakes and the Two Thousand Guineas, and I had far more on him than on April the Fifth, but I cheered myself hoarse when April the Fifth swooped down to beat the Aga Khan's Dastur by three-quarters of a length, with Miracle a short head away third.

Lord Rosebery had paid only 170 guineas for Miracle, who was bred by Lord Beaverbrook. As Miracle had previously won the Newmarket Stakes, and subsequently won the Eclipse Stakes, Lord Beaverbrook might not have taken such a jaundiced view of racing had he been a little more patient.

Seldom can the first and third in the Derby have cost as little as 200 guineas and 170 guineas respectively, a perfect example of the glorious uncertainty of racing. I do not subscribe to the view that April the Fifth was one of the least distinguished of our Derby winners. He was still immature when he won at Epsom, and having subsequently fallen lame, he ran well in the St Leger for a long way, though Tom Walls had been unable to give him a preparation.

I was delighted at April the Fifth's victory, not only on account of the fact that I had had a good win. Tom Walls was a friend of mine, and remained one till his death in 1949. He was a delightful man with a great sense of humour, which cannot be said of all comedians, and his success in the Derby was a triumph for the little man over the big battalions, which is always popular with a British crowd. Tom trained at Epsom, and the locals, who were on his horse to a man, gave him a terrific reception. April the Fifth was the first Epsom-trained Derby winner since Amato in 1838.

I had first seen Tom on the stage during the war in *Watch Your Step* at the Empire, but it was not till, in conjunction with Leslie Henson, he produced a farce called *Tons of Money*, which ran for two years, that he made his name as a leading comedian. He called one of his horses Tons of Money, but having been heavily backed for the Lincoln Handicap, he finished last.

His greatest stage triumphs were in a series of farces at the Aldwych Theatre, in company with Ralph Lynn and Robertson Hare. I often went round to see him after the show, and he never seemed in a hurry to go to bed, though he was always up on Epsom Downs at 7 a.m. to work his horses.

# 14 *Back in circulation*

Felix Leach jun. was a most successful trainer. Still in his twenties when he died, he had a stable of over fifty horses. None of them were up to classic form, but he entered them most astutely, and very few members of his stable failed to win a race. What was even more to the point, he had a very shrewd idea of when they were going to win, and we profited accordingly.

Gerald Wellesley was knowledgeable on the subject of racing. He liked to bet and landed a number of coups on horses of his own, and those of his friends. On my recommendation he sent a couple of horses to be trained by Felix, one of them, a little chestnut filly, he called Joy to See, named, I assume, after Betty. She was no world beater, but Felix was a past master at finding races for his less distinguished horses, and he rang me up one evening in 1930 and told me that she was in a selling race at Chepstow on the following Saturday. 'They're a poor lot, and though she is not much good she could fall down and still beat them, so tell your friend Wellesley to let me have all his wires.' This meant that the opposition was negligible, and that even if she met with interference in the course of the race she would still win. The 'wires' referred to telegrams; in those days most bookmakers would allow their clients to have up to £5 each way on a horse provided the telegram was handed in and timed before the start of the race. This facility was eagerly sought by those who betted at starting price, and Wellesley had a big supply of these mediums for speculation. I only had a few, but they included one of £10 each way from a Scottish bookmaker.

On the afternoon of the race all the telegrams were sent from a small post office in some remote village in Suffolk and in consequence did not reach their destinations till long after the race was run. This was known as a starting-price job, and the bookmakers did not appreciate these methods of obtaining a better price than if the commission had been worked on the course.

Joy to See started at 4/1 against, but the market at Chepstow was so weak in those days that, had we had all the money on her on the course, she would have started at 4/1 on. Neither owner nor trainer went to Chepstow, and I travelled there with Chubb Leach who was to ride her. My instructions were not to breathe a word to a soul and to buy her in after she had won. When I arrived on the course a number of people asked me if she was fancied, but I put them off by saying 'She wouldn't win an egg and spoon race', which, of course, was true.

She was an excitable filly and played up a bit, but Chubb got her well away, and drawing out a furlong from home she won by two lengths, cheered home lustily by me. Those I had dissuaded from backing her gave me some dirty looks, but there's an old saying on the racecourse, 'Don't ask questions and you'll hear no lies.' I bought-in Joy to See on behalf of Wellesley for 150 guineas, but she never won another race. I backed two other winners and had one of the most profitable days of my career.

On my return to London that evening, Betty, who had spent the day with the winning owner, told me she wanted to marry him, so would I 'behave like a gentleman' and give her her freedom. This I agreed to do, but as I was returning to India early the following month, while she was going to visit her parents in the States, I thought we should wait till we met again in November. Few things infuriate a woman more, when she has given you the air and expects you to weep on her shoulder and go down on your knees begging her not to leave you, than to find that you are just as keen on regaining your freedom as she is hers.

I had fortunately refrained from destroying my address book, and though some of the telephone numbers were now obsolete the news that I was once again in circulation soon got around, and I had an enjoyable time before I caught the *Kaisar-I-Hind* at Marseilles. On the train I met a charming girl, married to an officer in the Indian Army, and we spent an enjoyable day together in Marseilles before the ship sailed. We spent much of the time in each other's company till we docked at Bombay.

The *Kaisar-I-Hind* was the only coal-burning ship still in service with the O & P, and I shall never forget watching her being coaled at Port Said. She was connected by pontoon bridges with the shore, along which the coolies carrying baskets of coal on their heads ran in an unbroken stream for hours on end. It was one of the most inhuman spectacles I have ever witnessed, and as the day wore on the cloud of coal dust was so thick that the ship was invisible from a distance of a hundred yards.

Bombay, during the monsoon, is hell, even for the well-to-do, and everyone who can get away goes to the hills. I shudder to think what it must have been like for the slum dwellers, and the thousands who sleep on the pavements.

I took the first train available up to Poona (the Aldershot of India), where I spent the next three months. It was wet and humid enough in all conscience up in the hills, and my chief recollection of Poona was the vast number of insects, from a huge horned beetle, which nearly decapitated me on my first evening, to the fleas which nearly bit me to death in the Club of Western India, an uncomfortable, unfriendly establishment, populated almost exclusively by Anglo-Indians with yellow faces, cirrhosis of the liver, a blind faith in the British Raj, and a desire to hang Gandhi. One and all ate curry for breakfast.

All sorts of stories have been told about Poona, and they are mostly true. Had the Sahibs and Memsahibs appeared on the stage they would have been accused of 'hamming' their parts. There was no plumbing in the Club of Western India and one bathed in a tin tub.

I played squash with Jack Sadler, a fellow stipendiary, several times a week, and I invariably defeated him. I never played with anyone else, and when I returned to England and was asked by a friend if I played squash I replied 'Yes, I was never beaten in India.' He was very impressed, but we decided to play level and I scored one in the first game and none in the second. No one appreciated this story more than Jack.

I developed 'Poona tummy', a euphemism for dysentery, soon after my arrival. In western India racing takes place in Bombay from the middle of November till late March, and in Poona from

July till late September. I told the Turf Club authorities that I must return to England at the end of the Poona season to get divorced, but I lacked the moral courage to tell them that I had no intention of returning to India; this was surely a lamentable way to treat people who had shown me the greatest kindness and consideration.

I had received a lot of hospitality which I decided to return by giving a large dinner party at the Turf Club a week before I sailed home on the *Comorin*. Beauty is a relative attribute, and while a girl must be a knockout in order to shine when parading clad, in a bikini, before the judges in Europe, a very ordinary female could work up the sex-starved males in Poona into a state of frenzy.

She was about twenty-three and her husband was a railway executive, and when I was introduced to her, a few days before my party, she seemed to be all the lovely women I had ever met, rolled into one.

I was leaving India, never to return, so what the hell? I therefore placed her on my right at my dinner party, with the General's wife on my left, and the other worthies strung out along the table according to their rank in the Poona social register. I did not visit the Club the following morning, but those who did told me that no incident in India's history had given rise to such indignation since the Black Hole of Calcutta, so it was fortunate I was leaving the country.

The consensus of opinion was that the husband, who was a very nice chap, should horsewhip me for what was tantamount to an avowal of my dishonourable intentions. Like the sensible young man he was, he did nothing of the sort, and asked me round for drinks, and that was the last I saw of him or his wife.

On board the *Comorin* I met a very pretty girl, who had been visiting Australia and had become friendly with one of the ship's officers on the journey between Sydney and Bombay. The object of one's admiration becomes twice as desirable when she appears to belong to someone else, and I determined to cut the young officer out, and succeeded. I had an unfair advantage in that I had twenty-four hours at my disposal, while he, poor chap, had his duties to perform.

In the Mediterranean I received a cable from Betty saying that her decision was irrevocable, and would I behave like a gentleman at the earliest possible moment. 'Behaving like a gentleman' was a contradiction in terms, and entailed behaving in an unseemly manner by taking some strange woman to a hotel, registering as Mr & Mrs Gilbey, and spending the night with her.

I had given a dinner to some of my racing friends before my departure for Poona, and I was very touched when I arrived at the Guards' Club to find a message to the effect that they were giving me a 'welcome home' party in a private room at the Piccadilly Hotel that evening. The organisers were Francis Egerton and the jockey Bobby Jones, and it was a joyous occasion.

My chief concern, on my return, was to meet my 3-year-old son, Robin, and after a series of letters between the respective solicitors I located him in a small village in the Marseilles area. I therefore arranged to go and see him and take him and his nurse out to lunch.

I had recently made the acquaintance of Sir Robert Throckmorton, and he agreed to accompany me as far as Paris, where we spent a few days before I travelled south. Robert was known as the dormouse, or 'the sleepy Bart', but beneath that somnolent exterior was an extremely agile brain which missed very little. As Robert had not found suitable employment since leaving the Grenadiers, and my journalistic career was in the doldrums, we were seldom apart.

He had not liked soldiering any more than I had, and when he was interrogated by his commanding officer as to why he wished to leave the Regiment, he answered: 'In order to better myself.'

I spent a happy day with Robin, who had grown into a most attractive little boy; and had I any idea that I should be debarred from seeing him for thirty years, despite the fact that I was paying for his education, I should have refused point-blank to provide his mother with evidence of my 'adultery', which she considered to be her right.

My solicitor and Francis Egerton pleaded with me not to accede to her request, which they declared to be tantamount to asking me for a blank cheque. They urged me to divorce her.

and to cite Wellesley, which of course I could have done. But I was adamant. To be fair, I had to admit that it was my fault that a marriage which should never have taken place had begun to go wrong some time before Wellesley appeared on the scene, and that I was every bit as keen on securing my freedom as she was. I therefore felt that it was up to me to supply the evidence; I still think so.

As Wilfred Egerton had introduced us and acted as my best man, he felt it was up to him to find a young woman who would accompany me to the Grosvenor Hotel for the sum of £20. I had a flashy green and red Delage which delighted the detectives whom I found awaiting me at the Guards' Club, as they said that there was no chance of losing sight of it in the traffic. At the hotel my new-found friend went upstairs, while I took the detectives for a drink at the bar. They told me what a real pleasure it was to be associated with someone so co-operative, explaining that from time to time they came up against some proper bastards, and that recently an irate husband had set about one of them and given him a black eye.

My friend's first words, when I joined her upstairs, were 'No funny business'; I took this to mean that the £20 did not include sexual intercourse, and I assured her that that was quite O.K. by me. We had twin beds, and when the detectives arrived the following morning they asked me to get into my friend's bed, adding, 'We mustn't leave anything out; we might get old Judge So-and-So. He's an awkward bugger, and unless we can swear we've seen you in bed together he'll say adultery hasn't been proved, and you'll have to go through this lark all over again.' My friend was engrossed in the *Daily Mirror*, which she was asked to put down for a moment 'just to make it seem more life-like'.

When Robin returned to London I saw him once a week and we both enjoyed our times together, but from the time Wellesley placed the ring on Betty's finger everything changed. I had bent over backwards to enable her to marry Wellesley, and there was no reason why we should not all have behaved in a civilised manner. Instead of which, Wellesley conceived a pathological hatred of me, and wrote to my brother Geoffrey, who had been his lifelong friend, telling him that he would never speak to him or Mollie again so long as they had anything to do with me. I need hardly say what their answer was.

Instead of my seeing Robin once a week Wellesley's solicitors sent me a list of available dates, which invariably clashed with the Derby, Grand National or some big race. In course of time I had to give up the unequal struggle, hoping that when Robin grew up he would realise that it was his stepfather who was responsible for my disappearance from his life.

I have read somewhere that deserted husbands do one of two things: either they go into a decline or they make up for lost time. I did not go into a decline. I was earning regular sums from articles in weekly and monthly journals including the 'Shinies' – the *Tatler*, the *Sketch* and the *Bystander*, and for once in my life I was quite affluent.

Social gossip, rather than racing, was the subject of most of these articles, and as people love to read about themselves, no matter what they may say to the contrary, the articles were quite successful, though inevitably they made me some enemies.

Robert Throckmorton and I were caught in a raid on the Silver Slipper Club in Regent Street. This was one of Mrs Meyrick's more respectable clubs. It was Boat Race Night, or some such undergraduate festivity, and when a number of hearty young men came clattering down the stairs, a man at the next table said, 'Don't take any notice of the silly bastards, this is only a rag.' I fell for this, and when the police arrived at our table I raised my glass and drank their health.

At Marlborough Street, the next morning, most of my fellow revellers, including Robert, got off with a caution, but I was charged with drinking in defiance of the police and my case was adjourned.

On the day it was down for hearing at 3 p.m. I gave a buffet luncheon at Quaglino's to thirty of my gayest friends, including Tom Driberg, Lord Donegall, Charles Graves and 'Bunny' Tattersall, all of whom wrote a society column in those days. All my guests accompanied me to the Magistrates' Court, which might have been mistaken for the Embassy Club or Ciro's when I entered the dock.

The presence of such beautiful women in his court as Romie Drury-Lowe, Margaret Whigham, Lady Bridget Poulett, Rose Bingham and Oonagh Kindersley may have softened the judge's heart, as he was content to bind me over not to enter a club for the next twelve months.

As he had not stipulated what sort of club I was to steer clear of I explained I was living at the Guards' Club and asked him if I should have to change my quarters. It seemed to me a natural question, but it brought titters from my friends in the court and a stern rebuke from the magistrate, who informed me that any future attempt to raise a laugh at his expense would result in a charge of contempt of court.

I met Romie Drury-Lowe, as she was then, at a joint coming-of-age party given by Lady Bridget Poulett and Emerson Bainbridge, a Subaltern in the Scots Guards. Two years earlier Bridget, with Margaret Whigham and Rose Bingham, had taken London by storm. They made a big fuss of debs in the thirties. Bridget and Emerson each gave a dinner party at the Embassy and joined forces afterwards at a night club hired for the occasion. I was one of Bridget's guests, and Romie and her husband, Johnny, dined with Emerson.

Jack Harris had replaced Bert Ambrose as band leader at the Embassy. His music was very similar, and he was just as obliging when requested for a particular number. Margaret Whigham asked so often for 'Trees' that Jack used to play it when he saw her enter the club, to save her the trouble of asking for it.

I was an inveterate party-goer in those days, but Bridget's and Emerson's twenty-first birthday party was a landmark in my life; from that time I was a hundred per cent certain that Romie was the girl for me.

I had recently met Tim (Sir Henry) Birkin of motor-racing fame, one of the great drivers of his or any other generation. Tim asked me to stay the week-end and go to Brooklands with him, where he was driving Dorothy Paget's vast green Bentley in the long-distance event. This was the only occasion on which I have been motor-racing, and I was completely out of my depth, but I remember that Tim's car conked out early in a race which seemed to go on for ever, and that John Cobb, driving a Delage, won from George Eyston. Sylvia Ashley, who was involved with Tim at that time, was also in the house party. Dressed in overalls, she watched the races from the pits with the mechanics, lending glamour to the occasion, though probably not much practical help.

A few weeks later I turned in my Delage for a Speed 6 Bentley, simply and solely because I thought it would impress Romie. I bought it through Tim, but I do not hold him responsible for its shortcomings. I was so anxious to take delivery of it that I failed to notice that the tyres were worn down to the canvas, that it required two men and a boy to lug it round a corner, and that it developed a terrifying wheel wobble at 70 m.p.h. It went ten miles to the gallon, but as the cheapest petrol was a shilling a gallon I could fill its 20-gallon tank for £1. It consumed oil at approximately the same rate as petrol. Nevertheless, it impressed Romie, and so achieved its objective.

As Rosemary Hope-Vere, Romie had been the deb of her year; with her golden hair, blue eyes and perfect skin she was staggeringly beautiful. Moreover, she was a wonderful companion with a strongly developed sense of humour.

I met Margaret Whigham with Robert Throckmorton soon after my return from India, and we became very good friends. She often dined with me, and went racing with me at Folkestone, where my horse, Wearing A Crown, was running. As she was with an owner she was allowed in the parade ring, which delighted her, and when press photographers heard she was attending this humble meeting they descended on us. I had told Margaret she could lead in Wearing A Crown if he won, but unfortunately he could only finish fourth. The most sought-after invitation, next to one to Windsor Castle, was an invitation to stay for Royal Ascot with the Whighams. I therefore felt very honoured when Margaret invited me, adding, 'I haven't told my parents you're divorced, so you and Robert mustn't make jokes about it.' In the years to come her two marriages were dissolved.

As Robert and I drove up to the house in my Bentley, two men in morning coats were fighting on the lawn. They turned out to be press photographers, each of whom claimed that Margaret had promised him the exclusive right to photograph the house party. Margaret explained that this was always happening, and she ordered a footman to pacify the contestants with a glass of champagne, and her permission for both of them to photograph us.

As Margaret Whigham, Mrs Charles Sweeney and the Duchess of Argyll, Margaret has been photographed more than any woman in this country, excluding members of the Royal Family, and the click of the cameras has been music to her ears. She was fabulously beautiful, and still is. Both Margaret's husbands were friends of mine, but divorces only concern the people involved. As a girl, some thirty-five years ago, Margaret had the glamour of a film star with the carriage of a duchess, and was the perfect hostess. Her craze for publicity was shared by many girls of her age, but that is something we all outgrew.

Every night, a large dinner party was followed by a ball in one or other of the neighbouring stately and not so stately homes, and we never got to bed before 4 a.m. Charlie Sweeney, who was a member of the house party, was very much in love with Margaret, but Margaret and Max Aitken were in love at the time, though she married Charlie a year or so later. One of the best parties was that given by Max's sister, Janet, who was married to Ian Campbell, the future Duke of Argyll, though they were separated.

Despite the fact that I was unable to devote as much time as usual to studying the form book, I had a very successful week, which was just as well as this was to be my last appearance on an English racecourse for a very long while.

# 15 *Sir Gordon*

Neither Sir Gordon Richards nor I can remember when we first met, but it was a very long time ago, and I suspect it was around 1925 that I first interviewed this boy with the unruly black hair which had earned him the nickname of 'Moppy'.

I recall seeing him ride a winner at Kempton, however, very early in his career. The horse's name was Squarson, and the little lad had ridden with tremendous vigour to beat a senior jockey by a narrow margin. But the pundits would not stand for him, pointing out that his technique would shame a butcher boy, and that although he had won he had broken every rule in the jockey's textbook, except that of falling off. When driving his horse through the last furlong he had pivoted so far round in the saddle that he seemed to be facing its tail, and he had finished with a loose rein. 'Danny Maher and the other great jockeys of the past must be turning in their graves,' I was told.

But Gordon's unorthodox methods prevailed, and in the final analysis it is results that count, and at the end of 1925 this remarkable young man in a cloth cap, and without an ounce of conceit behind those intelligent brown eyes which looked you straight in the face, was champion jockey with 118 winners, a position he was to occupy on twenty-five more occasions before a serious injury put an end to his career as a jockey in 1954.

On my retirement in 1966, the man who beat all existing records and then went on to beat his own, wrote me the following letter. 'Well, Quinny, it comes to us all, some time or other, but reading you no more in the *Sporting Chronicle* will leave a blank, for me anyway. We have been good friends for over forty years. I recall our little week-ends in Paris and Ostend (what a bastard you were) but it was all great fun. You were never afraid to criticise, or give credit where it was due – that is why you were so popular with us all. See you soon, all the best, Gordon.'

I must explain that, with Gordon Richards, 'bastard' amounted almost to an endearment, and when he had stayed up late the previous evening and drunk a glass or two more than usual – he was very abstemious and was always superbly fit – he would explain, 'It was that bastard Quinny, he got me at it.'

At the end of every season Gordon gave a dinner at which I was one of his guests, but it was not till he broke the great Fred Archer's record of riding 246 winners in one season, at Liverpool in November 1933, that we became close friends. For the past weeks, not only English journalists but those from every country in which racing takes place had been following him around, in order to get a first-hand story when he accomplished his remarkable feat. When it actually happened the little man had to be given police protection to prevent his being trampled underfoot. Knowing him so well and guessing what he was most likely to have said, I was able to lead off with a couple of quotes, but it was not till after dinner at the Adelphi Hotel that evening that I met him and told him how much I wanted something exclusive. 'Right, Quinny,' he answered. 'Fill up your glass and I'll tell you a story, which you can have all on your own.' For the next quarter of an hour he talked, but it was an evening of jubilation and then more jubilation, and it was 4 a.m. before I finally went to my room. The next morning I could not recall a word Gordon had said, and neither could he, so the great story was never told, and after thirty-five years I suppose it never will be.

From then on our friendship ripened, and whenever he rode abroad, which was not often, he invariably took me with him. I spoke French fairly well, but I have a feeling that the chief reason that Gordon liked my company on these jaunts was that he could always blame 'that bastard Quinny' when he had a hangover.

Although evening racing did not become popular till after Gordon retired from the saddle, he more often than not rode in all six races, and he considered that six races a day and a six-day week was enough for anyone. It was this belief, rather than any great concern for the Fourth Commandment, that caused him to turn down many lucrative rides in the big races on the Continent, which are nearly all run on Sundays.

If, however, a horse from one of the stables for which he was retained was running, he naturally rode it. On several occasions we went to Ostend for the big international race which was run there in those days, and one visit stands out in my memory. Gordon invariably hired a private plane, and on our arrival from Gatwick, where we had been racing, the first person we bumped into was Charlie Elliott, who was to ride Corrida for M Boussac in the big race the following day. She was a previous winner of this race, and had proved herself the best of her sex in Europe, but early that year she had given reason for believing that she might be on the down grade. At her best, she was a certainty, and over a bottle of pink champagne Charlie told us that she was back at her best, to which Gordon exclaimed, 'In that case mine's got no bloody chance, we'll make a night of it.'

Our party included Tom Reece, the ex-billiard player, who was Gordon's devoted slave, Steve Donoghue, trainer Donald Snow and Archie Burns, who ran Gordon's bath, while old Tom put the links and studs in his evening shirt. We had an excellent dinner, after which we went to the casino. Gordon was to ride a horse belonging to Jimmy Rank and about 3 a.m. we met Jimmy and his wife Pat, who had been playing at the big table. We were all stone-cold sober, but I noticed that Jimmy was less genial than usual.

Corrida won the big race the following day, as she was almost sure to do, but a few days later Gordon received a letter from Jimmy Rank saying that he did not pay a jockey a large sum of money to spend the night before a big race in the casino, and that he did not think he had ridden a particularly good race. Gordon was incensed and consulted his solicitor, but it was smoothed over and Jimmy and Gordon became as good friends again as they had always been. Jimmy Rank was a great sportsman and a wonderful supporter of racing under both rules, and that letter to Gordon was completely out of character.

Corrida, who was five years old at that time, was probably the best mare ever owned by M Boussac, but she met with a tragic end. When the battle in the Falaise Gap was at its height a party of Germans arrived at M Boussac's stud and seized the first three horses they saw, one of them being Corrida. At the end of the battle, with the Germans in full retreat, the other two horses were found wandering among the shell craters, but there was no sign of Corrida.

The visit to Paris of which I have the most vivid memory was for the Grand Prix de Paris of 1938 in which Gordon was to ride the Epsom Derby winner, Bois Roussel. After Bois Roussel had won his first race by a narrow margin Aly Khan bought him from Léon Volterra, who was always prepared to buy or sell if he thought the price was right. By this time Aly had earned himself the reputation for being a pretty astute 'coper', and though it was not suggested that he had taken his friend Peter Beatty for a ride when he passed Bois Roussel on to him for £7,000, those who knew the form thought that Peter had paid plenty for a colt who had won a race, for horses that had never raced before, only by a short head. Peter sent him to be trained by Fred Darling, who had won the Two Thousand Guineas with the brilliant Pasch, ridden by Gordon, who of course rode him in the Derby, in which Bois Roussel was ridden by Charlie Elliott. Jimmy Rank's Scottish Union, about whom Pat Rank had laid me 100/7 to a tenner each way a few nights earlier at the Four Hundred, having got the better of the non-staying Pasch, looked home and dry, when Bois Roussel came out of the clouds to beat him by four lengths.

In the field for the Grand Prix was the Italian colt Nearco, the unbeaten winner of thirteen races, who was regarded by his owner trainer, Signor Tesio, as the best horse he had ever had in his stable.

Gordon was to ride Bois Roussel. There were long faces when we arrived at Northolt Airport, and we were told that Le Bourget could give us no idea when we would be allowed to land. It seemed that we might be grounded indefinitely, when our pilot had a brainwave. We would land at Villacoublay, but as there were no Customs on this airfield we should have to land first at Le Touquet to declare Customs. This we did, and as we were waiting while the formalities were being gone through, Steve Donoghue ordered two bottles of what he always called 'the Rosie' – pink champagne. After we had checked in at the Chatham Hotel, an Edwardian establishment, all gold and red plush, which for generations had been patronised by racing men from all over the world, Gordon asked me to ring up Maxim's and reserve a table for twelve. I knew that our only hope was for me to go round and plead with my old friend Albert.

One of France's most famous *maîtres d'hôtel* (he was also the guiding light at Ciro's in Deauville), Albert shook me warmly by the hand, but when I said I wanted a table for twelve in an hour's time, he gave me the sort of pitying look one gives to the very old when they can no longer be treated like other people. In his kindest voice, and with tears in his eyes, he remonstrated with me for my folly. Did I, with my experience of Paris, not know that on the eve of the Grand Prix every table at Maxim's had been reserved a month ago. 'It isn't for me, Albert,' I explained, 'it's for Gordon Richards.' 'Gordon Richards,' he echoed, with the reverence normally reserved for a reigning monarch, 'I will see what I can do.' When we arrived, the small space on which dancing would have taken place was occupied by a table for twelve, bearing the name 'Gordon Richards'.

On our way to dinner we had stopped for a drink at Frank O'Neill's bar. The great American jockey looked much as he had done when he won the Derby on Spion Kop eighteen years earlier. After dinner, John Bisgood, a successful trainer for many years, and I went to the Sphinx, and as far as I know Gordon went to bed. Soon after our arrival I saw a very attractive girl saying goodnight to a man, and I asked her to join us, which she did, and that was how I met Arlette. As the crowd began to thin out, we invited more girls to our table, and having supplied them with all the champagne they could drink, we organised a sing-song and very well they sang. Their favourite song was the still popular 'J'attendrai', and they sang it a dozen times, John and I joining in after we had been taught the words.

At around twelve o'clock on Sunday morning my telephone rang, and it was a very irate Gordon at the other end. What the hell was I doing? We were going to lunch before we left for the racecourse, and would I come down at once. So I packed Arlette off home, with the promise that I would contact her when I next came to Paris, which I did. The promise was not hard to keep. Although Gordon had ridden Bois Roussel a canter on Longchamps racecourse at some ungodly hour, he said he still had a hangover, and of course it was my fault, though I hadn't seen him from the moment the party broke up at Maxim's. For once Gordon rode a bad race, though it made no difference to the result. Nearco was a horse and a half, and he won like one. Had Gordon steered clear of trouble, Bois Roussel might have finished second instead of third, but in no circumstances would he have won. If Bois Roussel had won, we were to have stayed in Paris for another night, but after the race Gordon couldn't get home quick enough. When the Customs official, on landing, asked us if we had contracted anything while we were abroad, Gordon replied 'I haven't, but Steve Donoghue, Commander Bisgood and Mr Gilbey won't know till next Wednesday – at the earliest.'

It was not till 1939 that Gordon rode for the first time in Ireland, his mount being Lord Astor's Plymouth in the Irish Derby. Racing on the previous day was at Folkestone, and we flew from near-by Lympne. A reception committee was awaiting the champion, and after a few words of welcome we were hustled into a large car driven at breakneck speed to the Dail (Irish Parliament). A debate was in progress as we arrived, but the Speaker announced that there would be a suspension 'while we welcome Mr Gordon Richards, the greatest jockey in the world, who in tomorrow's Derby will be riding in our country for the first time'. I cannot believe that a jockey had ever been honoured in this manner before, or ever will be again. As always, Gordon, from out of the blue, found the right thing to say, and not only charmed the politicians, but even more important, he made them laugh. A vast amount of Irish whiskey was consumed by one and all, and I should have liked to have heard the continuation of the debate, but it was getting late, and Gordon had not eaten since breakfast. Although beautifully bred, as were all Lord Astor's horses, Plymouth was very moderate and never looked like being concerned with the finish; the race was won by the great Irish jockey Joe Cantly on Montagon.

Early in 1941 Gordon sustained a broken leg, when he was kicked at the post, and did not ride again that season. Fred Darling saddled the first two in the substitute Derby at Newmarket – Owen Tudor and Morogoro. Owen Tudor, the easy winner, ridden by Billy Nevett, started at 25/1, and Morogoro ridden by Harry Wragg, at 11/2, so had Sir Gordon had his pick he would almost certainly have chosen the wrong one.

Gordon had a long and highly successful association with the Welsh shipping magnate, Lord Glanely. Stout, with a walrus moustache, Lord Glanely was known as 'Guts and Gaiters', though why I have never discovered. He was a lavish supporter of racing, and year after year was a most prolific spender at the yearling sales. 'Bluff but cordial' best describes him. He was no courtier, and this was possibly the reason why he was not elected to the Jockey Club till a few years before his death which occurred in an air-raid – at Weston-super-Mare, of all places. He liked to have a bet if he considered one of his horses had a few pounds in hand, and he was reported to have landed a big *coup* when his Royal Salute won, ridden by Gordon in the Royal Hunt Cup of 1931. The result of this victory was that he, his trainer and Gordon were up before the Stewards, who considered the horse had made abnormal improvement. The following day his Singapore, also ridden by Gordon, was beaten by a short head by Trimdon, the mount of Joe Childs, in the Gold Cup. I thought that Singapore had been interfered with and that Gordon would object, but those who were in much closer contact with the stable than I was told me, 'Guts and Gaiters got such a rocket from the Stewards yesterday that he is determined to have no truck with them again.' Lord Glanely had a number of trainers and still more jockeys, but he never fell out with Gordon, and put him up whenever he was available. The Oaks, with Rose of England in 1930, and the St Leger with Singapore 1930 and Chulmleigh 1937, were the classics won by Gordon in the black jacket with a red, white and blue sash. All these horses were trained by Captain Tommy Hogg. Hogg, an Australian, was a close friend of Marty Hartigan, with whom Gordon served his apprenticeship, 'and to whom I owe everything', he has often told me, and it was Hogg who trained Squarson, previously referred to in this chapter.

I have often been asked whether Gordon was a good judge of a horse's potentialities. The answer is 'Yes'. Despite the fact that in many seasons he was retained by five stables, there were any number of races in which he was free to pick his mounts from half a dozen offers, and the number of occasions on which he picked the right one testifies to his judgement. He used to tell stories against himself as a tipster, and I have heard him relate that when he rode eleven winners in a row at the two-day Chepstow meeting, the only one he really fancied was the twelfth, which got beaten. I have an idea that this may have been propaganda in order to stop people pestering him for tips.

Except on the occasions when I was staying with him, and we went through the day's card together before racing, I seldom had any idea what his views were, but I do know that on the rare occasions Gordon said a horse would win it usually did. On the other hand he would often find two or three horses which might beat his mount. In this way he enjoyed the best of both worlds, in that he would be delighted if he won, while if one of the dangers beat him, he could say 'What did I tell you? I knew that damn' thing of so and so's would beat me.' If Gordon had marked your card every day of the twenty-six years during which he was champion jockey you would not have backed many losers, but you also would not have backed all that number of winners. Some of the winners you would have been certain to back which come to mind are Tudor Minstrel, in all his two-year-old races, and also in the Two Thousand Guineas; Pasch in the Two Thousand Guineas and Eclipse Stakes; Pinza in the Derby; and Tehran in the St Leger. After his runaway success in the Guineas Tudor Minstrel started at 7/4 on for the Derby, but Gordon wasn't a bit happy, in fact he was worried sick whether he would be able to settle him down, as he was such a hard puller, and even if he could, he doubted whether he would get the trip. His fears were only too well founded, and Tudor Minstrel was a beaten horse at Tattenham Corner.

I had a wonderful stroke of luck in that Derby despite my having £75 on Tudor Minstrel at a decent price before the Guineas. About ten days before the Derby I met the French jockey Roger Brethés at Hurst Park, where he was to ride Chanteur for Mr William Hill, who had just bought this very high-class horse from France as a stallion. Roger had never ridden at Hurst Park before, and asked me to explain to him the layout of the course and the pitfalls to beware of. He thanked me, and having ridden Chanteur to victory in the big race on both days of the meeting, he advised me to 'have a save' on Pearl Diver in the Derby. 'He may not beat your Tudor Minstrel,' he told me, 'but he stays, and I'm sure he is improving.' I therefore had £2 each way on him at 40/1, and won £25 on the race, instead of losing £75. Chanteur was the sire of Pinza, Gordon's mount in the 1953 Derby. Gordon's ill luck in the Derby was proverbial, and a number of people went so far as to say that when he went to the post for the most famous race in the world he was so hot and bothered that his skill deserted him. This was, of course, utter nonsense, and year after year, when summing up the race, I wrote 'Gordon Richards has never won the Derby for the simple reason that the horse under him has never been good enough.' There is no doubt, however, that Gordon's continued ill luck in the Derby worried him. He was fifty, and time was running out, but Noel Murless, who had succeeded Fred Darling, having no runner, Gordon was free to ride Pinza, trained by Fred Darling's former travelling head lad, Norman Bertie, for Victor Sassoon. A big heavy-topped horse, Pinza had shown brilliant form as a two-year-old, but he had not the best of legs to carry his huge body and was difficult to train. Norman Bertie had been unable to give him much work in the spring of his three-year-old career, and when he cantered down to post for the Newmarket Stakes he looked more like a candidate at the fatstock show than a racehorse. Notwithstanding this he won the race in a hack canter, and one asked oneself, 'What kind of a horse will he be when he's fit?'

A few days later, I said to Gordon, 'I bet you wish the Derby was run at Newmarket', as it seemed to me unlikely that such a big heavy horse would be able to negotiate the turns and gradients on Epsom Downs. I remember Gordon's answer as if it were yesterday, 'I wouldn't give a bugger where they ran it, he's the best actioned horse I've ever ridden, and mark my words, Quinny, he'll win the Derby.'

I took his advice and napped him, though I was so keen on Gordon winning the Derby that my bet was a small one, and I stood to win more over the Queen's Aureole, ridden by another great friend of mine, Harry Carr, who finished second, beaten by four lengths.

Though he rode only 191 winners compared with 1947, when he rode 269 (an all-time record), this was Gordon's greatest year, as, in the week following the fulfilment of his only unfulfilled desire, he went to Buckingham Palace to receive his knighthood.

Some years earlier, Gordon had promised a society, known as the Sportsmen of Shropshire, that he would stand them a dinner at his birthplace, Oakengates, if he ever won the Derby.

Sir Gordon, Billy Wright, captain of Wolverhampton Wanderers and England, and I were the three speakers, and it was an unforgettable evening. Among the guests were Manager Stan Cullis and the whole of the Wolverhampton Wanderers team, and representatives of every branch of sport. I said to myself, as I rose to address this distinguished gathering, 'Lucky for Gordon he hasn't made a habit of winning the Derby or he'd be skint.'

# 16 *Cap over the windmill*

I have always believed it to be a mistake to re-visit a place in which you have been supremely happy, as I was at Sark and Bergenstock. Even if one is accompanied by the person responsible for one's happiness one can never recover the ecstasy of that first visit, while if, as in my case, the journey is to be made alone there will be reminders at every turn of one's folly in the years succeeding that time when one's heart sang with joy and one believed it would continue to do so as long as we both lived.

While I could understand the disapproval of my behaviour, it is ridiculous to label a man a home-breaker because he runs away with another man's wife.

One well-known journalist wrote that while Quintin Gilbey would be horrified at the idea of picking a man's pocket he had no compunction in stealing his wife. It is conceivable that a happily married woman might leave her husband for a Baby Pignatori, a Porfirio Rubirosa or an Aly Khan, but it is absurd to suggest that she would throw her cap over the windmill for a wine merchant's youngest son, who, at that time, was a far from successful journalist.

The price of newsprint has proved a blessing in that Editors of newspapers are no longer faced with the problem of how they are to fill all their available space. Social gossip is now confined to a few glossy periodicals. But in the twenties and thirties anyone who patronised the more elegant restaurants and night clubs was news.

The young of every generation since Cain and Abel have thought their parents a couple of squares and have been in no doubt that a wider gulf separated their two generations than in any period of history. I certainly am in no doubt that those of us born in the first decade of the twentiety century had a vastly different outlook on life and sense of values from our Victorian parents.

The only benefit the 1914–18 War bestowed on humanity was that it killed off the chaperone. When a girl had been a V.A.D. in a military hospital from the age of sixteen not even the Victorians could kid themselves that she would come to much harm travelling alone with her boy-friend in a taxi. Pre-marital experience was not as universally indulged in in the twenties and thirties as it is in today's permissive society, but virginities were no longer regarded as a priceless heirloom.

Divorce, however, was regarded as a terrible slur on a family's good name, and I have no doubt that had my mother been asked whether she would prefer her youngest son to be caught robbing a bank or cited as co-respondent she would have settled for the former, the Seventh Commandment being of more importance than the Eighth. My parents would have visited me in Pentonville, and on my release would have spared no pains over my rehabilitation, though they might have considered it better for me to have my dinner in my room when they were entertaining members of the aristocracy.

But for one's son to be cited as co-respondent! One could never live down the shame of it.

When my father announced that he had asked a Peer of the Realm, who had been divorced, to lunch my mother was reluctant to meet him, but my father was able to make her change her mind by explaining that his son and heir was at the front and that his daughter was a Sister in a hospital. But though he became a frequent visitor to our house and was a most genial man my mother never really took to him. I think it is a mercy that she did not live into old age, as had she done so I should have been a continual source of grief to her.

Bergenstock sprang into the news a few years ago, when Mel Ferrer and Audrey Hepburn went to live there, but in the early 'thirties few English people had heard of it. Thomas Cook, in Paris, recommended it to me as being off the beaten track and unfrequented by tourists from the United Kingdom, and so it proved to be.

Lucerne grows in profusion on the fertile lower slopes of the mountains around the lake of that name, and the scent of clover remained with us throughout our stay. The lake steamer, having stopped at half a dozen little villages, approached Bergenstock; to our dismay, it appeared to consist of a landing stage, a boat house, and one small cottage, but in response to my incredulous 'Bergenstock?' a fellow passenger pointed up the mountain side, and there on what appeared to be a narrow ledge, 1,700 feet above the lake, was a hotel.

The scent of clover grew stronger as the funicular climbed through enchanting orchards and woods, in which the trees grew so close to one another that one had the impression one was in a tunnel.

From our hotel, whichever way one looked, there was a view of breath-taking loveliness and there was so much to explore, both above and below us, that we felt we could never grow tired of this place. Neither did we, until the autumn rains sent us farther south in search of yet more sunshine.

Having missed the boat one evening, I decided to show my independence; I hired a light skiff in Lucerne. Although I had been a dry bob at Eton, I had spent quite a lot of time on the river and enjoyed rowing. We went everywhere in this narrow boat, despite the fact that Romie seemed to think that the men employed at the helm of the steamers were blind, and at them would shout when they were still a quarter of a mile away.

As the result of rowing, swimming, climbing the Rigi (shades of William Tell!) and walking for miles through the lovely countryside, I became fitter than at any time in my life, and had I ridden in a race in Switzerland I should not have run out of breath at half-way as I had done when riding poor old Wearing A Crown.

No one has been able to explain the extraordinary behaviour of insects, which will avoid a beautiful woman as if she had the plague, but will devour a very ordinary man as if he were a great delicacy.

On arriving late at night at Bari, where we were catching a

cargo boat for a Mediterranean cruise, we found our reservations had miscarried. Our taxi driver seemed a friendly sort of man, but was obviously a sadist, as he took us to a hotel where I was eaten by fleas, needless to say, Romie's fair skin was not punctured by a single bite.

We were the only human passengers as far as Sicily, but we had plenty of company in the shape of swarms of cockroaches and a herd of cattle which mooed incessantly. Near Marseilles the sea became very rough and our 800-ton vessel stood on its head. We were relieved to bid farewell to the cockroaches, the cattle having left us three weeks earlier. In Sicily, I should have liked to stay longer, but winter was drawing near, and six months, living in and out of suitcases, is long enough.

We were married by the Consul-General in Paris, and a number of our friends came over for our wedding. Nancy Mitford was Romie's bridesmaid, or whatever you call the girl who attends the bride in a register office, while Derek Blyth was my best man. I gave a luncheon party afterwards at the Cremaillière in the rue Faubourg St Honoré, and that evening all those at the luncheon, and a few others as well, came round for cocktails at our flat in the Avenue Henri Martin, where Nancy and 'Smut' were staying with us.

White Ladies (gin, Cointreau and lemon juice) were the fashionable cocktails at that time, and I must have shaken a hundred that evening. Someone or other had heard that a Russian restaurant, near the Place Pigalle, provided marvellous food, and Harry and Nell Stavordale,* Henry and Daphne Weymouth,† Nina Seafield and Derek Studley-Herbert (they were married though Nina retained her maiden name), Nancy, 'Smut', Hamish St Clair-Erskine, Derek Blyth and ourselves went to dinner there.

In the course of the day we had all consumed quite a lot of alcohol and this may have been responsible for our taking it for granted that in a Russian restaurant caviar would be cheaper than

*Lord and Lady Stavordale, subsequently Lord and Lady Ilchester.

†Lord and Lady Weymouth, subsequently Marquess and Marchioness of Bath.

in one run by the French. We ate jars of the stuff, washed down with vodka, before we embarked on champagne.

Some of us may have been a little tight, but after one glance at the bill we were all as sober as judges. We remonstrated with the management and gave them what we thought was a fair sum, which was, incidentally, all we had on us. But in a matter of seconds three very pro-Russian, anti-British gendarmes were at our table.

I must have been out of my mind in informing them, somewhat pompously, that I was domiciled in Paris and was the owner of a *carte d'identité*. As a French citizen, I protested at the exorbitant price demanded for our very simple meal. At this the gendarmes rubbed their hands with glee. They had assumed that we were all tourists, and as such they could not very well throw us into goal. But here was a member of the party stating that he was domiciled in Paris, and producing his *carte d'identité* to prove it. I was seized, and with a gendarme on either side of me, was marched down the street to the lock-up, with the remainder of the party trailing behind me.

I was pushed into an icy cell, and was told that I should remain there until the remainder of the bill was paid. Harry Stavordale took a taxi to the Ritz where he hoped, but not as devoutly as I did, that he could cash a cheque. He managed to do so, but there are few people in the world who can be so bloody-minded as the French police, and even when Harry returned with the money they kept me incarcerated for another hour in order to teach me not to try to cheat God-fearing restaurateurs.

When I was finally released we went on to a night club, and it was five o'clock when I arrived home. One way and another it had been quite a day. At Wormwood Scrubs, where I had spent my twenty-first birthday, I had been on the side of the law, a kind of auxiliary warder, but in the French gaol on my wedding day I was on the other side of the fence.

Ever since we left England I had managed to continue my career as a journalist, seldom writing less than three articles a week. Towards the end of our stay in Paris I was also writing an article for the *Weekly Despatch*. This was not so easy; it meant flying from time to time to England, where everyone was most friendly, though I had read in Lord Donegall's column that Johnny's brother officers had announced that I should return to England at my peril.

We had quite a lot of friends living in or near Paris, and during the season friends from England were continually turning up unexpectedly. Racing in France entailed no travelling. Auteuil was only a quarter of an hour's walk from our flat, and it took only a little more time to reach Longchamp by taxi.

On hearing that Buck's wife, Nellie Taylor, had died I wrote asking him to stay, thinking he might like to get away from England and so many sad memories. He arrived the day after the funeral, and stayed with us for a fortnight.

Like so many of my friends 'Buck' Buckmaster was much older than me, and had fought in both the South African War and World War I. After World War I, Lord Tweedmouth, his commanding officer in the Blues, suggested that he should start a club; Buck's Club is the result. Buck was a marvellous friend, the very soul of generosity with a delicious sense of humour. People said that he took offence easily, and that he evinced his displeasure by writing them letters in green ink, but I never received one. In his young days he was a man of tremendous energy, and once walked from London to Brighton for a bet. But in his declining years he was crippled by arthritis, and continually in pain. Although his marriage to Gladys Cooper was dissolved in the early 'twenties they remained close friends until his death. Their daughter Joan married Robert Morley, who I am also proud to number among my friends.

Constant visitors to our flat were Sylvia Ashley (Fairbanks by this time) and Basil Throckmorton, uncle of my friend Robert. Basil, who was in his seventies, had never married, and lived in the Palais Royal. He loved to talk of his numerous love affairs all over the world, invariably ending up with the words, 'I don't do much of it now, old boy, it makes my head ache.' I called him 'le vieux boul'vardier', and teased him about his sex life, to his enormous delight.

It was Basil who introduced us to Dick Grant Thorold who was of the same vintage as himself. A typical cavalry officer of the old school, Dick did not give one the impression of being romantically inclined, but his story was one of devotion to a single woman in the face of severe opposition from his family.

A future full of promise lay before him after the First World War, but Dick could not settle down, his thoughts continually returning to a young girl called Simone, whom he had met and loved during a slight respite from the front line. A year or so after the armistice Dick went back to France, and having met Simone again, took her to Maisons-Laffittes, where they set up house together. A year or so before his death they were married. Simone spoke very little English while Dick's French was typical of the French of most Englishmen of his day; but actions speak louder than words and they were blissfully happy.

Dick had friends in every walk of life, and at his luncheons, cooked by Simone, one met owners, trainers, jockeys, and on occasions a member of his family from England, who seemed a trifle ill at ease amongst Dick's racecourse friends.

The great English jockey, Charlie Elliott, who was first jockey for M Boussac, was a friend of Dick's, and together with Dick's trainer Sam Ambler they planned a successful *coup* in a handicap at Maisons-Laffitte. Charlie told me he had had some difficulty in preventing the horse winning his previous race, but fortunately it had been foggy, and this had not been apparent from the Stewards' box.

Although there were clandestine bookmakers operating in Paris at the time, it was impossible to put much money on a horse in a small race without its starting at a short price, and taking all things into consideration 4/1 was a satisfactory price for a racing certainty.

With Charlie Elliott and the Australian jockey Rae Johnstone to assist me, and plenty of time to study form, I did quite well betting, though our cast-iron 'good thing' came unstuck. When Charlie came round for a drink after racing at Longchamp one Sunday evening, he told me that one of the lesser lights of the powerful Boussac stable was a good thing for a minor race at St Cloud, adding, 'the only possible danger is the thing Rae rides, and if we can get him on our side it will be just a case of picking up money'.

Rae Johnstone had recently arrived in France via India, where he had ridden with great success, and he was not averse to investing a few francs on a 'good thing' in those days, though long before he became the most successful classic rider of all time he had decided that betting was a mug's game, at any rate where jockeys were concerned.

In his young days Rae played for high stakes in the casinos, and nothing gave him more pleasure than to 'Banco' M James Hennessy and the other French Stewards. After the war, however, he seldom touched a card. Of all the jockeys I have known, Rae was the most sophisticated. Always immaculately dressed, he was a connoisseur of good wine, good food and attractive women; in other words he knew his way around, and spent his holidays at such widely separated places as Acapulco and Tokyo. We were friends for many years, and he usually dined with me in London before the Derby, while I dined with him on my visits to France. He died very suddenly in 1964, since when my visits to Paris and Deauville have never been quite the same.

On the occasion in question, Rae agreed to play ball, adding that his mount wasn't much, and wouldn't beat Charlie's mount in any circumstances. It was nevertheless comforting to have Rae on our side, and I naturally betted accordingly.

All seemed to be going according to plan when Charlie's mount went to the front soon after entering the straight, opening up a two-length lead. The race seemed all over, and unfortunately this was Charlie's view, as he eased his horse entering the final furlong. Rae had to give the impression that he was trying for his life, but though he was rapidly closing the gap he still seemed to be no danger to the 'good thing'. Thinking that he had done enough, Charlie's mount slowed down to little more than walking pace, and before he could get him going again Rae had won the race by a head. It was the only occasion on which I remember seeing Charlie Elliott caught napping, but it would have to happen the day I had twice as much on him as I could afford to lose.

Soon after I had learnt the facts of life I was told by a hospital nurse that if it was left to men to produce babies, the human race would have died off several thousand years ago. I did not take this assertion very seriously, but ever since the birth of our son Anthony I have had a firm belief in its truth.

After about eighteen hours of sheer hell, Romie gave birth to a healthy son in the early hours of Sunday 2 April 1933, but her gynaecologist, Dr Bouffe St Blaise, insisted on her remaining in hospital for a month.

I spent most of my time when I was not at the hospital getting to know Paris. Although I had spent three years of my life there I was still a stranger to the real Paris which lies hidden away from the main thoroughfares and can only be explored on foot.

You may know the names of all the twelve avenues which run into the Place de l'Etoile, but you will never know the city till you have climbed the Rue Caulaincourt, where Toulouse Lautrec and Renoir lived, up to the Sacré Cœur, and having gazed over Paris you descend by a maze of alleyways and squares which have not changed since Sisley gave his landlord thirty of his paintings in lieu of a month's rent. Charpentier's music is sadly out of fashion, but one of these days they will revive *Louise* at the Opéra Comique and I shall be there for the first night and indulge in an orgy of nostalgia.

Dr Bouffe St Blaise told me at the Hôpital Américain in Neuilly, during those long hours waiting for Anthony's arrival, that he had been a close friend of the immortal Pierre Auguste Renoir, and had brought his son Jean into the world.

My hero Renoir had been born in 1841, four years after Queen Victoria came to the throne, and yet this little man with the white spade beard had officiated at the birth of his son in 1892, and of mine forty-one years later.

I plied him with questions about Renoir, and his eyes lit up with ènthusiasm as he described him to me as not only the greatest painter but also the most lovable man he had ever met. 'He was not only honest in his dealings with his fellow men, but also with himself, any form of pretence or affectation was abhorrent to him. He lived in an era of great painters, but there was never any jealousy among them. He had the greatest admiration for the work of Cézanne, an ill-mannered, irascible man, though Renoir assured me he had a heart of gold.'

Soon after Anthony's birth I received a most unpleasant communication from my bank in England and I realised that I should not be able to meet the hospital bill, which as a result of the complications would be more than twice the expected amount. I have always loved walking in Paris, which was fortunate as it cost nothing, and I realised that I must save every franc. A young American, George Ryan, had become a friend of ours, and when I met him at the Ritz bar one evening, having walked there from Neuilly, he told me his father was playing baccarat at the Sporting Club in the rue George V. Old man Ryan, who was a fabulously rich tobacco magnate, was sitting in the bar opposite a bottle of champagne when we arrived, and he told us that the Belgians running the bank had won every franc he possessed, and that he was going to pack it up for the evening. However, after the original bottle was finished and its successor half empty, old man Ryan decided to have another crack at the hard-faced Belgian industrialists, who were waiting and no doubt hoping to extract some more francs from the old gentleman who was in the process of cashing another colossal cheque.

As Mr Ryan resumed his seat, George, who was to be one of Anthony's godfathers, threw me 1,500 francs (about £12) with instructions to 'give it a run for the little fellow'. I betted on Mr Ryan's side of the table, and whereas he had lost consistently before our arrival he could now do no wrong, and I arose from the table the winner of just over £200. It was manna from heaven, and George and I went on to Bricktops and Le Bœuf sur le Toit, the two fashionable night clubs at that time. I'm afraid the 'little fellow' did not see much of my winnings, but they paid for his coming into the world, and but for this stroke of luck there would have been no little embarrassment at the hospital.

Anthony was six weeks old when we returned to live in England, and we took a furnished house at Churt, while we were looking around for a permanent home in the neighbourhood. Soon after our return, we visited Romie's parents in North Berwick, where press photographers had taken pictures of Romie on those famous links in her deb days. I had never had a golf lesson, but under the tuition of Ben Sayers I learnt to play well enough to obtain immense enjoyment from the game. Romie's father, Jim Hope-Vere, had previously been married to Marie Hope-Vere of Biarritz, and was one of the few men that I have met of whom I can say with certainty that he was loved by everyone who knew him. He had recently had a stroke and he could only speak with difficulty, but he gave me to understand that, as I evidently loved women, and he had heard that I also loved racing, he was sure we would have been good friends had we met a little earlier. This was the only occasion on which we met, as he died a few weeks later.

Romie's mother was not the easiest of people to get along with, but it is my experience that when a once beautiful woman has a beautiful daughter she unconsciously resents the daughter's success. Mabel Hope-Vere had adored her husband, and her unhappiness after his death was to some extent responsible for the friction which from time to time existed between us.

She was kind-hearted, and when staying with us for Christmas announced that she would like to take us on a West Indies cruise. We had, by this time, moved into a charming house just outside Haslemere, and Romie saw to it that I left for London early the following morning on a visit to the travel agents 'before Mummy changes her mind'.

A week before we were due to sail on the *Homeric* my mother-in-law, having read of the terrible storms in the Atlantic, asked me to cancel her reservation. This was a mercy; for although the *Homeric* was over 40,000 tons, and I believe the biggest vessel then afloat, she would not have been large enough to house Romie and her mother for a period of six and a half weeks without friction developing between them.

The *Homeric* was a legacy from the peace treaty. Previously known as the *Tirpitz,* she had been built to take the Kaiser on a tour of the world, after he had conquered most of it. We decided to re-visit the place we liked the best the next year, travelling on a banana boat and staying a month. We agreed that Jamaica was the loveliest island we had ever seen, and we sailed there on a 4,500-ton banana boat, which carried only a dozen passengers.

We had spent Christmas, as we did for three years running,

at Madresfield near Malvern, the country seat of Lord Beauchamp, who was living in Australia. The house was run by Lady Mary (Mamie) Lygon for her two sisters Lady Sibell and Lady Dorothy, and their brothers Hugh and Richard. I shall never forget the kindness we received from the Lygon family over the years, and Mamie included Anthony and his nurse in our invitation for Christmas.

Evelyn Waugh was also a frequent visitor, and he had Madresfield in mind when he wrote his book *Brideshead Revisited*. We were also frequent guests at the Lygons' house in Belgravia.

Although Romie was quite a good sailor, she invariably took to her bed on boarding a ship, declining to budge for forty-eight hours. When the Captain noticed her absence from boat drill he despatched a steward with his compliments, requesting Mrs Gilbey's attendance on deck, only to receive the following reply: 'Mrs Gilbey presents her compliments to the Captain, but has to inform him that she always goes down with the ship.'

I occupied the hours at sea by writing a novel about racing which I called *Cranberry Sauce*. Jamaica was completely unspoiled in those days, and having hired a self-drive car in Kingston we drove the 110 miles to Montego Bay. The roads were very rough but the scenery was enchanting, and we stayed at a comfortable hotel for 26*s*. a day each, all in.

We fell under the spell of the Caribbean, and we began thinking what fun it would be to fetch our small son and become beachcombers. However, with Cheltenham and another flat season just around the corner, I sailed home from Port Antonio with a cargo of 1½ million bananas in the last week of February, Romie following a fortnight later.

I have described how grateful I have always been to the Adjutant, whose insupportable treatment of the young officers was responsible for my sending in my papers, but I am equally grateful to Lord Nunburnholme for getting me the sack in 1935 from the *Bystander*, for which I had been writing a weekly article for over five years. It happened this way:

All journalists receive letters from their readers, and in reply to a correspondent who had asked me whether I thought that jockeys should be warned off for not trying, when in nine cases out of ten they were only carrying out instructions, I wrote: 'Yes, they should be, but it is an even worse offence when a man of means pulls his own horse in a race for amateur riders.' It so happened that Lord Nunburnholme had recently been before the Stewards and interrogated regarding his tactics when riding one of his own horses. His explanation had been accepted and he was completely exonerated.

To my astonishment, the Editor rang me up a few days after the publication of this article and informed me that Lord Nunburnholme took the view that my reference to an amateur rider pulling his horses referred to him, and that he was issuing a writ for libel. What had I to say about it? I replied that as Lord Nunburnholme thought the cap fitted, he could wear it as far as I was concerned, but as he had been exonerated, it could not possibly refer to him.

A few days later I received another call from the Editor telling me that he and our libel expert had had a satisfactory interview with the plaintiff, who, very sportingly, had agreed to withdraw his action on condition that Gilbey got the sack, and the paper donoted £100 to charity. So I was sacked after five years, in the course of which, without being unduly conceited, I think my articles had sold quite a number of copies.

Romie's reaction to my dismissal was short and sharp. 'Some women, I believe, like being married to failures, but I am not one of them,' she informed me, slamming the door behind her. At this distance of time I still regard those words as the most salutary I have ever received; they made me take stock of my achievements up to that time, and I decided that they amounted to very little. I had not libelled Lord Nunburnholme, but I had been content to muddle along, writing weekly articles here and there, instead of getting down to a real job of work on a daily or evening paper, and perhaps a Sunday paper as well. Smarting under Romie's well-deserved rebuke, I set about getting a worthwhile job at which I might realise any potentialities I possessed. I decided that the *Evening Standard* looked the best bet, so I wrote to Mike Wardell, one of the bosses, although I did not know him well at that time, asking him for an interview.

It all depended on my being able to convince him that I had something to offer that his regular contributor Jimmy Park, a magnificent journalist, wasn't giving him.

My suggestion was that I should do a short article each day dealing with personalities, and that on the days on which there was a big race I should write a diary under my own name, starting with the lunch edition and revising it throughout all the subsequent editions. As I entered Mike's office, I offered up a prayer that he would give me a chance, and my prayer was answered.

From that day my career prospered. The diary was an immediate success, it not only pleased the bosses of the *Evening Standard* office, but attracted the notice of other editors as well.

On big days I had little time to myself from 7 a.m. to 5 p.m., as I was continually ad-libbing stories over the telephone to catch the various editions, but I thoroughly enjoyed the work and it was a great satisfaction to me to feel that I was at last making a success in the profession of my choice.

I had a piece of luck on the morning of the 1936 Grand National. Having watched the forthcoming runners at early morning exercise I ran into Fulke Walwyn who was to ride Reynoldstown, who had won the previous year's race when he was ridden by Frank Furlong, son of the horse's owner-trainer Noel Furlong. I drove Fulke back from Aintree to the Adelphi Hotel, where we breakfasted together, after which I telephoned a story to the effect that Fulke had eaten a hearty breakfast, and was supremely confident that Reynoldstown would join the immortals who have won the Grand National two years running. I therefore urged all readers of the *Evening Standard* to go for a good win, and Reynoldstown duly won the race at 10/1. My *Evening Standard* diaries attracted the attention of Mr Harry Heywood, the London Editor of Kemsley Newspapers, and his recommendation to the Board that they should make me an offer fell on sympathetic ears, one of the directors being Sir Herbert Morgan, a business associate of my brother Ronald. Harry Heywood had been responsible for my getting the sack from Allied Newspapers ten years earlier, but he re-engaged me at a considerably higher salary, and from that time until his retirement he was to me a combination of Father Confessor and Fairy Godfather.

Jimmy Park was still in his prime, so my chances of advancement on the *Evening Standard* were nil, but if I gave satisfaction to the high-ups at Kemsley House I might work my way up to the star job of Kettledrum of the *Sporting Chronicle*. I therefore gave in my notice to the *Evening Standard*, and at the end of that month joined Kemsley newspapers, with whom I was to remain till my retirement over thirty years later.

I was as happy in our house in Haslemere as I had been unhappy at Hyde Park Square, and Romie furnished it, largely with money she had inherited from her father. Anthony was a lovely child, with flaxen hair and pink cheeks, and he was much admired by our friends.

My father gave me my first dachshund on my fifth birthday, and I have loved them ever since. When visiting the Heneages at Killochan Castle, for the Western Meeting at Ayr, we fell in love with a chocolate bitch called Coko belonging to our hostess, who was very fond of her, though her husband George threatened to shoot Coko if she continued to disturb his grouse or pheasants by hunting rabbits. George Heneage was a strange man; after dinner he would blaze away with a shotgun at the numerous heads which adorned the interior walls of the castle. A few weeks after our return from Scotland Romie received a frantic letter from Jean Heneage saying that George was going to murder Coko if she did not get rid of her within the next forty-eight hours. I was out when the letter arrived, but by the time I returned Romie had telegraphed for Coko to be put on the next train, and followed it with a cheque for £5. She was therefore technically Romie's dog.

We met her at King's Cross, and happy as we had been we were even happier after her arrival. Romie changed her name to Girleywoo, and by this name she was known to all our friends, as I never went anywhere without her. It was occasionally shortened to Woo.

Before myxomatosis, dachshunds were inveterate hunters, but

I have never met her equal for disappearing the moment my back was turned, in pursuit of the rabbits she must have known she would never catch.

If, after I am dead, my name crops up in the course of conversation, I have no doubt that I shall be best remembered for my obsessive love of my dachshunds. I derived constant pleasure from what some people described as my ridiculous and rather boring adulation of Girleywoo and her successors, and I like to think they in their turn enjoyed their all too short lives.

I had been engaged by Kemsley Newspapers to write a daily diary under my own name in the *Daily Sketch*, a far less strenuous job than was my diary in the *Evening Standard*, as the article handed in at 7 p.m. appeared in all the editions.

I was waiting for a taxi outside Victoria station shortly after joining the *Daily Sketch*, when four buses hove into sight, and on all of them were two posters bearing the inscription: 'Go racing with Quintin Gilbey in the Daily Sketch.' I had made it at last, the cards had forgiven me, and when opportunity knocked for the second time, I had grasped it.

But there was still one scare lurking round the corner. I was staying at Madresfield, and received a message to ring up the Editor immediately I came in. He informed me that an article of mine might cost the paper £10,000. A week or so earlier, at the instigation of the Sports Editor, I had written an article about selling races and had asked Bob Wigney, one of our senior auctioneers, if he had ever sold a horse to a purchaser who had been unable to raise the money. Bob said he had, and proceeded to tell me that a man had bought the winner of the selling race two days running; and when no money was forthcoming he had made routine enquiries; he discovered, so he alleged, that the man was bonkers and had escaped from a looney-bin. The sequel was that a gentleman appeared at the *Daily Sketch* office, and claimed to be the man who had bought the two selling-plate winners, and been unable to raise the wherewithal. He told the Editor that he had been suffering from amnesia, following a nervous breakdown, but that he had never been bonkers, and had never been inside a looney-bin.

Our legal expert took a serious view of the situation, as according to him there is no libel so damaging as that of accusing a man of insanity when he could supply evidence to the contrary. All ended happily, however, as on his next appearance at the office the gentleman who hadn't been in a looney-bin accepted a cheque for £25, and we all lived happily ever after.

Before the end of the year I was also writing articles for the *Sunday Times*, the *Daily Despatch* and the *Sunday Graphic*, so when Mr Chamberlain returned from Munich with a self-satisfied smile, and talked about 'peace in our time', as the result of selling Czechoslovakia down the river, I cheered lustily, instead of hanging my head in shame. I had made good at last, and I was earning more than twice as much as I had ever done before, and in order to go on doing so I was content for Mr Chamberlain to act dishonourably. Since our return to England we had been living far above our means, for which we were both to blame, being obsessed with a desire to be in the right place at the right time.

I had also made an unsuccessful speculation on the Stock Exchange. In racing, I would never dream of acting on the advice of a casual acquaintance, but I had done so over some West African gold shares and paid the penalty. In those days I knew nothing about stocks and shares, but did quite well backing horses; in the post war-years I have seldom had more than half a dozen bets a year, and when I have had some spare cash I have acted on the advice of my broker.

Matters came to a head when we returned from Deauville, and I found that the bank had returned my cheque for the rent of our London flat. This was the first and only time in my life that I have given a 'bouncer'. I had betted since before I was of age with Ladbrokes, and had always met my liabilities, though I often had to ask for time. I had also been able to give the firm, and in particular their representative Mrs Vernet, quite a lot of publicity in the *Bystander* and other 'shinies'.

I therefore paid a visit to the chairman, Arthur Bendir, who advanced me £750 at the trifling interest of 5 per cent on condition that I insured my life for £1,000. At the outbreak of war, I was broke again, earning 14*s*. a day as a lieutenant, Arthur thereupon not only declared a moratorium for the duration of the war, but also declined to accept any further interest on the loan. Arthur has been dead for many years, but I have never forgotten his generosity. 'I hear you're in the army, best of luck and pay me back when it's convenient', he wrote to me, which of course I did.

Funds were at their lowest ebb when I was due to go to Ostend for the week-end with Rupert Byass, a wonderful companion on a spree of this nature, which included two excellent days of racing, long hours in the casino, and the consumption of a vast amount of champagne.

I was covering the big race for the *Daily Sketch*, who were paying my overheads, but I would not draw these until my return. I therefore arrived at Rupert's house on the evening before we left with only £5 in my pocket, which I promptly lost playing dice. I was persuaded to continue, and I got it back and another fiver as well. At Ostend I could do no wrong, either on the racecourse or in the casino, and when I exchanged my Belgian francs I was handed £110!

Romie was so efficient at finding a house when we wanted one and disposing of it when we didn't that she should have been a house agent. As we seemed to be spending more and more time in London, she managed to sell our Haslemere house at a profit at the end of 1936, and we took a large and expensive flat in Bryanston Court. It had to be on the big side to house ourselves, a small child, his nurse and a maid. We could of course have chosen a less expensive neighbourhood, but such a thing never entered our heads.

I had exchanged the Bentley for a Humber Snipe through my old friend 'Pilks' (Sir Arthur Pilkington), and later swopped it for a Chrysler, which proved the most satisfactory car I had yet owned. Like all my cars, however, it was over-bodied and swung so violently rounding corners that my passengers were often sick.

Romie was responsible for these cumbersome vehicles. She invariably travelled with a vast amount of luggage, and when I suggested something smaller she replied, 'Where are we going to put Anthony and Nanny?'

We were invited to stay with friends so often at this time that had it not been for Anthony, a room in a hotel would have been all we needed. An unforgettable house party was the one at Wentworth Woodhouse for the St Leger Meeting. We had stayed with Peter and 'Obbie' Milton at Malton for York, and Peter had prevailed on his parents, Lord and Lady Fitzwilliam, to invite us for Doncaster. Wentworth Woodhouse was the largest, though not the most beautiful, of all the stately homes of England, and the house party, including the family, numbered seventy-six.

On our arrival Lady Fitzwilliam took us aside and told us that Mrs Hope-Vere of Biarritz was among the guests. 'That's splendid,' I replied, 'she and my father were great friends and she gave a party for me when I visited Biarritz with him.' Lady Fitzwilliam went on to explain that as the result of my marriage to Jim Hope-Vere's daughter by a subsequent marriage, Mrs Hope-Vere had announced that she would cut me dead as well as Romie. In a normal house party, Mrs Hope-Vere's hostility towards us might have been embarrassing, but in a party of seventy-six we only caught sight of her in the distance.

I subsequently visited Wentworth Woodhouse after the war. Peter had succeeded his father and he, 'Obbie' and his mother were living in one small wing of this vast house. The open-cast coal mines had taken the place of the spacious lawns, reaching almost to the dining-room windows.

Maud, Lady Fitzwilliam, who died in her ninetieth year, was one of the most remarkable women I have met. Although their backgrounds could hardly have been more different – Maud Fitzwilliam was the daughter of Lord Zetland – she reminded me in many ways of my grandmother. Her back remained as straight as a ramrod all her life, and she dominated any gathering by the magnetism of her personality. Although they were not at all demonstrative, she and Peter enjoyed a perfect relationship, and as a close friend of her son I became a close friend of hers.

Peter's death, in company with Lady Hartington in an air crash on their way to the South of France to visit Lady Hartington's father, Mr Joseph Kennedy, was a shattering blow, but his mother bore it with the fortitude which she knew he would have expected of her.

At the time of his death Peter owned the fastest two-year-old filly in training, Ballisland, which he bequeathed to his mother. I have never been more moved than I was after the filly won an important race on the July course at Newmarket, a few months after Peter's death. I was standing in the unsaddling enclosure, when Lady Fitzwilliam, having patted her filly and congratulated her jockey, came over to where I was standing and, having kissed me, said 'Wouldn't Peter have been thrilled?' She took me by the arm and said 'This calls for a glass of champagne'. I explained that I was not a member of the Private Stand, but seeing the Duke of Norfolk, she said to him, 'I am taking Quinny into the stand to celebrate, why don't you join us, Bernard?' and he did.

Munich had given us a year's respite and I suppose that someone as self-centred as I was could not be expected to worry about the fate of Czechoslovakia in view of the fact that Mr Chamberlain had enabled me to continue my career as a journalist for a few months longer. Not even a super-optimist, however, could believe that Hitler would be satisfied, while surely not even Mr Chamberlain could permit him to annex Poland without our taking action. We therefore let our expensive flat early in 1939 and Romie spent much of the spring and summer in Europe staying with friends, while I lived free at Ormonde Gate with Geoffrey and Mollie, in return for which I wrote an article for Geoffrey's paper, the *Sporting Record*. The exchange was very much in my favour.

From the racing point of view 1939 will be remembered for two great horses: Blue Peter, and Pharis II, owned by M Marcel Boussac and ridden by Charlie Elliott. Throughout this year I saw these two horses run in all their races; they were unbeaten, and I hesitate to say which was the better.

Blue Peter had finished second at Kempton in his only race as a two-year-old, and he therefore claimed the Maiden allowance in the Blue Riband Stakes. Knowing what a high opinion Jack Jarvis had of him, even money seemed a generous price and I had considerably more on him than I could afford to lose. I had few anxious moments, however, as it was evident that he had the race in his pocket when the field reached Tattenham Corner.

The Two Thousand Guineas was a triumph for Jack Jarvis. Blue Peter won cleverly from his stable companion Admiral's Walk, and he won the Derby as easily as he had won the Blue Riband over the same course.

Blue Peter's victory in the famous rose and primrose hoops was tremendously popular. This was Lord Rosebery's first and only Epsom Derby victory, though his father had won the race with Ladas, Sir Visto and Cicero.

Jack Jarvis, whose knighthood was so well deserved, had no doubt that Blue Peter was by far the best horse he ever trained. His only subsequent race was the Eclipse Stakes, in which he was less impressive. This was his third race in fairly quick succession, and he may not have been quite at his best. He won all right, but having laid £50 to £20 on him, I was relieved to seehim pass the post, Eph Smith having been hard at work a furlong from home.

I was spending the week-end in Paris when Pharis II made his début in the Prix Lupin. When I met Charlie Elliott before the first race at Longchamp he told me, 'We run a horse today who I think will win the Grand Prix. He's never run before but you'd better have your limit on him.'

In France, with no bookmakers and no Tote credit facilities as there are in England, one's limit is confined to the money in one's pocket at the moment. Leaving myself enough to pay for a taxi back to Paris, I invested the lot, and when this heavily built coal-black colt lost his action coming down the hill, and entered the straight half a dozen lengths behind the leaders I foresaw an embarrassing interview with the manager of the Hotel Scribe when I was presented with my bill the following morning. But my anxiety was short-lived, as when he reached the straight, Pharis II accelerated, and passed his opponents as if they were standing still.

In the French Derby he stumbled in the straight, and his knees actually hit the ground, Charlie Elliott told me, but he picked himself up to win comfortably.

He looked a certainty for the Grand Prix, but remembering how badly he had acted down the Longchamp hill when making his début, I was a little worried as to what would happen in a much larger field, in what was still, in those days, France's most important race.

In the circumstances Elliott would have been better advised to keep to the outside, as his inability to stride out down the hill resulted in his being hemmed in behind a wall of horses nearing the straight. It was not till he was well inside the last furlong that Charlie was able to extricate him, and as he started to eat up the ground I said to Frank More O'Ferrall, 'That's the unluckiest loser we shall ever see.' But such was Pharis's acceleration at the end of this 1 mile 7½ furlongs race that he took the lead inside the last hundred yards to win by three lengths. I have never seen anything like it before or since, and on that particular day Pharis II was the best horse I had ever seen. Twenty-seven years later I saw another French-bred colt, Sea Bird, win the Derby on the bit, and the Prix de l'Arc de Triomphe by six lengths from Reliance II, who had won the French Derby and the Grand Prix de Paris. But the careers of these two horses were so brief that in point of merit they cannot be compared to the two Italian champions, Nearco and Ribot, who were never beaten, winning fourteen and sixteen races respectively.

Pharis II was sent over to take on Blue Peter in the St Leger, but the race was never run. Had it been, Pharis II would not have been in the field, as on the day before the declaration of war he went so badly in a gallop that it was decided not to send him to Doncaster. Had they met on perfect going with both horses at their best, we might have seen one of the greatest races of all time, but on firm going Blue Peter would unquestionably have won, while in heavy going I think Pharis might have proved too good for the English colt.

Lord Rosebery intended to keep Blue Peter in training as a four-year-old, but as there were no races for him to win in the restricted programmes in 1940 he was sent to stud.

During the war Lord Rosebery received tempting offers for Blue Peter as Lord did Derby for Hyperion, and it was fortunate for British breeders that these two horses were not the property of the Aga Khan.

Pharis II was stolen by the Germans when they overran France, but they took great care of him, in fact when he was restored to M Boussac's stud in Normandy at the end of the war he was so fat that he had to undergo a diet.

Frank More O'Ferrall and I spent the week-end of the 1939 Grand Prix at Claridge's in the Champs-Elysées, a hotel of which the management held very broad views when I was a bank clerk. Frank and I were therefore a trifle taken aback when he answered the telephone at around 2 a.m. when we were drinking a bottle of champagne with my friend Arlette and a friend of hers, and heard the concierge complain 'You have ladies in your room.' Frank's reply, 'Of course I have, what the hell do you think I came to Paris for?' was typical of a man who in a highly successful career has seldom come off second best in a battle of words. This Paris jaunt took place several years before Frank married lovely Angela Jackson, who was only a year old when her father took me down the coal mine.

As the senior partner in the phenomenally successful Anglo-Irish Bloodstock Agency, with Paddy Prendergast acting in an advisory capacity, Frank More O'Ferrall has bought, sold and syndicated some of the most successful horses of the post-war era.

I paid one more visit to Paris before the outbreak of war. I was due to cover Deauville races for the *Daily Sketch*, and as it could not be more than a matter of weeks before Germany invaded Poland I flew to Paris in order to spend an evening with Arlette, taking the train on to Deauville the following morning. But Arlette was on holiday in the country, and the manageress of the Sphinx night club told me, over a bottle of champagne, that France had no stomach for another war, that she was unprepared morally and physically, that the Maginot Line was a bad joke, and that the fall of Paris would be swiftly followed by the capitulation of the French armies. She asked me questions concerning Britain's preparedness, and thinking that her pessimism could only emanate from someone with pro-German sentiments I told her the lie that the year since Munich had given us time to build up our resources, and that we had never in our history been so powerful on land, on sea and in the air.

In the light of subsequent events I can only believe that this good woman had had her card well marked, and that my suspicion that she was a German agent, or at least pro-German, was without foundation. She, in her turn, must have thought that either I was a great fool or a great liar. I never saw Arlette again, as although I scoured Paris after the liberation in 1946, I could find no trace of her.

Although authors and playwrights sentimentalise over the tart with the golden heart, most English people are convinced that all girls who work at joints like the Sphinx are cold-hearted, sexless money-grubbers, incapable of feeling any affection for the opposite sex. But Arlette was none of these things, and at the risk of being considered gullible to the point of naivety, she was to me a lovable person, who for some reason became attached to a man she met in the course of her job. She used to write me affectionate little letters in a childish hand, and her greatest treat was to be taken out to dinner on Sundays when the Sphinx was closed. She refused to dine at smart restaurants, preferring the bistros and cafés where we were likely to run into some of her colleagues to whom I would be proudly introduced as 'mon cher ami'. She was not in the least mercenary, and after an evening in which she and her friends had prattled away about their jobs, with no more inhibitions than if they had been seamstresses, she was offended when I offered her money. She told me that there were, of course, occasions when it was *comme il faut* for a girl to accept a present from her gentleman friend, but this was not one of them.

There was an air of forced gaiety about Deauville that August, when it was obvious that war was inevitable, and there was even an absence of urgency around the tables in the casino. One evening I found a normally heavy gambler sitting disconsolately at the bar drinking brandy and when I asked him how the luck was going he answered, 'What does it matter if one wins or loses when in a week's time everything we care about will be swept away?'

# 17 *The gentle Beaver*

It was in 1935 that June introduced me to Lord Beaverbrook, and if I had not refused to allow her to cut me I should not, in all probability, have made his acquaintance till my post war visits to Jamaica. I was in Paris on a story concerning the strength of the coming French invasion at Epsom and Ascot, and was walking along that long corridor, full of show cases displaying the wares from all the most expensive shops, which leads from the Place Vendôme side of the Ritz in Paris to the rue Cambon side, when I encountered June. Her response to my greeting was the barest flicker of an eyelid as she hurried by. This was too absurd, and so I did an about-turn and asked her what the frozen mitt was in aid of.

She explained that she had heard I had been staying at Castle Wemyss with Alan Inverclyde, when his first wife Olive was also staying there, so she assumed I was 'on the other side'. I must explain that three years earlier June's marriage to Lord Inverclyde had been dissolved after one of the most widely publicised divorce cases of the present century. June had subsequently written her life story for the *Sunday Express*, so although she had retired from the stage on becoming the chatelaine of Castle Wemyss in 1929, she had remained very much in the public eye.

Over a champagne cocktail I explained that I had never expected people to take sides over the two divorces in which I had figured, and I had, most certainly, not taken sides in her divorce. Alan and I had been together at Eton and in the Brigade, and his first wife Olive and I had been friends for years. We had been fellow guests but the divorce had not been mentioned.

Having straightened things out, we had a most enjoyable lunch, and arranged to dine together the following evening. Next morning, however, June rang up to say we were both dining with Lord Beaverbrook if that was O.K. by me. She had run into him the previous evening, and he had asked her to dine, and when she said that she was dining with me he had told her to bring me along as he already had a business associate dining with him. I was to discover in years to come that Lord Beaverbrook abominated rich food, but the sole and the chicken at Philippe – he seldom dined anywhere else in Paris – were superb, as was the Krug '21, though he himself drank whisky.

Perhaps it was because I only had eyes for June that evening that my first impressions of my distinguished host are very vague, and the only occasion on which he addressed me, so far as I can recall, was to ask me if I was related to Geoffrey. The fourth member of the party made even less impression; I can't remember his name. After dinner we went on to a box at the Casino de Paris, where more champagne was produced. Half-way through the show Lord Beaverbrook said he was tired and left the theatre, taking his friend with him. June and I saw the show out, and went on to a night club, where she told me that she thought Max one of the most fascinating men she had ever met, and her eyes shone with enthusiasm as she went on: 'I know he's as ugly as sin, but is he attractive! – and he knows it.' I flew home the following day and a few weeks later June went to America, where she married again.

A year or so later I joined the *Evening Standard*, and although Lord Beaverbrook was not in the least interested in racing, after an unsatisfactory venture as an owner in the 'twenties, he asked Romie and me to a very swagger dinner party at his London residence, Stornaway House, St James's. All the men with the exception of Aneurin Bevan, who wore heavy shapeless tweeds, were in tail coats and white ties. Lord Beaverbrook had met Romie in the South of France, and as he subsequently told me how much he admired her, I think that her looks and charm, rather than my recent appointment to one of his newspapers, were the reasons for our invitation.

Lord Beaverbrook, Brendan Bracken, Valentine Castlerosse and Aneurin Bevan shouted at one another throughout dinner. This deafening interchange of words was the result of Mr Bevan being placed towards the kids' end of the table which was presided over by Lord Beaverbrook's daughter Janet. Previously married to Ian Campbell (subsequently Duke of Argyll), Janet was now married to Drogo Montagu, brother of Lord Sandwich.

Max Aitken and one of his first two wives, I forget which, was also at our end of the table, and as we all knew one another well we had a most enjoyable evening and drank a lot of champagne.

It was not till I became a regular visitor to Montego Bay in Jamaica in 1947 that I became intimately acquainted with Lord Beaverbrook. He had a fantastic memory, as not only did he never forget a face, he never forgot anything he was told, no matter how trivial it might have been.

We had not exchanged more than a couple of dozen words on the occasions on which I had been his guest in Paris and at Stornaway House, but on my first day on the beach at Doctor's Cave I heard my name being called. On looking round I saw that the voice emanated from an outsize straw hat which crowned an outsize dressing gown. The owner of the voice was invisible, but as I approached, an arm shot from the dressing gown, and a hand grasped mine. I could distinguish a wide mouth, grinning at me from beneath the hat, though the eyes were still invisible.

After an exchange of trivialities he embarked on a series of interrogations, one of the first being: 'How are your two lovely wives?' I replied that so far as I knew they were both very well and happy; that I had not communicated with number one since our divorce, but that I was on the very best terms with number two and her husband, and that we corresponded every week. 'I have never met a young fellow [I was in my middle forties] who married two such beautiful women; there must be something about you which is not immediately apparent', he told me, and throughout our friendship this subject was a puzzle to him. On a number of occasions, he introduced me to fellow guests in his house as 'My friend Quinny Gilbey, he's got two beautiful wives.' I would, whenever possible, point out that both were 'ex', but as Lord Beaverbrook had used the present tense I have no doubt that his visitors often went home firmly convinced that they had been introduced to a bigamist.

Having satisfied himself that my ex-wives were in good health, the straw hat was pushed back revealing a countenance of puckish good humour, though those probing eyes never left mine, and it seemed to me that my soul was laid bare. 'What about a swim?' denoted that the scrutiny was over and the result not altogether unfavourable, and from then onwards our morning swim together became a ritual. If he could not see me when he considered the moment for immersion had arrived, he would bellow: 'Where the hell is Quinny, has anyone seen Quinny? God damn it, where's he got to?'

I never discovered why he insisted on my company on his morning bathe, as I am not a strong swimmer and would not have been of the slightest use to him had he got into difficulties. As we seldom swam more than a few yards out of our depth there was little danger of this.

The weather on the north coast of Jamaica in January and February is for the most part ideal for bathing, but occasionally the temperature drops and a strong wind blows. On one of these occasions we pondered as to whether we should brave the elements, before he finally decided we should climb down a ladder – no diving for us – from the groin into deep water, as the waves were breaking on the beach. As we reached the ladder a small boy, looking the picture of misery, climbed up it. 'You look very sad, my little man, what makes you so unhappy?' Lord Beaverbrook asked him. It was very cold on the groin so I remarked, somewhat petulantly: 'What the hell has he got to bellyache about? He's been in.' I am not suggesting that this was a great witticism, but it appealed to Lord Beaverbrook as an apt appreciation of the situation, and he often referred to it.

A number of people in Jamaica used to say that I could say anything to him and get away with it, but that was not so. As our friendship ripened, I knew how far I could go, and that the barrier separating that deep-throated chuckle from a silent rebuke, more terrifying than any words, was a very narrow one. It did not take me long to discover that Canada and all things Canadian, and *Express* newspapers, were sacrosanct, and that any derogatory remarks on these subjects would incur lifelong displeasure.

I shall never forget his rage when a woman, who with her distinguished husband had long been friends of his, spoke disparagingly of the *Daily Express* at a dinner party. He gave her a murderous look but said nothing. On the next day he asked me: 'Did you hear what that stupid bitch had the impertinence to say about the *Daily Express*? What did you think of her remarks?' I replied quite truthfully that I thought they were very silly. She had known him far longer than I had, and as she was an intelligent woman I can only attribute her indiscretion to too much champagne.

He was quick to anger, and it took him a long time to forgive. I think that his fantastic memory kept words and deeds fresh in his mind, so that the passing of time failed to erase an incident, as it does with most people. I once incurred his displeasure. Although his judgement was often proved wrong, his policies invariably made sense at the time, though they did not prove acceptable to the electorate. But on the subject of racing he talked complete nonsense. He claimed to have spent £200,000 as the result of his two years as an owner of racehorses, and he attributed most of his misfortunes either to the incompetence or to the dishonesty of those in whom he had placed his trust. 'They must have been either knaves or fools, and I prefer to think they were knaves.' A fool, in his eyes, was a more dangerous enemy of society than any, except the most dangerous criminal.

France has had three great equine empires in the present century, those belonging to the Rothschilds, to Marcel Boussac and to François Dupré. François Dupré had taken a house in Montego Bay, and he, Lord Beaverbrook and I were dining together one evening when the subject turned to racing. M Dupré and I should have been warned to change the subject when Lord Beaverbrook informed us that Lord Rosebery, for whom he had a warm regard and whose opinion he valued, had failed to convince him that the turf was not peopled by rogues and vagabonds, and that we were unlikely to succeed where this most eloquent of elder statesmen had failed.

Undeterred, M Dupré and I made a concerted attack on what we described as his gross slander on racing men, pointing out that horses are not machines, and that his failure was the result of ill luck, in that the well-bred horses, bought by experts on his behalf, had failed to realise expectations. I think that we made our point so well that our host realised he had been talking nonsense, a most damaging blow to the self-esteem of a man of power. He bade us a curt goodnight, and the only occasion on which he again laughed heartily in my presence during that particular holiday was when I stepped on a cactus plant, when walking barefoot.

On meeting someone for the first time he would make a snap decision, and in the case of a pretty girl the first impression was invariably favourable. On the beach one morning, I introduced him to a very pretty girl who was staying in my hotel. He had obviously taken a very favourable view of her, and at the end of five minutes he said: 'Quinny must bring you up to dinner tonight.' He placed her next to him, and his first words when we met the following day were: 'She's a most charming girl, you should marry her.' I could think of half a dozen good reasons against the suggestion, but I knew he wouldn't listen so I answered that I was so glad he liked her, and left it at that. Twice more that week I took her to dine with him, but on the morning after the last occasion, he announced: 'That girl's a bore, you'd better get rid of her.' Once, however, he had accepted you as a friend, his loyalty never wavered.

In Europe, he had always worn very sombre clothes, and even in Jamaica his only concession to the prevailing fashion of light colours was a white jacket. I could therefore hardly believe my eyes when he arrived at a cocktail party, given by Constance, Duchess of Westminster, wearing a light-blue linen jacket. It was evident that he was self-conscious at his own sartorial splendour, one of the very few occasions on which I ever saw him not in complete control of the situation. Few men have cared less what image they created in the opinion of the multitude, though he minded very much what people thought of his newspapers. But on this occasion he was far from certain that he had not made a fool of himself.

I thereupon walked over to him and said: 'What a magnificent coat, it suits you splendidly.' He was obviously delighted at my words of commendation, and even more so when I called over several mutual friends who also expressed their approbation. At lunch time, the following day, he rang me up to tell me that on his way back from the beach he had bought me a length of the same material and given orders to my tailor to make me the self-same coat, and charge it to him. I still have it.

This story reveals a side of his character unsuspected by the millions who read his newspapers, and only knew of him as the greatest backroom boy of all time, the man who made one government and helped to unmake several others, who as Minister of Aircraft Production worked twenty-four hours a day, and whose unorthodox methods were largely responsible for our eventual supremacy in the air.

Although he had accepted a peerage, he was opposed to hereditary titles, and it infuriated him that our hostess should still call herself Duchess of Westminster, though she had divorced the Duke more than thirty years since. The Duke had remarried three times and she was happily married to Commander Lewis, a highly amusing character who delighted in telling stories at the expense of his wife, whom he declared to be the original Mrs Malaprop.

One that delighted Lord Beaverbrook concerned a recent incident at King's House, at a reception given by the Governor. The Duchess, finding herself in the company of one of Jamaica's magistrates, asked him if there was much crime in the island, to which he replied: 'Not of a serious nature, mostly petty larceny, though recently we have had a number of cases of arson.' At this the Duchess gave him a withering look and stamped out of the room followed by the Governor, the Lord Chief Justice and a couple of A.D.C.s, all beseeching her to tell them what had occurred. For a long time she declined to mention the offending words, but eventually she pointed an accusing finger at the offending magistrate and explained. 'That horrible little black man talked to me about larceny and arson.' 'But your Grace, there's nothing shocking about these words,' the Lord Chief Justice assured her. 'Nothing shocking!' replied Her Grace. 'Am I wrong therefore in interpreting them as meaning those disgusting things which men do to one another?'

Of all the people I met in Lord Beaverbrook's company I think that Bea Lillie, Lord Boothby, Aneurin Bevan, Clare Boothe Luce and Sally Cooper were the only people who were not in awe of him when they were guests in his house.

Sally Cooper was aged seventeen when she took her fifteen fellow diners' breaths away. In reply to her host's query as to whether she did not consider the meat, which had been flown from Canada, to be the best she had ever eaten, she prodded it for several seconds before looking steadfastly at him through her glasses, and giving her awful verdict: 'If it is, your knives must be blunt.' Sally was Gladys Cooper's daughter by her marriage to Neville Pearson, and for that reply I award her the prize for courage over any girl of her age I have ever met. She was great fun, and didn't give a damn for anybody. The following day Lord Beaverbrook asked me if I had heard Sally's verdict on the meat. I told him I had, and that as he regarded courage as one of the greatest virtues he should not hold it against her. He looked at me for several seconds before he burst out laughing, and I knew that Sally had got away with it.

There is no twilight in Jamaica, and I was swimming one evening when the sun disappeared below the horizon, and in a moment it was dark. A few minutes later I heard a girl's voice singing 'Someone to watch over me'. I looked over my shoulder and saw a brightly lit barge being rowed towards the hotel where it came to a halt. The singer was an attractive coloured girl, and she was singing this song, made famous by Gertie Lawrence, extremely well. None of the other performers were up to her standard, but it was good entertainment, and when I told Lord Beaverbrook about them he asked me to arrange for them to come up to his house and sing to his guests after dinner. This I did and they were a great success.

About a week later he told me he had a large house party arriving next day, including Clare Boothe Luce and Henry Luce, and would I arrange for a gala performance. The answer to this request was the addition to the usual cast of half a dozen very young girls, who joined in the choruses, accompanying the words with some very obscene gestures. Mrs Luce was horrified at what she described as the corruption of small children, and at the end of the performance she distributed money amongst them on the condition that they never participated in the act again. When he heard this Lord Beaverbrook gave vent to one of his loudest roars of merriment: 'What a racket, what a racket, here am I paying the little bastards to sing, while Clare Luce is paying them not to sing.'

The leading singer's name was Hortense, and I toyed with the idea of sending her to England as she had considerable talent, but I knew no one who would take on the job of looking after a semi-educated coloured girl, who had only once been in a train, and knew nothing of the outside world. Lord Beaverbrook always referred to Hortense as 'Quinny's black girl friend', and when I protested my innocence he feigned incredulity. He did not believe in platonic friendships, and he enjoyed few things more than an earthy conversation on the subject of the love lives of our acquaintances. I have already referred to his prodigious memory, and when I once expressed the view that two people, well known to us both, were only friends, he snapped back: 'That wasn't your view a year ago.'

Winston Churchill's visit was a memorable occasion. He had not yet received the Garter and was still Mister. The great man had been spending a holiday with Harold Mitchell near Ocho Rios, about sixty miles from Montego Bay; Harold Mitchell was to motor him over to lunch with Lord Beaverbrook, and he was to catch the plane to New York in the afternoon.

In the course of the morning Lord Beaverbrook received a message to the effect that owing to engine trouble the plane would not leave till late that night. Sir William and Lady Wiseman put their private beach at Mr Churchill's disposal, and in addition to the luncheon party a dinner party was laid on. Willie and Joan Wiseman were old friends of Lord Beaverbrook and they had become friends of mine. They had an enchanting house and garden a thousand feet up, overlooking the sea and reached by a precipitous road. They were most hospitable, and I always enjoyed their parties. It was at one of them that I met Irving Berlin. and managed to steer the conversation round to his 'shop'. He expressed surprise that I was familiar with at least ninety per cent of the songs he had written. Little more than five feet tall, he peered short-sightedly through very strong glasses and mistook Sir Alfred Butt for Lord Beaverbrook. Apart from wielding considerable power in their different spheres, the two men could not have been less alike.

Having taken it for granted that he would be in New York in plenty of time for dinner, Mr Churchill made no attempt to conceal his impatience at the enforced delay, behaving like a spoilt child. 'Why had the bloody plane gone wrong, and if it had gone wrong why hadn't they sent another one to take its place?' In response to our host's introductions to his fellow guests, Mr Churchill pushed out a limp white hand in several directions, but soon grew tired of it and I, together with the other less important guests, failed to get a handshake.

'What about a drink?' Lord Beaverbrook asked him, and proceeded to busy himself with his new gadget. This was a cocktail shaker which, when plugged in, did the job for him. His recipe was approximately 90 per cent ice, 5 per cent rum and 5 per cent lemon juice. This was not to Mr Churchill's taste, and after one sniff, he asked if there was any rum in the house. A bottle was produced and he helped himself to half a tumbler, drinking it down neat without blinking. He was asked whether he would like champagne for lunch, and he said he would. A bottle was placed in front of him and he drank the lot. After lunch he consumed several brandies.

Soon after his arrival, Willie and Joan Wiseman told him that they hoped he would bathe from their beach, but he said he would prefer to bathe from the public beach (Doctor's Cave). It was pointed out that as it was known that he was arriving in Montego Bay he would be mobbed, and that the police might not be able to control the crowd which would flock to see him. He therefore accepted the Wisemans' invitation, but it was obvious that he was disappointed.

He spoke very little during lunch and his few remarks were

directed at Lord Beaverbrook and Willie Wiseman. The rest of us, pretty girls and all, might not have existed as far as he was concerned. I have never met a man between the ages of nineteen and ninety who appeared so uninterested in feminine society. If he addressed a remark to any of the women I must have been looking the other way at the time, and he talked about nothing but the tiresome delay, and how much he disliked flying in the dark when it was totally unnecessary.

After a brief rest he set off with the Wisemans for their beach, taking a bottle of whisky with him, as he sometimes felt cold on emerging from the sea. That was the last I saw of him, but I gathered that dinner was a replica of lunch and that he departed for the airport, carrying a bottle of whisky, as he often felt cold when flying at night.

When I met Lord Beaverbrook for our daily swim the following day, and remarked that Mr Churchill had seemed very disgruntled at the delay, he replied that his ill humour was rather the result of his not being allowed to bathe from the public beach. 'He was looking forward to rolling over and over in the sea like a porpoise,' he said 'and making the V-sign to the crowd every time he came to the surface.'

I cannot recall ever having taken such an instinctive dislike to anyone. My cousin Frank Gilbey was also unfortunate in his one association with the great man. One of the best 'whips' in the country, Frank was chosen to drive the P.M. in the Coronation Procession in a carriage drawn by horses belonging to W. & A. Gilbey, who still owned a coach and four at that time.

All the cheers were of course for the Queen, and the P.M., unnoticed by the crowd as he emerged from Westminster Abbey, was obviously in an ill humour as he entered his carriage. The procession had progressed only a few yards when the P.M. ordered Frank to drive straight to Downing Street instead of to the Palace. My cousin could hardly believe his ears but did as he was told, and the P.M. alighted without a word and let himself into his official residence.

Later that day the P.M. explained that the horses drawing his carriage were out of control, and that he had no alternative but to leave the procession. This was a gross slander on both Frank and the horses, who had been used to London traffic all their lives. Frank consulted me as to his course of action, and I advised him to write a letter to *The Times* explaining exactly what had happened. Had I been in his position I should have demanded a withdrawal of the P.M.'s statement and an apology, but Frank is a much nicer person than I am and he decided to forget all about it.

My Jamaica holiday of 1951 was the most memorable of all my West Indian holidays; it was the year that Max Aitken married Vi de Trafford in the Presbyterian Church at Montego Bay, and Ivor Novello arrived with a party of theatrical celebrities to stay for a month in his house which stood on a hill half a mile from the hill on which Lord Beaverbrook's house 'Cromarty' was situated. My friend Harry Carr, the Queen's jockey, arrived with his wife Joan and daughter Anne, and one way and another I had a wonderful time.

Lord Beaverbrook was not at all pleased at the prospect of his son and heir embarking on matrimony for the third time, and I did not envy Vi her task of winning over her prospective father-in-law. I did my best by pretending I knew her far better than I did, and saying that she was one of the most charming and intelligent girls I had ever met. On the day she and Max left on their honeymoon, Lord Beaverbrook told me that my description of his daughter-in-law had been correct in every detail.

Soon after his arrival on the island, Max asked me to be his best man, and the wedding was a very small one, only Lord Beaverbrook, Willie and Joan Wiseman and two or three other close friends being present. Before the wedding Lord Beaverbrook made over his country estate, Cherkley, to Max, in the presence of the butler and myself, who signed the deed as witnesses.

A few nights earlier Max and Vi gave one of the best beach parties I have ever attended. They had become very determined to repay the hospitality they had received. They certainly succeeded.

I was appointed to recruit the cabaret, and I secured additional talent from St Anne's Bay and other villages. I informed the artists that Mrs Luce would not be present, and after several glasses of rum any inhibitions they may have possessed were cast aside.

The marriage was to take place at 4.30, and after lunch Lord Beaverbrook was in one of his most capricious moods, stalking round the house singing 'Walter, Walter, lead me to the altar'. Max seemed to be rather on edge, so as his best man I suggested we drive down to Sunset Lodge and partake of something to steady our nerves. The bar clock had stopped weeks ago at 4.45, but Max, thinking it was the correct time said: 'Good Lord, old boy, look at the time, it must be all over and we've missed it.' In the course of a speech he gave at a dinner, at which I was a guest, Max told this story against me, but I am convinced that it was he who said it. After dinner, on the night of the wedding, Lord Beaverbrook said: 'Quinny, you're tight.' As usual, he was right.

Although he seldom consulted a colleague, he soon tired of his own company, and it was on this account that I came to know him so intimately in the course of the five years during which we both spent part of the winters in Jamaica.

I invariably stayed at the Casablanca Hotel, and the only occasion on which I slept at his house was when an attack of gout prevented his accompanying me on a visit to Kingston after I had vacated my room at Montego Bay. His butler telephoned me at lunchtime to say that his Lordship's gout was very troublesome, and would I visit him after my afternoon swim and stay the night. Having had some experience of his irascibility when suffering from asthma, I feared the worst, but he thanked me for my kindness in visiting him in his sorry plight. I dined with him in his room and we talked till it was time to go to bed. Except for an occasional oath, when his gouty foot gave a more than usually painful twinge, he did not refer to his discomfort and our conversation embraced a variety of subjects.

I discovered, early in our association, that he resented being asked questions when other people were present, but on this occasion he was more expansive on the subject of his own life than at any time during our friendship.

He told me that his greatest satisfaction and one of his biggest disappointments were both concerned with the same post. 'I was summoned to 10 Downing Street,' he told me, 'and on my arrival

I was shown into the Cabinet Room, where Lloyd George was talking with Bonar Law. He immediately offered me the post of High Commissioner to the General Assembly of the Church of Scotland. As the son of a Scottish Presbyterian Minister this was the post, above all others, that I had coveted, but my private life at that time was not in my opinion compatible with such a post, so with the greatest regret I declined it. Lloyd George then turned to Bonar Law and said: "So Geordie gets it." And you know as well as I do that, compared with Geordie [the Duke of] Sutherland, I had led a positively cloistered existence.' He continued, 'I had been dining at the Criterion with the Dolly Sisters when I was summoned to Downing Street, and when I returned to the restaurant, whom should I find dancing with one of the Dolly Sisters but Geordie Sutherland.' This story was told me in strict confidence, but several years later it appeared in a modified version in his book, *The Decline and Fall of Lloyd George*.

Often we would spend an hour or more gossiping like a couple of old washerwomen. He once described Lord Birkenhead to me as having a biting wit at the expense of his fellow men, but a very soft heart where women were concerned. My comment was that this applied equally to the proprietor of the *Daily Express*. He was obviously pleased, but said he had never thought of himself in that light, though of course he had.

For years he had been telling the world that he no longer directed the policy of his newspapers. If that was true, he wasted a lot of money on telephone calls, for if one happened to call on him between 6 and 8 p.m., he was invariably talking to Fleet Street.

He told me, unasked, that he regretted his acceptance of a peerage, but his biggest disappointment was his failure to win over the electorate to his policy of Empire Free Trade. His greatest triumph was the success of his newspapers, but in reply to my question as to the extent of his influence on the affairs of the nation in his role of backroom boy, he only grinned.

He often said: 'I am not a very ardent Royalist', though he declined to expand on this subject, except to say that he hoped that Lord Mountbatten, as Prince Philip's uncle, would not be allowed to poke his nose into affairs of state. He made no secret of his dislike of Mountbatten, holding him responsible for the death of so many Canadians in the raid on Dieppe. 'The Canadians were used as guinea pigs in an ill-conceived experiment,' he told me, and tears of rage filled his eyes as he thumped the table.

'I was a King's man over the Abdication,' he said, 'and had the King followed my advice we would have won, but you can't keep a man on the throne against his will.' I think that his dislike of Baldwin, rather than his allegiance to the reigning Monarch, was the driving force in his participation in this sad affair.

He made no secret of his dislike of Lord Curzon, Ernest Bevin and Stanley Baldwin, and though he declined to place them in order of detestation, I think that Baldwin was his *bête noire*. As he had been largely responsible for Bonar Law's appointment as Prime Minister, at the expense of Curzon, he no longer had any bitterness in his heart towards the man he referred to as 'that pompous ass'. He respected Ernest Bevin as an honest man, and I formed the impression that Bevin disliked him more than he disliked Bevin.

I failed in my endeavour to make him draw comparisons between Lloyd George and Winston Churchill as war-time Prime Ministers. The furthest he would go was to say that Churchill's task was by far the easier. 'With the exception of a few cranks, everyone was behind him, but Lloyd George had to fight not only the Germans, but the Generals, Northcliffe and the *Morning Post* as well.'

No detail in the lives of those around him was too trivial to be of interest, so it did not surprise me when he asked how much I was paying for my self-drive car. When I told him I didn't know, he commanded me to bring along the papers when I came to dinner that evening, adding: 'I expect the bastards are cheating you.' He handed the papers back to me the following day, and when I opened them I found his cheque for the entire amount. When I thanked him he protested that the car had been used largely for the transport of his guests, but spontaneous acts of generosity were typical of him, and this was far from the only occasion on which I was on the receiving end.

Early in 1950 he bought a lovely Colonial house in Nassau, which he occupied for a month after leaving Jamaica. I arrived to stay with him in Nassau on the day King George VI died, Lord Beaverbrook having contacted Lord Kemsley, who was my boss at that time, and secured his consent to my extending my holiday. Mr and Mrs Paul Martin were the other house guests; we had become friends in Jamaica a year or so earlier. They were a charming couple: Paul was Minister of Health for Canada in the Liberal Government when we first met, and he subsequently became Secretary of State.

After breakfast one morning, Lord Beaverbrook announced that he was giving a dinner party that evening and that his guests were Lord and Lady Kemsley, Ghislane Alexander (now Lady Ashcombe), Sir Victor Sassoon, Mr and Mrs Charles Clore and Roy Thomson.

'And who's Roy Thomson?' I asked. If there was one fault Lord Beaverbrook would not tolerate it was ignorance, and he shouted to Paul Martin in the next room, 'Paul, this ignorant bastard has never heard of Roy Thomson, but he will, my God, he will', a prophecy which was fulfilled. In the course of the next two years Roy Thomson bought out Lord Kemsley, lock, stock and barrel, and therefore became my Lord and Master. This was the first occasion on which he and Lord Kemsley had met, so it was quite an historic evening.

My only recollections of the man who, I was told, owned forty-five newspapers in Canada, were his embarrassment when he found the other men at the party wearing dinner jackets whereas he was in a lounge suit, and his assertion that he never bothered about the members of his staff on minimum wage, as if they were any good they wouldn't be on minimum wage. Although I worked for him for over ten years we never met again.

Lord Beaverbrook enjoyed the company of stage people, and when Ivor Novello arrived with a large number of friends he gave a dinner party in their honour. Gladys Cooper was staying at a near-by club with her son John Buckmaster and daughter Sally, and it was she who introduced me to Ivor. I had seen him in dozens of shows but strangely enough we had never met, though I knew the other members of his party. Few men have possessed more charm, and on the two occasions I dined at his house he and his guests put on an impromptu cabaret after dinner which would have cost many hundreds to stage in a public place. Olive Gilbert sang like a lark in several languages, having previously cooked an excellent dinner, but Bea Lillie was the star performer, and as a Canadian she was of course an old friend of Lord Beaverbrook, who was always in cracking form when she was around.

He seldom drove a car, and having heard from his passengers of their terrifying experiences it seemed just as well. But one day he announced that he was going to take Bea to visit some friends for drinks, and that they were going alone. He always dined punctually at eight, but eight o'clock struck and there was no sign of them. Eventually, his elderly car hove in sight, and it was noticeable that the occupants had changed hats and were singing. The road up to his house was steep, and Lord Beaverbrook's efforts to change into bottom gear resulted in the car grinding to a stop. Nothing these two intrepid Canadians could do would induce it to start again, and their merry song having given way to fearful oaths, they disembarked and made the steep ascent on foot, arm in arm.

Ivor was recuperating from a bad go of flu, which had caused him to retire temporarily from the cast of *King's Rhapsody*. If ever a man was dedicated to the theatre, that man was Ivor Novello, and he seldom talked of anything else. I spent much time in his company, and one day he said: 'We talk our shop all day long, but Quinny never mentions his.' I explained that I enjoyed listening to their conversation about the theatre; not only would my racing 'shop' be unintelligible to them, but there could be no greater infliction than for a racing professional to discuss racing except with experts.

Gladys Cooper had been a friend of mine for many years, and she, Sally, John and I went on a number of expeditions together into the interior of the island, taking a picnic with us.

Shortly after my return to England I went to see *King's Rhapsody*, and visited Ivor and Bobby Andrews in their dressing rooms after the show. Ivor was in great form, and said he hadn't felt so well for years, thanks to the Jamaican sunshine. Three days later I was working in the press room at Cheltenham, when I overheard a colleague say: 'Very sad about Ivor Novello.' He had collapsed in great pain after the evening performance and died a few hours later from coronary thrombosis. I had only known him for a few weeks, but such was his charm that I felt I had lost a lifelong friend.

Lord Beaverbrook's kindness and hospitality were largely responsible for my Jamaican holidays being some of the happiest of my life, but with each succeeding year I became more aware of the poverty in the midst of so many riches. Every year, men and women of fabulous wealth spent vast sums of money in the island, and luxury hotels were springing up like mushrooms. Bauxite had been discovered and, judging by the scars which were beginning to disfigure the countryside, it must have yielded a sizeable revenue, but little, if any, of this money reached the slum dwellers in Kingston and Montego Bay.

The following letter, which I wrote to Jamaica's leading newspaper, *The Gleaner*, speaks for itself. It was later the subject of a leading article and evoked a response of over a hundred letters, many of them very moving, from coloured people all over the island. The reaction of the proprietors of the hotels and big stores, however, was by no means favourable, and the owner of one hotel, at which I had stayed a couple of nights, accused me of biting the hand that fed me.

'To the Editor of *The Gleaner*, February 1953.

'I have recently returned from a holiday in Montego Bay from which I have derived much benefit, though I do not believe that anyone with the glimmering of a social conscience could be entirely happy in a place in which a small part of the community is living in the lap of luxury, while others spend their lives in dire poverty in slums which are a disgrace to the name of Jamaica.

'A few yards from the hotels, where guests are charged up to fifteen guineas a day, is situated the only hospital, so inadequate that in many cases two patients occupy one bed. The Poor House cannot accommodate more than fifty per cent of the needy who clamour for admission, and in the grounds of this institution are a number of patients in the last stages of tuberculosis. Large sums of foreign capital are being invested in the island, but there seems to be no increase in the money available for social services. I can see little improvement in the conditions in the slums of Montego Bay compared with when I paid my first visit sixteen years ago, whilst conditions in Kingston are even worse. Those whose hearts permit them to view these conditions with equanimity may, however, be roused to indignation if they reflect that they constitute the most fertile breeding ground for Communism anywhere in the world.

'The raising of hands in horror is of no avail if unaccompanied by some constructive suggestion, and the remedy I put forward to the Jamaican Government is the imposition of a tax of five per cent on all hotel bills, this tax to be borne equally by visitors and management. Judging by the number of hotels that are being built, the catering for visitors is a profitable business, and I do not think that those responsible for the comfort of tourists like myself would suffer undue hardship by having to pay sixpence in the pound of the money they receive from their guests. As for the tourists, I am sure that anyone who can afford a holiday in Jamaica will not be deterred from visiting the island on account of the fact that he is asked to contribute a trifling sum towards the relief of the people with whom he is making his holiday.

'My own hotel bill was approximately one hundred and twenty pounds and I am forwarding my cheque for six guineas to Archdeacon Fox of Montego Bay, with the request that this small sum shall be expended in succoring the poor in his Archdeaconry.

'I understand that last year the tourist trade realised five million pounds, and if my scheme came into operation poverty in Jamaica would be a thing of the past, and this happy state of affairs would have come about without imposing the slightest hardship on anyone.

'Yours faithfully,
'Quintin Gilbey.'

# *18 Aly and the Aga*

A friend once confided to me that he had irrefutable proof that Aly Khan had been to bed with his wife and his girl friend in the same week, and that he was going to kill him. But when I met him a week or so later he told me that Aly had been so charming when he had run into him at Epsom that he couldn't bring himself to refer to the matter, especially after Aly had told him to back one of his horses which had won.

He went on, however, to tell me that he had spoken very sharply to his two erring women, who had admitted their guilt, and promised not to do it again. In point of fact it was most unlikely that either would have had the chance, at any rate for a long time. Aly never forgot a face or a body, and seldom a name, and if he had met either of them in a different environment in the years to come he would most likely have suggested a repeat performance. But for the time being they were on a par with yesterday's paper.

This story typifies much of Aly's love life, the one-night stands, the irate husbands who refrained from reprisals on account of Aly's charm, and the erring women who readily confessed because it was Aly, though they would have strenuously denied the charge had it been anyone else.

It became a status symbol among the international set to have been to bed with Aly. It would be incorrect to describe most of these romps in the day as affairs, as an affair suggests that the couple have spent at least a week together, while in Aly's case the majority of his girl friends considered themselves lucky if he was still with them when dawn broke the following morning.

For a period of three or four years, in the middle 'thirties, I suppose I knew Aly as well as any man could know this mercurial descendant from Mohammed; judging from the varying descriptions of him given after his death by his best-known mistresses, they too found him a complex character.

Aly had more charm than any man I have ever met, and this sums up his entire character. His desire to please and to extend hospitality were genuine, but he was selfish and self indulgent, and like Steve Donoghue, he thought that rules and regulations were made for others. So long as it was only Aly Khan who was out of step, all was well in the best of all possible worlds.

I think he was barely eighteen when Michael Beary introduced us at the Newmarket sales. Michael, who was riding as first jockey for the Aga Khan, was not only a great rider but he also knew his way around the West End of London, so he was an ideal mentor for this fabulously rich young man, whose chief ambitions were to meet as many pretty girls as possible and to learn to ride well enough to compete successfully in races for amateur riders. Both ambitions were very quickly realised.

In my book, *Racing for Fun*, I compared Michael to oysters; you either liked him very much or you didn't like him at all. I liked him very much, but he was his own worst enemy. He was very hospitable but extremely tactless, especially with his fellow jockeys. He and Aly hunted in couples for six months, and having fallen out, presumably over some woman, they never made it up.

In course of time Aly became an authority on the Stud Book and a good judge of a horse, but when I first met him he was chiefly concerned with the betting side of racing and he told me that one of his aims was to bring off a colossal *coup* at the expense of the bookmakers. He had no personal animosity towards them, but like most punters he regarded them as the enemy, and therefore there to be shot at.

During his career on the turf Aly landed some very big bets indeed, but I should be surprised if he was a winner on balance. He was alleged to have lost the best part of a hundred thousand pounds at a Royal Ascot meeting a year or so before his death, and I can well believe it. He was far from being a shrewd backer of horses, being more inclined to chase his losses than play up his winnings, while if a horse was a shorter price than he had anticipated, he would increase his bet.

Although we were close friends, I was never particularly keen to execute his commissions as he was a very slow settler, not realising, apparently, that his agent would have to settle the account on the following Monday, and that it might be very inconvenient for him to fork out a large sum of money for Aly, who by that time could well be on the other side of the world.

He always paid his debts in the long run, though on occasions it was a very long run indeed. Fortunately, most of the bets I made for him won, and on the few occasions when he was a loser on the week I was able to nab him before he left these shores in pursuit of someone who had taken his fancy.

At one of the Autumn Meetings at Newmarket, he rushed up to me – he was always in a hurry – as the horses left the paddock and said: 'I am told our horse [it was one of his father's] is a 2/1 on chance. I haven't got nearly enough on; put me on another thousand.' The English winter held few attractions for Aly, and it occurred to me as I made my way to Tattersall's ring that I might not see him again till the following spring. I therefore approached Jack Burns and laid a thousand pounds to five hundred on, adding: 'And put it down to Prince Aly Khan.' The horse won by a short head, thanks to Gordon Richards having ridden one of his most brilliant finishes, but I should have had heart failure if the bet had been struck in my name.

Only the Ismailis, the Moslem sect which regarded the Aga Khan as holy, and Aly as his successor, could pretend that Aly's faults did not outnumber his virtues, but such was his charm that he made a generous contribution to the happiness of his fellow beings in the forty-nine years of his life. Apart from the thousand or more women to whom he had made love, Aly was the friend of all with whom he came in contact. It was always fun to be with him, and he had the priceless gift of making one feel that he was enjoying one's company. As he had never been subjected to any real discipline, and was the possessor of an indulgent father with a bottomless pocket, it was surprising that he was not a great deal more spoilt than he was. A young Englishman who had only to ask for the moon to have it handed him on a plate would almost certainly have developed an insufferable arrogance, but this son of the greatest living Muslim and an Italian mother was completely natural, and without an ounce of conceit, excepting where women were concerned.

On one of the few occasions on which we dined alone together, we got on to the subject of our childhood, and he told me that he had been lonely and often frightened, and had suffered from bad dreams. I told him that my childhood had been a blissfully happy one, but that I too had suffered from nightmares, and that when I awoke from one I crept into my nurse's bed, where I knew I would be safe, to which he replied: 'Good for you, old boy, you started getting into other people's beds long before I did.'

From that, our talk turned to sex, and he told me he attributed his success to a course of study under an old Arab doctor in Cairo who, forty years earlier, had given his father similar instruction. The technique is known as *Imsac*, which means 'retaining', and no man who has mastered it will ever reach his climax till his partner has derived full satisfaction. He told me that by exercising mind over matter, he could prolong sexual enjoyment almost indefinitely. This was confirmed to me by four women, all married, who told me that they had not known the meaning of sex till they experienced it with Aly. Aly concluded the discussion by saying, with a twinkle in his eye: 'I picked up more useful information from that old man in Cairo than you ever did in all the time you were at Eton.'

Aly was a member of our house party at Carvers near Haslemere for Goodwood in 1934, and he was a wonderful guest, though he was apt to monopolise the telephone with calls to such widely separated places as New York, Paris, Deauville and Cannes. He was delighted to find that a very beautiful, very young, titled woman, whom he greatly admired, was a member of the house party, and I thought it was as well to inform him that we expected our guests to be in their own beds when they were called with early morning tea at 8.30 a.m. As our somewhat prudish housemaid did not hand in her notice at the end of the week, I assumed that he had acceded to my request.

After dinner, on the last evening, Aly made a little speech in which he said: 'Romie and Quinny have given us a wonderful time, and now I am asking you all to be my guests in my villa at Deauville.' Of course we all accepted, and we had an unforgettable week. We had never been to Deauville before, and though I have paid many subsequent visits to this best of all seaside resorts, our week as Aly's guests stands out in my memory. As all too rarely happens at Deauville, the sun shone throughout our stay, and we lived in the greatest luxury, in the gayest possible company. Beautiful Thelma, Lady Furness, was our hostess, and she and her equally beautiful twin sister, Gloria Vanderbilt, were as charming as they were decorative.

On the last day of our stay, Aly told us that his father was bringing his house party to dinner, and would we all be on time, and on our best behaviour. Among the Aga's guests was Mrs Loel Guinness, whom Aly placed on his right. They appeared to get on extremely well, but it nevertheless came as a surprise to us when, a few weeks later, we heard that Loel was divorcing Joan, citing Aly as co-respondent. Although we all knew that Aly must get married sooner or later we had thought he was having too good a time to contemplate matrimony for at least another ten years, but marry he did. Joan presented him with two sons, of whom the eldest, Karim, is the present Aga Khan.

Aly drank very little, and I only once stood him a drink, except at lunch or dinner. The Aga Khan owned the Derby favourite Bahram in 1935, and he also had three other runners in the race. Unbeaten as a two-year-old, Bahram won the Two Thousand Guineas when not fully wound up, and on all form he looked a good thing. As the horses left the paddock for the parade at Epsom, Aly appeared breathless, and with his hand on my shoulder said: 'I can't stand the strain, I need a drink.' There was a champagne bar near at hand, and over a bottle of Bollinger he told me he had the biggest bet of his life on Bahram.

He didn't tell me how much, and I doubt whether he knew within two or three hundred of the exact sum, but I am sure that, relatively speaking, that my eighty pounds was the bigger bet as it was eighty pounds I didn't possess at the time, while Romie was also heavily involved. All ended happily, however, as Bahram, ridden by Freddie Fox, won in the style in which all hot favourites for the Derby should win, and that night we attended the celebration party given by the Aga Khan at the Embassy Club.

As Aly's life was lived at breakneck speed, it was only in the nature of things that he should drive fast cars as fast as they would go. I was driving Romie back from Newmarket at around 65 m.p.h. when Aly passed me as if I was standing still. The Gilbeys had had a losing week and were not in the best of tempers. Romie remarked that while some wives might like crawling along the road, she was not one of them: in other words, my driving compared unfavourably with Aly's.

Between Baldock and Stevenage I saw people running towards a field on my near side where a car was lying upside down. A dazed Aly, suffering from concussion, and making no sense, was walking up and down beside it. I persuaded him to enter my car and dropped him off at the Ritz, where I told the head porter George to call a doctor. All the way home Aly had talked of the good thing he was to ride in an amateur riders' race on the following day, but he was not well enough to ride it, though he had suffered no serious damage.

I did not see him during the war, in which he served with considerable distinction, chiefly in Syria, and after it we saw far less of one another than we had done in the 'thirties. He spent very little time in England, but when we met on one of the Paris racecourses or at Deauville, he was as friendly as ever.

I was, however, working very hard, and casinos and the other night spots no longer held the same glamour for me as they had done in pre-war days. I had, in fact, given up playing *chemin de fer*. Currency was an insuperable problem for me, though many of my acquaintances seemed able to lay their hands on all the francs they needed.

If any man could introduce his girl friends to his men friends with impunity, that man was Aly Khan, but he was always loth to do so. You could, however, bet your life that if you were escorting an attractive girl friend and Aly was around, he would bear down on you with his most enchanting smile, and a 'Dear old boy, how wonderful to see you', in order to be introduced.

Although he delighted in brief encounters, Aly had a number of long affairs, though I doubt whether he was faithful for more than a week to anyone.

I met his second wife, Rita Hayworth, only once and as an introduction he said: 'Darling, of course you know Quinny.' We looked blankly at one another, muttering something unintelligible, while Aly plied me with a series of questions on the merits of the horses opposed to his father's representative in one of the big races.

Aly paid scant attention to his wives and mistresses on the racecourse, and all, except Bettina, a philosophical and resourceful young woman, appeared bored and neglected at even such glamorous spots as Ascot and Longchamp.

It was shortly after Aly and Rita had split up that I was walking back from the casino to the Hôtel Normandie at Deauville, when I heard an unmistakable voice calling 'Quinny', which he always pronounced with the accent on the second syllable, followed by hurrying feet. As always, an arm was around my shoulders as he said: 'Dear old boy, I've been looking for you in the casino all evening, but I bet you've been in the hay with a lovely girl.' Both these statements were untrue, as I had seen him playing at the big table for the past three hours, and he knew perfectly well that if I had been as fortunate as he had suggested I should not be pacing the street between the casino and the Normandie at 1.30 a.m.

He went on to tell me that he was giving a supper party at the night club, and he wanted me, above all people, to be a member of his party. Would I therefore go along to his table and he would join me in a few minutes.

I smelt a rat, but one always accepted Aly's invitations. At the table reserved for him were his son Karim, another man whom I took to be his tutor, and five gorgeous, though obviously infuriated, women.

No one was saying a word, and my announcement, in my best French, that I had just seen Aly and that he wouldn't be long, evoked no response. Having grabbed a bottle of champagne, and knocked back half a glass, I asked one of the young women to dance, to which she responded, 'Merci, non', through clenched teeth.

It did not require the powers of observation of an Inspector Maigret to realise that Aly had asked five women to supper with him, having given each one to understand that it was to be a tête-à-tête, but that he had met someone in the course of the evening who had taken his fancy and with whom he was now dallying.

When he joined us, half an hour later, he ignored four of the women, and devoted his attention to a beautiful young girl who wore so much jewellery that it couldn't have been real. Aly was not in the habit of giving expensive presents to girls he hardly knew, and it was evident from the manner in which he was dancing with her, that this was something quite new. He asked me whether I didn't think she was the dead spit of Rita, which seemed to please the girl, though in point of fact she wasn't in the least like Rita and was only half her age.

Cold as the other four women had been on my arrival, they had been little rays of sunshine compared with what they were after Aly joined us. After an hour of this glacial treatment I took my departure.

The next day Aly appeared at the races with a black eye. He told me that it was the result of a collision with a horse's head, but I don't think he expected me to believe it, and of course I didn't. I never discovered who struck the blow, but I like to think that the four scorned women set about him, and that three held him, while the fourth delivered the blow. I did not mind in the least his standing up four women, all of whom were quite capable of taking care of themselves, but I did object to his casting me in the role of eunuch in a discontented harem.

I have no idea whether he would have eventually married Bettina had he lived, but he always seemed more married to her than to either of his wives. She realised that in order to keep him she must agree to his terms, which few women would have done.

The last time I met him was at Longchamp, two weeks before his death. He was with Bettina and Bill (Lord) Astor, and he asked me to join them on a visit to the stables to inspect the horses running in the big race. He was, as always, in cracking form, but he was beginning to show his years, having gained weight and lost a lot of hair, and I got the impression that his gaiety was less spontaneous than it had been before he learned that his father had cut him out of his spiritual heritage in favour of Karim. Aly never discussed this subject with me, but I think it was a terrible blow to his pride, though he did not take his religion seriously, and he could hardly have visualised himself in the role of Imam.

I met the Aga Khan at approximately the same time that I met Aly, though in a strictly professional capacity. As usual, the Aga had a dozen horses in the forthcoming classic races, and in the course of an interview I asked him which of them would be his representatives. Dick Dawson, who trained for him at that time, could have given me a more accurate idea of stable plans, but a quote from the Aga Khan was highly prized by editors.

It was our wives who were responsible for our subsequent friendship. Sadruddin had been born in the Hôpital Américain at Neuilly a month before the arrival of Anthony, and the Begum had been attended by the nurse who was now looking after Romie. The Begum had become attached to her nurse, and when she paid her a visit one day she introduced herself to Romie saying: 'I am Andrée Khan, I think our husbands know one another.'

Born Andrée Carron, daughter of an Aix-les-Bains restaurateur, she was the Aga's third wife, and was as charmingly unassuming as her manner of introducing herself would indicate. She was running a dress shop with her sister, in the Boulevard Haussmann, when the Aga met her, and she never sought to conceal her bourgeois origin.

We became very fond of her, and I think it was as a result of her influence that the Aga asked us to stay at their villa at Deauville two years running. As there was not sufficient room in the villa to house all his guests, we, and our friends Ralph and Cynthia Raphael, slept at the Hôtel Normandie.

Andrée and Aly were studiously polite to one another, but we did not think there was much love lost between them. I heard it suggested that Aly considered his father had been disloyal to his mother in marrying again, but I ridiculed the idea. Aly had many faults but hypocrisy was not one of them, and I think his resentment was directed at the infant Sadruddin. Aly believed that even the richest man in the world could not afford two sons, if one of them was himself.

There were seldom less than a dozen people lunching and dining at the villa, and dinner never took less than one and a half hours, often longer. The food and wine were superb, and the Aga, who had a very large appetite, would often demand a second helping. He talked throughout every meal, often laying down his knife and fork while he related some anecdote or the latest story to reach him. His guests were invariably as cosmopolitan a collection as one could find anywhere in Europe, which necessitated his telling his stories in a number of languages. One story, which I had first heard told by Gertie Lawrence fifteen years earlier, was told in English, French, Italian, and Urdu and he laughed louder after each recitation. I don't know where he got his stories from, but I had heard several of them at my private school.

I shudder to think what his highly respectable trainer, Frank Butters, and his wife must have thought of the Aga's ribaldry. Café society is unshockable, but Mr and Mrs Butters belonged to a social circle in which the lavatory is known as the toilet and the sex act is carried out in the dark by God-fearing people solely for the procreation of the species.

Like so many highly intelligent men, the Aga had an adolescent's delight in practical jokes, He would have large quantities of potent Normandy cider served during the first course at lunch, as the result of which his guests would be fidgeting in their seats long before the end of the meal. Romie, however, rather spoilt this joke; when she felt the need to spend a penny, she had no hesitation in saying so, and emboldened by her example, the other guests would follow her to the loo.

Although the Aga and Aly seldom exchanged confidences, a very real affection existed between them. Even in his most flippant mood Aly never spoke of his father except with the respect due to one of the most remarkable and influential men of his day, while the Aga was proud of Aly's popularity and success with women. 'He has me to thank for that,' he told me and confirmed Aly's story of the old man in Cairo.

Although he weighed over seventeen stone, the Aga was still extremely active, playing a round of golf every day; moreover, although he had a beautiful blonde wife, thirty years younger than himself, we were soon to discover that he was also carrying on with a six-foot brunette beauty queen in the South of France.

The Aga had many sides to his character, one of the less attractive being that he was what is known in India as 'a box wallah', which means that he had a never-failing eye for the main chance, and that everything he owned was for sale, provided the price was right.

Although he had a genius for finding the right man for the right job, his judgement of character could not have been more at fault than when he lauded Hitler to the skies after visiting him at Berchtesgaden in 1937. He came away with a signed photograph of the Führer, and wrote to *The Times:* 'Hitler is a firm pillar of peace. Why not take him at his word?' This was particularly unfortunate in that earlier in the year he had been unanimously elected President of the League of Nations.

Although he loved England he took the view when war broke out that Germany would win, and consequently sold all his horses in training and went to live in Switzerland. After El Alamein he wondered if he had not backed the wrong horse, and began to replenish his stud.

Aly was to dine with us one evening, a year or two before the war, at the Embassy Club, and at about seven o'clock he rang me up and asked me if 'Father could join us after dinner and bring his girl friend'. We felt very honoured but also not a little surprised. In the first place we had no idea that the Aga had a girl friend, and secondly, it was owing to Andrée that we had become friends.

The party was, I think, a great success, though we were not greatly enamoured of Yvette Blanche Labrousse, who in due course was to become the fourth Begum Aga Khan. She spoke little English, but Sir Richard Sykes, who was placed next to her, fortunately spoke good French. As Andrée had paid only infrequent visits to England a number of people that evening thought that the statuesque Yvette was the Begum, and addressed her as 'S'Altesse'. She did not correct them, no doubt realising that the honour would not be long deferred. That Cairo doctor can have had no more apt pupils than the Aga and his son.

Like Lord Beaverbrook, the Aga loved earthy conversation, and no detail concerning the lives of members of the international set was too trivial to be of interest to him. Lord Rosebery once described him to me as the greatest living authority on the Stud Book, but racing played only a small part of his life.

When, shortly after the end of World War One, he decided to found an equine empire on a larger scale than any in the history of the turf, he employed George Lambton to purchase him the best female blood. Given a blank cheque, Lambton did as he was told, and in the space of fifteen years, horses carrying the Aga's chocolate and green hoops had swept the board. In 1932 his horses finished first, second, fourth and fifth in the St Leger, and in 1936 his Mahmoud (Smirke) and Taj Akbar (Gordon Richards) finished first and second in the Derby. His greatest triumph, however, was with Bahram, who in 1935 won the triple crown (Two Thousand Guineas, Derby and St Leger), the last horse to do so.

With all his knowledge of breeding, the Aga did not know one horse from another, and when he won his first Derby in 1930 with Blenheim he is reputed to have patted him on the neck as he led him in, cooing: 'Good old Rustom Pasha', the name of his other runner in the race. Reggie (Earl of) Pembroke teased him about this in my presence one day, but the Aga furiously denied it. As Reggie was of the same vintage as the Aga, and claimed to have been his 'bear leader' when he was a young man, he could take liberties with him which few men dared.

As it was not more than twice that I spent any length of time in the Aga's company after the war I can only hazard a guess as to when it was that he finally decided that Aly was unfitted to succeed him as the Aga Khan.

Aly was married to Joan when we stayed with the Aga for the

second time at Deauville, and he spoke in glowing terms of his daughter-in-law, which was not surprising since they had met when Joan was a guest in his house. 'Her background and erudition are the ideal qualities for a Begum Aga Khan,' he told me, though he himself had married an Italian member of a troupe of dancers, the daughter of an Aix-les-Bains restaurateur, and was subsequently to marry the daughter of a bus conductor. Had Aly remained married to Joan, it would never have entered his father's head to pass him over in favour of his son Karim.

The last occasion on which I talked with the Aga was in his car on the way back to Paris from Longchamp. I had met him as he walked to the racecourse gates, and he offered me a lift. Our conversation chiefly concerned racing, and the Aga deplored the dearth of good stallions, making no allusion to the fact that having sold his three Derby winners Blenheim, Bahram and Mahmoud to the United States, he was to no small extent responsible for the shortage.

I said that I had met Aly and Rita and that they seemed very happy, to which he replied that he hoped they would remain so after causing him so much embarrassment by the publicity and ballyhoo preceding their marriage. He went on to say that though Rita had no social background and no knowledge of any subject other than motion pictures, he liked her and thought she would make Aly a good wife. 'As Aly never reads a book and lives entirely for the present her ignorance will not worry him,' he concluded.

He seemed to think that Aly might now settle down, but when his marriage to Rita ended, and he straightaway started an affair with the beautiful actress Gene Tierney, whom he also expressed a desire to marry, it was then, I think, that the Aga realised that Aly was not fitted for the role of Imam, the spiritual ruler over countless Ismailis, who have limitless faith in his divine power.

When I had met the Aga, also at Longchamp, towards the end of 1946, a season in which the French horses had proved themselves immeasurably superior to our own, he told me he attributed this superiority to the German oats on which they had been fed during the occupation. This was a scoop for me, and I telephoned the story to the *Sporting Chronicle*, without comment. The French were very touchy about their activities during the Occupation, and the suggestion from a man who had spent the war in Switzerland that their horses had been fed on oats imported from Germany raised a storm of protest.

The story was reproduced in French papers which did not normally carry even the racing results, and I was interrogated over the telephone by the French racing authorities as to whether the Aga had made any further allegations, and if I knew what the basis was for his assumption.

I told them that he had made no other reference to French horses, and that I thought that he based his assumption on the fact that his former trainer, Dick Dawson, had once imported a load of German oats, after which the stable had enjoyed unprecedented success. The excitement died down in due course, and as the German horses are normally very much inferior to our own and the French horses, I am sure that German oats had played no part in the success of the French horses. The Aga was so knowledgeable on so many subjects that it was inconceivable that he should express so controversial a view on a matter on which he had no first-hand knowledge, though personally I am glad he did, and so was Bill Clarke, my Editor.

Although Aly played an occasional game of tennis, I never saw him participate in any other outdoor sport except riding in races for amateur riders. His father, on the other hand, was a tremendously keen golfer. I had never played against him, but I had a shrewd idea that a number of his opponents allowed him to win, a view which was strengthened when he announced at dinner, one evening at Deauville, that he had never been beaten off his handicap of eighteen.

Ralph Raphael, who had a handicap of sixteen, but often played down to twelve, told the Aga he would like to take him on in a friendly game. He suggested that they should play for a small stake, and after a deal of discussion they agreed to play for a hundred pounds. The following day, Ralph and I were playing a single, and at a dog-leg hole to the left, his drive, with just sufficient draw on it to bring it round the corner, was probably the best of his life. He was picking up his tee, when the Aga's head popped up from the far side of a near-by hedge. He had obviously been lying in wait, 'touting the gallop' as we say in racing parlance.

As Ralph holed out for a birdie four I told him that it would prove to be the most expensive hole he had ever won, and I was prepared to bet him a fiver that the Aga, having ascertained the form, would call off the bet. Sure enough, he announced that evening that having thought it over, he had come to the conclusion that friends should not play one another for money.

Someone suggested that as he had scratched he was liable for a forfeit, so he magnanimously offered to give Ralph's wife, Cynthia, a set of golf clubs. I told her not to expect too much as she might be disappointed, though, knowing how much he admired her, some of our fellow guests expected him to present her with clubs of the latest design, autographed by a famous player. The half-dozen clubs which eventually arrived were the product of a bygone age, and must either have been some old ones of his own or some he had found lying about in the locker room.

When a man is fabulously rich, money ceases to have any real meaning, and had the match been for five shillings the Aga would have called it off just the same. He had paid hundreds of thousands of pounds in order to create his equine empire, which paid handsome dividends, but after his horses had finished first and second in the Derby, he debated as to whether he should tip his caddy two shillings or half-a-crown.

# 19 *War and peace*

I was racing at Manchester on 2 September 1939 and so deep was the gloom, that there was virtually no betting and the races were run in dead silence. The only laugh I heard was when the winner of the selling race was led into the ring, and the auctioneer asked 'Any bid of a 100 guineas?' Who but a raving lunatic would buy a racehorse on the eve of Judgement Day?

We had been ordered to draw gas masks and paint our car lights, but as I had been away racing all over the country I had done nothing about it. I could not get back to London in daylight so I rang up my friends Sir Arthur and Lady Pilkington at Melton Mowbray, and asked if I could stay the night.

As always, I had Girleywoo with me, and while we were at breakfast she went off hunting. I did not expect her back before evening, but as Liz and I were sitting in the garden, having switched on the wireless, she re-appeared, and throughout Mr Chamberlain's speech stood gazing up at me. I am absolutely certain that her uncanny instinct told her that something was afoot which would disrupt our lives; and she never left my side for the remainder of the day, though there were any number of rabbits in the vicinity.

In my boyhood, an elderly schoolmaster told me that if the human mind could comprehend a thousandth part of the suffering resulting from a world war we should all go raving mad. Human nature being what it is, there is little fear of this happening; although at the age of forty I was fully aware of the fearful implications of our decision that Hitler could no longer be allowed to ride rough-shod over Europe, I was chiefly concerned, that sunny morning at Melton Mowbray, with my own personal problems.

I had had only three years in which to inhale the sweet smell of success, and here I was, back again where I started. My length of service with Kemsley Newspapers did not entitle me to any compensation, and though I should probably get three months' pay in lieu of notice from the *Daily Sketch*, my articles for the *Daily Despatch, Sunday Graphic* and *Sunday Times* were regarded as contributions, and were paid for as such.

I hoped the Germans didn't drop gas bombs on us until I had drawn my gas mask, and I was longing for news of Romie and Anthony. I knew that they had left Cannes, but had heard nothing since. Geoffrey rang up to say that the air raid sirens had sounded, and they were expecting the bombing to start at any moment. I wondered how much of London would be standing when I arrived there the following morning.

The office rang up to ask me if there was any truth in the agency story that Gordon Richards had joined up as a dispatch rider, and was going to the front with the first draft. I was not aware that Gordon could ride a bicycle, much less a motor bicycle, but as I had been instructed to write a story on how the wonderful spirit of 1914 had been re-born twenty-five years later, I painted a graphic picture of the champion jockey dodging the shells on his motor bicycle, as he sped from Army headquarters to the front line, carrying orders on which the fate of nations might depend.

Unfortunately it only made the first edition, after which it was superseded by an even more unlikely tale, written by someone else. On arrival in London I had news that Romie and Anthony had reached Southampton, and having been told that all children were being evacuated from London, Romie had taken rooms at Canford Cliffs, near Bournemouth.

Having drawn my gas mask in its cardboard box and had my car lights painted, I set off with Woo in the Chrysler to join my wife and child. After a few days we went on to Devonshire, but when at the end of a couple of weeks it seemed unlikely that the Germans would drop anything more sinister than pamphlets for the time being, we returned to London. We took a furnished house in Fairholt Street, Knightsbridge. As I was on the reserve, I paid a visit to the Regimental Orderly Room, and asked the

Adjutant, who must have been still at the breast when I joined the Grenadiers, when I should be needed. Having ascertained that I had left the Grenadiers as an Ensign, nineteen years earlier, he looked at me as if I was some obscure fossil, recently unearthed, and replied 'Not before next July, at the earliest.'

He acceded to my request to join another regiment, if I so wished, and when I was lunching at Buck's the same day I was approached by a Brigadier whom I did not know, who asked me if I would accept a commission in the Durham Light Infantry. I readily agreed.

I had begun to feel rather conspicuous in my blue suit now that nearly all my friends were in uniform, and though Romie hadn't mentioned it I thought it was only a matter of days before she informed me that although some women were proud of non-combatant husbands in wartime she was not one of them.

It was therefore with more relief than pride that I put on uniform for the first time since 1920. The phoney war was at its height, if that is the correct expression, but everyone knew that this state of affairs could not continue indefinitely, and although I did not hear of anyone being presented with a white feather, those who had not answered the call of King and Country were the target of unfriendly looks.

I was informed that I should be attached to Brigade Headquarters, and that just as soon as the Brigade was issued with anti-tank guns I should command the section, platoon or what have you, responsible for wiping out the Panzer division which might be threatening us.

They could hardly have picked a more unsuitable man for the job. I had so little knowledge of ballistics that I had only a vague idea as to the workings of a Lee Enfield rifle or a Lewis gun; moreover, my courage was decidedly suspect, as we say about a racehorse who declines to do his best when the money's down. Thank goodness, I was never put to the test. We were stationed at Chester-le-Street, one of a number of particularly unattractive towns dotted about Co. Durham. The pub, however, where I was billeted, was comfortable, and I had a room to myself, a blessing beyond all price to someone who loathes communal life, and whose idea of purgatory is sharing a room with anyone.

On my first day as duty officer I overheard two private soldiers discussing the officers as I made my tour of the latrines. I was heading for the almost equally insanitary butcher's shop, when one of them asked 'What's new bloke like?' 'La-di-da, and you can't understand a word booger says,' was the reply. So much for my expensive education!

One evening our Transport Officer, Duncan McNicol, and another officer asked me to join them at dinner in Newcastle. We had no transport, but a civilian friend of Duncan's was to drive us there. He appeared somewhat flushed on arrival at our mess, but consumed two large gin-and-frenchies (no ice) in the space of five minutes before taking us to his car and asking me to sit in front with him.

The black-out was bad enough in London, but it was far denser among the coalfields, and it struck me that my new-found friend was driving much too fast. However, it needed more moral courage than I possessed to tell a man I had only met a few minutes earlier that he was driving dangerously.

We had gone little more than a mile when it happened. The outline of a stationary lorry appeared for a fraction of a second, the car swerved violently, there was an ear-splitting crash, followed by a stab of pain.

I lost consciousness for the moment, and my next sensation was one of choking. Rough hands were trying, ineffectually, to undo my collar in the darkness, but it had tabs which were attached to the stud under the tie, and they were making no progress. Although only semi-conscious I managed to unfasten it myself, and felt my breath returning. The driver, who was unhurt, had succeeded in getting his side of the car clear of the stationary lorry, but had hit it with the near side, and our car finished up with its nearside front wheel and bonnet partially under the lorry. I had been struck by the rear of the lorry after it had penetrated the windscreen. My uniform was soaked with blood and I realised that those of my front teeth which had not been knocked out were broken off close to the gums, while my nose was also smashed.

The rough hands fumbling at my collar belonged to miners, and I was sitting in the parlour of a miner's cottage, whose owners could not have been more concerned, or shown me more kindness, had I been their son.

An X-ray at Newcastle Infirmary revealed a hair-line fracture of the skull, and I was told to keep as still as possible.

Romie and I had not been getting on too well, for which I was at least 95 per cent to blame, but when she received the telegram informing her of my accident, she caught the next train, which was due to arrive at Newcastle at midnight. This was a pretty good effort on her part, as she was by no means certain to secure a seat, and she would arrive in a strange city in the black-out with the prospect of spending the remainder of the night in the station waiting room. She was not to know that my friends, Duncan and Ethel McNicol, would meet her and take her to stay with them at their house.

Romie was, and still is, a most efficient person, and having made up her mind that something needs doing you can bet your life that it will be done in the shortest possible time. By next midday, she had secured me a room in Newcastle's best nursing home, with a nurse of my own, and that afternoon I was transported to the peace and quiet I so urgently needed. I was indeed fortunate in my nurse, and under her care I made good progress.

I had been in the nursing home only a couple of days when a man arrived, to ask for my signature in order that I should receive third party damages as soon as possible. My head was swathed in bandages, with only my good eye visible, but I was capable of signing my name and muttering my thanks for the trouble he was taking on my behalf.

It transpired that I had signed a prepared statement completely absolving the driver of the car, saying that the accident was the result of the stationary lorry carrying no tail lights.

Two weeks after my accident my Brigade went to France. The men were only half trained but as most of them were miners they had been chosen to supplement the Pioneer Corps in building an airfield. They had nothing to defend themselves with in the face of the German advance, and only half of them returned from Dunkirk. But for my accident, therefore, I might well have spent five and a half years as a prisoner of war.

When the swelling subsided, it was a great relief to find that my eye had suffered no damage. Facial injuries can jeopardise the career and future happiness of an attractive woman, but in the case of a 40-year-old man it is only the eyes that really matter. Teeth can be replaced, a nose remoulded, while the deepest cuts heal, leaving only a faint scar.

For over a week I was fed through a tube. I could not take solids, while liquids, drunk from a cup, would have leaked through a hole in my chin.

My only permanent disability was the result of an injury to my left ear, of which I was not aware at the time. The doctors told me that I should become increasingly deaf with the passing of the years; they were right.

I spent the spring and much of the summer of 1940 in and out of hospitals having operations on my teeth and nose, though before the broken teeth could be extracted my broken jaw had to be given time to heal, and for over a month my jaws were fastened together with wire.

I spent my convalescence with a friend, Humphrey Fulford, at Fulford House in Devonshire. The Germans were bombing Plymouth every night, and one night I was woken by a terrific bang, and I heard an aeroplane circling above us. A few seconds later there was an even louder crash. It was a moonlit night and it seemed that the pilot had mistaken this imposing white house, on the edge of a lake, for a military objective.

As there was nothing to stop him dropping bombs till he had demolished it I was never more frightened in my life, and my fear conveyed itself to Woo, who lay pressed against me rigid with terror. To my intense relief, however, the sound of the plane grew fainter, and it did not return. We found two large craters less than a hundred yards from the house, but the only casualties were a dozen chickens.

By a coincidence my Brigade was stationed near Exeter on its return from Dunkirk. Its function was to guard the coast between

Plymouth and Lyme Regis, and when I rejoined, one of my duties was to inspect the weapon posts. These were cunningly hidden, but unfortunately they were devoid of weapons, and although we were prepared to obey Mr Churchill and fight on the beaches, we were very little better equipped than the Home Guard. One day I inspected a post near Dawlish, which I was told had received some weapons. They turned out to be two brass cannon dated 1898. I asked the Sergeant if he had the necessary ammunition, to which he replied devoutly 'God forbid, sir, we should ever let them off.' Towards the end of August we received orders to proceed to Iceland at the end of September. It was all very hush-hush, and we were supposed not to tell even our wives, but of course we did,.

We were promised a full complement of equipment, but as it was slow in coming I was sent on frequent visits to the War Office. This suited me well as I had taken to playing *chemin de fer* at the gambling parties which had sprung up in the West End.

Fear is unquestionably the strongest sensation known to man or beast, but when we are assailed by two conflicting terrors they cancel one another out. On one occasion I arrived at Paddington, at about 9 p.m. when a savage raid was in progress, to find one taxi under the glass roof, with its driver deep in a book. In answer to my request to drive me to the Mayfair Hotel, he replied, 'I don't much like going out in this', but for double fare he agreed to 'chance it'. The guns in Hyde Park were blazing away and every now and then I heard the thump of falling bombs. On reaching Hyde Park Corner he pulled up. 'What the hell's the matter?' I asked him, fearing he had been hit, to which he replied, 'Can't you see the lights are against us?' There was not another vehicle on the streets for miles, but we remained stationary till the little cross, to which traffic lights were reduced in wartime, changed to green.

Ambrose and his orchestra were playing in the underground restaurant at the Mayfair, and over a large drink I asked him if there was a gambling party that evening. He told me of one in Upper Brook Street, and after an excellent dinner and sufficient alcohol to supply me with the necessary Dutch courage, I cashed a cheque, which was far from certain to be met, and sallied forth.

I had lost most of my cash, when I started to run a bank, and my opening £2 had swollen to £30. In my impecunious state I should have taken it in, but when a man from the big table sauntered over and bancoed me, I decided to let it run. He was agonisingly slow, licking his fingers as he picked up the cards, and I could not resist the temptation to take a peep at my own. I had a nine and a court card, so I was unbeatable, but at that moment it happened. There was a deafening roar, the house rocked on its foundations, and there was a tinkle of broken glass, but my only concern was the safety of my £30 on the table, which, short of my opponent also holding a nine, would become £60. The raid had become of secondary consideration, and I prayed 'Please God, leave the cards as they are, and don't upset the table'; my prayer was answered.

My financial affairs were at a very low ebb, but this time it was not my fault. The war had reduced my earnings from over £2,000 a year, plus expenses, to £260 a year with no expenses, while I had not yet received one penny damages in respect of my accident. As I had been travelling in a civilian vehicle I was not eligible for one penny from the Government, while although it was almost certain that I should receive a large sum in due course, no one had any idea when that would be. I had paid the nurses, the nursing homes and the surgeons in Newcastle and London out of my own pocket. My bank manager was sympathetic but a problematical sum for damages in the distant future could not be regarded as security for a loan.

Iceland, therefore, seemed to be the answer to my immediate problems. I could live there for next to nothing. Had we not occupied Iceland there is no doubt that the Germans would have done so, and if they had, all contact between ourselves and the American continent would have been lost. With submarine bases in Iceland, in addition to Norway, the Germans would have been in complete control of the North Atlantic. Owing to the eccentricity of the Gulf Stream the sea round Iceland is always free of ice, except on rare occasions in the extreme north. There had been no physical opposition to a landing party of marines, followed by troops from this country and Canada, though the Icelanders, not surprisingly, were indignant at our high-handed behaviour, which deprived them of their newly-won independence from Denmark of which they were so proud. They had, however, an additional grievance, which affected the comfort of every citizen in Reykjavik. A year earlier, a German firm had contracted to harness the geysers which abound in Iceland, so that every house in the capital would be provided with free hot water, but the first action of the landing party had been to clap the German engineers into gaol.

My constant companion on the voyage out had been Ian Akers-Douglas, a Gunner. He was one of the best cricketers produced by Eton between the wars, and was captain of Kent. He had a wonderful sense of humour and an appreciation of good wine, so he was a most entertaining companion. Drink on board was so cheap that Ian thought that any time spent without a glass in his hand was time and money wasted. I lost sight of him on our arrival in Iceland, but met him when I was accompanying the Brigadier to an out-of-the-way station on the north-west coast, within a few miles of the Arctic Circle. The cold was intense. We slept, or tried to sleep, in flea bags on the floor, and the following morning I found my dentures frozen solid in a glass by my bed, much to the amusement of Ian and the others. I have never discovered why dentures should be the object of such ridicule. One does not make fun of an artificial limb, but any mention of false teeth evokes peals of laughter.

With daylight reduced to four hours it became a problem to keep the troops usefully employed and amused. There was no likelihood of an invasion till the spring, and Iceland was fortunately just outside the range of German bombers, though from time to time long-range planes would fly very low over the various camps and fjords, and having taken all the photographs they needed, would spray us with machine-gun fire.

We did not possess a single aeroplane or ack-ack gun so when the first Hurricane arrived we gave it an ovation. Christmas day was so mild that we drank our pre-lunch drinks outdoors. But in January we experienced the kind of weather we had expected would be our lot throughout the winter. After a severe frost, it snowed without ceasing for two days; this was succeeded by a hurricane, measured at over 100 miles an hour, though the temperature remained around zero.

As Camp Commandant, I made a twice daily tour of the huts, but took the precaution of taking two men with me, which was fortunate as on one occasion I was blown into a snowdrift, from which I could not have extricated myself unaided.

By and large, however, we had little to complain of; we were performing a useful if unspectacular job, and – most important, as far as I was concerned – there were no opportunities to spend money. Drink was scarce, but thanks to my brother Ronald, Chairman of W. & A. Gilbey, we were never short of whisky and gin at 4/6 and 3/6 a bottle respectively. This reached us by Icelandic trawlers, and on occasions I was able to supply other units than my own. I therefore achieved a popularity which I could not attribute to my qualities either as a soldier or as a companion during those long nights. Even when it was light, the sun did not appear above the horizon.

In the years just before the war I had been suffering from spasms which rendered me incapable of swallowing anything. The only cure was to lie down and wait for the spasm to relax, and I was not very popular with my hostess when I spent most of the evening lying prone and gasping for breath.

After an evening at the Gunners' Mess as the guest of Ian Akers-Douglas, I had an attack which did not relax; I was removed to hospital where an X-ray showed the passage between my gullet and my stomach to be completely blocked. After three days, the M.O. told me he was sending me back to England by the next ship.

After nine months away from my family, my friends and last but not least my dog, I was overjoyed at the prospect, though I was sad at leaving my men to whom I had become very attached and they were kind enough to show that they reciprocated my feelings.

The voyage was uneventful till we were within about 100 miles of the Clyde, though we never moved without our life-jackets. It was a glorious morning, and we had taken our pre-lunch martinis on deck, when our escort vessels, consisting of two semi-obsolete American destroyers, which we had acquired in return for naval bases in the West Indies, started to dart hither and thither. One of them ran up a black flag, denoting that a torpedo attack was imminent. They then proceeded to drop depth charges, which rocked our ship, spilling our martinis.

Alone in the darkness, the prospect of attack from the air, the ground or under the sea would fill me with alarm, but on this lovely morning, with the sea shining like silver, a martini in my hand, and my homeland only a hundred miles away, the presence of an unseen foe seemed unrealistic and absurd.

After about twenty minutes, during which the ancient American destroyers, manned of course by British sailors, revealed unexpected agility, the black flag was lowered, and a sailor informed me that the German submarine had been destroyed. This I very much doubt, though we did not hear of it again.

Next morning we anchored in the Clyde, and I managed to smuggle in a thousand cigarettes with a perfectly clear conscience. The Naafi in Iceland was fairly bursting with cigarettes, at twenty for 8*d.*, while in England they were becoming scarcer every day.

Romie was waiting for me at the Dorchester, where we dined, and went on afterwards to a night club called The Nut House. London had taken a terrible hammering since I last saw her, and as I walked around the familiar streets I had the feeling that I was visiting a very dear friend who had been gravely ill and was not yet out of danger.

When, day after day in Iceland, we received the news that London had received yet another savage attack, my heart had bled, not only for the people subjected to this ordeal, but for London herself, the city which had been my home since boyhood. Most of my fellow officers were from the north, and they could not understand my concern, nor my feeling that I had deserted a friend in need.

In June 1941 the worst of the Blitz seemed over, at any rate for the time being, and I was home again. Romie had taken a flat on West Hill, Putney, where Woo was waiting for me. It was around 2.30 a.m., and her cries must have awoken the entire neighbourhood. As she had been my constant companion for nearly five years I am sure that she had missed me far more than my family had done.

However intelligent a dog may be, you cannot make it understand that you can't help going away, that you hate leaving it, and that you will come back as soon as you can. All it knows is that it is terribly lonely and sad. Dachshunds are very possessive, and the idea that the loved one has deserted them is more than they can bear. Woo was never separated from me again for more than a week or so.

I believe Romie's and my divorce to be the most civilised in the history of British jurisprudence. This was largely due to the fact that we were still devoted to one another, according to our fashion, though most people thought that we had a strange way of showing it.

After our divorce Romie married Naps Brinckman, a regular soldier in the Grenadiers. I did not know him well, but we subsequently became very good friends and we have all enjoyed many happy times together in Barbados, where he and Romie have built themselves the most attractive house in that island. Naps could not have been kinder to Anthony had he been his own son, while their daughter, Theadora, now married with two sons of her own, has been my favourite girlfriend since she was old enough to walk.

My only stipulations were that I should have the custody of Woo, and that Romie should find me a suitable flat. Woo was nominally Romie's, but she realised that she had become much more my dog than hers. She set about house-hunting in the Chelsea district, and the flat she found me in Tite Street is where I am still living.

When my marriage broke up my cousin Derek Blyth asked me what I was going to do now. 'Look for a girl with a 17-year-old face and a 32-year-old mind,' I told him. It took me 27 years to find her. Alas by then it was too late. Having been over-housed throughout my adult life I was now installed in a flat, the rent of which was within my means.

My financial situation was further improved as the result of another visit to the Law Courts. This time I had to travel to Newcastle, where at long last my case for damages for the injuries that I had received in the motor accident two and a half years earlier was down for hearing. Before we went into court the insurance company of the car in which I was being driven and that of the stationary lorry agreed that the loser should pay me £1,350. The case dragged on for nearly two days, but I was sitting pretty as it was highly unlikely that the Judge would decide that it was an unavoidable accident. He finally decided that the driver of the car was to blame.

Of the four divorces in which I have been concerned, this was the only one in which I was the innocent party, and therefore had to be present at the hearing. I think it is only fair to say that my two wives were blissfully happy with my successors, from which my readers can draw what conclusions they choose.

Marriage, in my view, should be a civil affair, and I consider it sheer blasphemy for a couple to have to swear before God that they will remain faithful to each other 'till death us do part' before they can secure a licence to set up house together. No matter how much in love a man or woman may be, they cannot be certain that they will rejoice in each other's company for the remainder of their lives. It is surely common sense that when the breach is irreparable the parties should face up to it, and make a clean break. Remaining together for the sake of the children is condemning themselves to living a lie, and one which will not deceive those whom it is supposed to benefit. My own parents never expressed a difference of opinion in front of me, but had they been forever quarrelling I would far sooner they had separated and I had visited them in turn, and I am sure most children feel the same.

At about that time I decided to try and supplement my income by writing a play and also a eulogy of Gandhi, who since my second visit to India had become one of my heroes. I had the good sense to realise I was no playwright before I had finished the second act, so no-one had to endure my outpourings. With the country fighting for its life and large sections of our cities in ruins from the German bombers, it was not surprising that I failed to find a publisher for my article on 'The aspostle of non-violence' even though it contained an altercation I had had with Lord Lloyd, ex-Governor of Bombay, who told me he was the first person to put Gandhi in gaol.

Recently, I was placed next at dinner to a lovely young girl who told me that she was shortly to be married to an eligible young man at a fashionable church, that the reception for 500 guests was to be held at an equally fashionable hotel, and that her wedding dress was being made by Balmain. I asked her if she believed that marriage was a sacrament. From her look of blank astonishment it was evident that she hadn't a clue, but after a pause she asked me if I meant all that jazz about 'for better for worse, for richer for poorer'. 'Sort of' I replied, to which she told me that what with arrangements for the bridesmaids' dresses, going to Paris for fittings, and writing thank-you letters for wedding presents, she hadn't had time to bother about things which didn't matter, and anyhow her fiancé was an agnostic.

I replied that in those circumstances she should be married at a registry office, at which her lovely mouth fell open, and when it closed again it had become a thin, pale pink line, while from the set of her jaw I formed the opinion that although she might love and honour the young man of her choice, he was the one most likely to do the obeying. Fixing me with a look which was likely to become more daunting with the passing of time, she told me that if I thought that she was going to cancel her wedding dress, and get married in a filthy registry office in her old tweeds, I was out of my mind.

I attended her wedding, and very lovely she looked, though my pew was too far back for me to hear how she and her handsome young husband got on when the time came for them to repeat 'all that jazz'. Surely a conscientious priest cannot derive much satisfaction from joining together an agnostic and a bride who does not know the meaning of the word 'sacrament', or, for that matter, officiating at any marriage in one of the fashionable churches in the West End of London?

My finances remained under control as long as I was in Iceland, but shortly after my return to London I borrowed £25 from both 'Buck' Buckmaster and my brother Oliver, and pawned Romie's engagement ring. I went from hospital to medical board and back again to hospital. Eventually the President of the Board became sick of the sight of me, and returned me to civilian life. I managed to secure a job as a Press Cable Censor at the Ministry of Information, where I remained for the last three years of the war. 'Censorship' is rightly considered a dirty word in peacetime, but it is a necessary evil when a country is at war. The salary was no great shakes, but as the hours were long, my opportunities for spending money were curtailed. Woo and I were now on our own, cared for by my elderly Austrian housekeeper Maria Karasek, I was approaching freedom from financial worries for the first time for as long as I could remember. After I had become a senior censor at the end of a year, I was appointed resident censor to Associated Press of America, whose office was in Reuters building in Fleet Street.

In one respect I was at an advantage over most of my colleagues; being a journalist I could appreciate how infuriating it must be to have one's story held up. The aim of a censor should be to deal with the stories as expeditiously as possible, having satisfied himself that they contain no items of news which could assist the enemy. In order that there should always be a censor available we worked in 12-hour shifts, but after the flood of work following D-day had subsided I staggered the work, with my assistant, so that we each worked only six hours. The work was simple, provided that one did not get lulled into a sense of false security, resulting from a succession of innocuous messages.

I was fortunate in having as my chief a charming Old Etonian named Kenneth Rea, and immediately I told him that I was on very friendly terms with one of the editoresses at A.P., he appointed me their permanent censor.

The editoress's husband was a conscientious objector and was on the run, so she had reverted to her maiden name. I watched her pound a typewriter for a week or so before I plucked up courage to ask her out to dinner. Subsequently, I found myself censoring with one eye on this 24-year-old girl.

Eleanor or El, as she was always called, was unflappable, and when the buzz-bombs arrived in their hundreds, soon after D-Day, she didn't appear to give a damn for them. While the rest of us were diving under the desks when we heard one cut out, El would go on hammering her typewriter, only stopping to remove her cigarette when it began to burn her lip.

I did not find the V1s and V2s as frightening as the Blitz as there was an impersonality about them, and one did not get the impression of being their No 1 target, as one did when one heard an enemy aeroplane circling overhead. I realised, however, that I must find some place out of London in order to get some sleep, and it was Romie, of course, who came to my rescue. She and Naps were staying at Maidenhead, prior to his departure with the military mission to Moscow, and Romie heard that a mutual friend, who had a house within a few yards of Windsor racecourse, thought it too near London. I got in touch with her, and a couple of days later, Maria, Woo and I moved to this haven on the banks of the Thames. Woo was gun-shy, so the buzz-bombs terrified her, and even had I been able to get the requisite sleep I could not have kept her in London in a permanent state of terror. It was typical of Romie to find me a house when I needed one so badly, and thanks to Naps, who lent me his bicycle, I was able to commute without any trouble. I bicycled to the station, and took my bicycle in the train with me, riding it from Waterloo to Fleet Street and back again. Without it I should often have been stranded at Waterloo, as the tube did not run under the river when a raid was in progress. I used to feel very vulnerable on my bicycle, when a V1 cut out, but I never came to any harm, though I was once blown across the road by the blast from one which must have dropped fairly close.

El spent several week-ends at my house at Windsor. She had never known a dachshund before, but she fell in love with Woo. Much later, she told me that she had known that there was not much future for her with me if she didn't. The house was situated a few yards from a wood, which was full of rabbits, and in which Woo spent many happy hours. Windsor was one of the few courses on which racing was taking place fairly regularly, and while I was living at Windsor racing was re-started at Ascot on Saturdays.

After I had had a good win, El and I used to stay at the Savoy, which was very handy for the office at which we both worked. We were dining in the Savoy Grill one evening when a friend came over. After he had gone I told El that we had been at Eton, Sandhurst and in the Grenadiers together, to which she replied, 'Taking into consideration the appalling disadvantages under which you suffered in your youth, you are surprisingly human.' A very liberal-minded girl was El, and I like to think that some of her liberalism rubbed off on me.

I moved back to London that autumn. There were still sporadic raids by both aircraft and V bombs, but I could not keep two establishments going indefinitely, even though it meant that Woo would be frightened from time to time.

Anthony, who was eleven years old, spent most of his summer holiday with me at Windsor. Naps had left for Russia and Romie was staying at a hotel in Windsor, so the three of us and Woo were together again.

I went racing as often as possible, and though I had been unable to back a winner on my return from Iceland, 1944 was proving a highly profitable season. Providing one was prepared to take a short price, something which has never worried me if I thought it was value for money, it was easier to make money when racing was regionalised in wartime than at any time in my experience.

I was also fortunate in being on very friendly terms with Gordon Richards, with whom I stayed on several occasions at his house at Marlborough for Salisbury races. Early in 1944 Harry Heywood wrote me asking if I could find time to write a weekly racing article for the *Empire News*. I replied that although I was a civil servant I went racing whenever possible, and had plenty of time to write an article on the lines he suggested.

The article was a success, and in the 1944 St Leger, run at Newmarket, I tipped the first four, Tehran, Borealis, Ocean Swell, and Hycilla in the correct order, and, what was even more to the point, I had the biggest win of my life, entirely thanks to Gordon Richards, over Tehran.

From the time Gordon was engaged to ride the Aga Khan's

colt, following its defeat in the Derby when ridden by another jockey, he was emphatic that there was no danger to Tehran, and on each occasion that he returned from Newmarket, having ridden him in a gallop, he told me he had gone better than ever. I therefore kept having a bit more on him, and I shall never forget listening to the race on the wireless in my house at Windsor with Romie and Anthony.

Whenever I got a few days' leave from the M.O.I., El and I and Woo spent them in Devonshire or Cornwall. We loved the West Country, in addition to which the vet who had successfully operated on Woo when I was in Iceland lived in Penzance. She was getting on in years, and dachshunds are delicate animals.

Although it took the Allies two years longer to defeat the Germans than it had done in World War I, V-Day could not compare with Armistice Day for glamour and excitement. We were as thankful for the end of the killing as we had been twenty-seven years earlier, but whereas in 1918 the enemy's capitulation had been so sudden that I was one of thousands who had to read it in black and white before I could believe it, in 1945 it had been realised for months past that it was merely a question as to how much longer the Germans could hold out.

On the day after the last shot was fired I received a letter from Harry Heywood engaging me to write a daily article for the midday edition of the *Sporting Chronicle*, concluding with the words 'Can you begin at once?' Nothing goes against the grain in the civil service to the same extent as closing down a department, and those at the top made a stern fight for the survival of censorship. We were still at war with Japan, and though I could not believe that any material a journalist might cable abroad would prove of much use to the Japanese, we were informed that censorship would continue for the time being. I therefore wrote to Admiral Thomson saying I had a lucrative job awaiting me, and requesting my immediate discharge. I received a charming letter by return of post acceding to my request, and thanking me for my three years' work.

Had I had the courage of my convictions, I should have won a lot of money over the postwar General Election, but with the

*Daily Express*, presumably acting on the advice of Lord Beaverbrook, predicting a Tory majority of over 100, who was I to pit my scanty knowledge of politics against the pundits? I reckoned that in the eyes of the electorate the capitalist system had failed ignominiously from the moment that Lloyd George had been returned to power with an overwhelming majority in 1918. Although his was ostensibly a Coalition Government, with a Liberal Prime Minister, it was a Government of the Right, and within six months of it being returned to power there was widespread unemployment, and the railwaymen had gone on strike. I have described the appalling suffering inflicted on the miners and their families during the lock-out which followed the General Strike, and I had commanded men who joined up in World War Two at the age of 25, having never had a job. I had also watched the unemployed from Jarrow and the Welsh coalfields march into London, and I remembered how food had been destroyed in order to keep up the price of it while thousands starved.

Lloyd George had been the nation's hero in 1919 as Churchill was in 1945; in fact, the situations after the two wars were almost identical, the only difference being that while Lloyd George had proved himself a stalwart defender of the people's rights in times of peace, Churchill's record, in this respect, was uninspiring and he had never concerned himself with domestic affairs. He still referred to coloured people as 'blackamoors' and said he did not like them.

It seemed to me that all the signs pointed to a landslide to the Left, and this view proved correct. Right-wing die-hards accused those who shared my view of base ingratitude to the man who had led us to victory, but Mr Churchill was in his seventies, and not in the best of health; it therefore seemed a propitious moment for him to sing his Nunc Dimittis.

There was yet another group of people who voted Labour, for the only time in their lives. They held the view that the problems facing any Government at that time were insoluble, and that in consequence it would be thrown out on its ear at the next election. The worst possible result for either party would be to be returned to power by a narrow margin. Labour was welcome to try its hand in 1945, and when it had failed to accomplish the impossible the Tories would come back for a long innings.

The 1945 Derby, like the four previous Derbies, was run on the July course at Newmarket, and was won by Dante from Midas and Court Martial, the latter of whom had beaten him narrowly in the Two Thousand Guineas. Owned by Sir Eric Ohlson, trained by Matt Peacock, and ridden by Billy Nevett, this result was a great triumph for the North. Dante went wrong, and could not run in the St Leger, which he must surely have won, since Chamossaire, who won the final classic, had finished a long way behind him in the Derby.

Dante had been unbeaten as a two-year-old, and was the best of the wartime Derby winners. His career provides an example of the luck of racing. Eric Ohlson sent him up to the yearling sales with the modest reserve of 1,000 guineas on him, but nobody wanted him, so he sent him to be trained by Matt Peacock. Eric also owned his brother, who when he came up for sale at Newmarket fetched the record sum of 28,000 guineas. He was bought by the Maharajah of Baroda, a very free spender at that time, who called him Sayajirao: as he won the St Leger he was well worth the money.

Eric and his wife Marjorie became very good friends of mine, and a coloured print of the portrait of Dante, by Haigh, a present from Eric, hangs over my desk.

The Ohlsons were most hospitable people, and I stayed with them for York races on a number of occasions at their house at Scarborough. I know of no one who was more fun to spend an evening with in Paris than Eric, his favourite night club being the Jarret-Catch in Montmartre, at which attractive young women gave exhibitions of all-in wrestling, the object being to remove the other's garter. We became friendly with several of the contestants, who would drink champagne with us after their performance. Sturdy young women, they were well capable of taking care of themselves, and I should have hated to get on the wrong side of one of them.

The 1945 St Leger was run for the first and only time at York. I stayed with Geoffrey and Mollie, who were living there at the time, and my fellow guests were Martin Gilliat, who was subsequently knighted after many years as Private Secretary to the Queen Mother, and Tom and Tigie Nickalls.

Tom subsequently became Man on the Spot in the *Sporting Life,* and he and I were opposite numbers on our respective newspapers for many years, in the course of which we always regarded our friendship as more important than scoring off one another.

From a social point of view the York meeting was the greatest fun, but I had the worst week of my life; my crowning piece of folly being to lay £90/£40 on Rivaz in the Gimcrack only to see her beaten in the last stride by Gulf Stream. I got half my losses back at Brighton the following week, where Gordon Richards came to my rescue, as he so often did, by riding three winners. But by the end of the season I began to wonder whether it was possible to do two jobs simultaneously and make a success of both.

El and I and Woo were staying at St Ives in February 1946, when I received the most satisfactory communication of my life. It was from the Managing Editor of Kemsley Newspapers, Manchester, informing me that the Board had appointed me Kettledrum of the *Sporting Chronicle*. The *Sporting Chronicle* had ceased publication soon after the outbreak of war, but now that it was over it had been decided to resume publication, and I was appointed as leader writer.

For several years after the war, like the *Sporting Life,* it purported to cover all sports, but this was found not to be an economic proposition, and it became solely a racing paper.

The resumption of publication was to coincide with the opening of the flat racing season at Lincoln, and it seemed too good to be true that six months after the end of the war I had been appointed to the job I had always hankered after. Good old Harry Heywood! as, although my letter of appointment had not been signed by him, I had no shadow of doubt that it was he who was responsible for my good fortune.

In Manchester, where I stayed for the Grand National, I paid a visit to the Managing Editor, Mr Booth, or Natty as he was known throughout the newspaper world. I had never met him before, and when I was shown into his office I could not see him, as he was so small that only his head was visible above his huge desk.

He spoke softly, with a broad Lancashire accent, and I was to find out that his bright little eyes missed nothing. He told me he was well satisfied with my first four articles, and that was the only occasion on which he ever referred to my work, except to give his consent when I thought that in the interest of the paper I should cover a race in Ireland or on the Continent. Although I wrote under the *nom de plume* of Kettledrum, the Derby winner of 1861, my articles also carried my own by-line.

There was a long waiting list for the few cars which were beginning to trickle off the assembly lines, and second-hand cars were fetching double the price paid for them ten years earlier when they were new. In my job a car was essential, and Jean (Lady) Throckmorton (subsequently Lady Ashcombe) was kind enough to use her influence to get me one of the new Morris Tens. I took delivery of it on Derby Day, and drove it day in and day out for three years, when I sold it for £75 more than I had given for it.

The Derby was won by the 50/1 chance Airborne. He was the only horse in the field who really stayed 1½ miles, thereby sowing the first seeds of suspicion that stamina had been sacrificed for speed during the war years. Blood-stock breeding is a question of supply and demand, and during the war there had been very few long-distance races, while there was a lot of money to be won by two-year-olds, who would be unlikely to stay more than six furlongs at any time in their careers. Owned by John Ferguson, Airborne was trained by Dick Perryman and ridden by Tommy Lowrey, who had been associated with the St Leger victory of Chamossaire in the colours of Mr Stanhope Joel. John, Stan and I had been at Eton together, but I neither tipped nor backed Chamossaire or Airborne, though I did nap Airborne when he won the St Leger, which was run at its rightful home on the Town Moor at Doncaster for the first time for eight years.

Racing took place on the Rowley Mile course at Newmarket

for the first time for six years in the autumn of '45, and the Champion Stakes was memorable in that M Boussac sent over Priam, one of the lesser lights of his powerful stable, to take on Court Martial. He was the first French horse to run in this country since the fall of France, but he did not seem to be greatly fancied. I laid £35/£20 on Court Martial, and received the fright of my life when Priam battled it out neck and neck with him all the way to the winning post. The camera had not yet been installed, but the judge, God bless him, decided that Court Martial's nose was in front where it mattered.

The fact that a horse who ranked only fifth or sixth in M Boussac's stable should run the horse who had won our Two Thousand Guineas and finished third in the Derby to a nose left one with the inevitable conclusion that we were in for some humiliating experiences when M Boussac and the other leading French owners sent over their best horses.

From the moment that Paris had been liberated I had longed to return to the country in which I had spent so many happy days, and which I regarded as my second home. My first visit was to Deauville. Charlie Elliott was now based in England, but he still rode for M Boussac when required, and he asked me to accompany him to Deauville, where he was to ride Nirgal in the Prix Kergolay, and it won very easily. It was a lovely day, and I have experienced few thrills comparable with that of the moment when our plane touched down on French soil and I heard the sounds and inhaled the smells peculiar to France and France alone. We lunched at the Casino with Rae Johnstone, and another great Australian jockey Wally Sibbritt, and as I ate my sole meunière, washed down with a deliciously dry white wine, the years rolled back and it was hard to believe that seven years had passed since I had bade farewell to France at this very spot.

Harry Heywood liked my story, and when I told him that I thought that the French horses would sweep the board from then onwards he urged me to go to France whenever I considered there was a story to be had. I was not slow to take advantage of these instructions, and I take pride in the fact that not once in over twenty years did my Editor suggest that my fairly hefty expenses did not constitute money well spent.

I spent several weeks in Deauville, covering not only the racing but also the principal Normandy studs. Marcel Boussac invited me to visit his magnificent stud at Fresnay-le-Buffard, and his racing manager, François de Brignac, who became a very good friend of mine, accompanied me on several visits.

Unlike M Boussac, who assured me that he spoke no English, though I should not have cared to say anything unfavourable about one of his horses in his hearing in my own tongue, François de Brignac spoke perfect English. A handsome man with great charm, and a confirmed Anglophile, he was a splendid ambassador for his country.

Fresnay-le-Buffard is situated in the Falaise Gap through which the Germans had retreated. There were still the remains of a German gun in the pond in the front of the house, and several of the mares carried scars as the result of shrapnel wounds. I also visited Caen, which had suffered so grievously from the shelling of both sides. Although nearly all the streets had been reduced to rubble, every street bore its original name, awaiting its rebuilding. The inhabitants were living in primitive huts, and I found their courage and philosophy in the face of the loss of their homes and cherished possessions very moving.

El's husband gave himself up when the war ended and, having received a savage sentence, was sent to Dartmoor. So convinced was he that in no circumstances is a country justified in going to war that he had declined to make any compromise. One must admire a man who had the courage of his convictions, whether or not one agreed with him, which I did not at that time. Only when the world becomes converted to the cause of peace, and the conscientious objectors become the cowboys and the belligerents the Indians, will there be no more wars.

El accompanied me on my visit to Paris to cover the Prix de l'Arc de Triomphe. I was the only English journalist present, and therefore got a scoop. How different things are today, when all the leading newspapers send journalists to cover not only the principal races run on the Continent but also the races leading up to them. We had a splendid evening at the Bal Tabarin, but we both had a feeling of guilt as we ate in the plush restaurants, knowing that the food, for which I had paid through the nose, had come from the black market; in eating it we were depriving French people of the food they needed so desperately.

France, being an agricultural country, recovered rapidly; but in the autumn of '46 thousands of those who lived in the towns were suffering from malnutrition. Coffee and sugar were unprocurable, except at a few of the most expensive hotels, and the ersatz coffee, made from acorns, which was sold in the cafés, was undrinkable.

I had made a grave error in asking my brother Ronald, who was in Paris on business, to secure me accommodation at his hotel. He wired me that he had done so, but he had always prided himself on his inability to speak French; when we arrived at his hotel we were met with the spreading of hands and shrugging of shoulders, which I knew from past experience meant that no room was available.

I managed to secure one of the few taxis then on the streets, and asked the driver to take us on a tour of Paris in search of a room. We started at the Ritz, and descended the social scale till we reached the somewhat sordid quartier near the Gard du Nord. We had met with fifteen 'plein partouts' and 'tout complets', but at a hotel, with a blue light above the door, I was welcomed by the stout *patronne* with a 'mais oui, monsieur' in reply to the question to which I had despaired of receiving a favourable answer.

But on seeing our suitcases her face fell and on hearing that we wanted to stay the whole night she gave me to understand that this was a very different kettle of fish, and she must consult her husband. She returned with a somewhat unattractive man, unshaven and with no collar, who rapped out the words 'deux mille, cinq cents' (approximately £5), and when I suggested that this seemed rather steep for a room with no bath, he made it very clear that he couldn't care less if I took it or not.

Speaking slowly, as one does to a small child, he explained that it was a Saturday, and that on Saturdays he could let the room in questions four or perhaps five times in the course of one night, at a charge of 1,000 francs, plus 10 per cent for the *femme de chambre*, and that in allowing us to occupy it for the whole night for 2,500 francs he was doing us a great favour.

I saw his point, and was sure that every other hotel, with a blue light above the door, would take the same view. As it was a 100/1 against getting a room in a respectable establishment, we took it.

The Prix de l'Arc de Triomphe was won by Boussac's four-year-old Caracalla, ridden by Charlie Elliott, who beat that year's French Derby winner Prince Chevalier after a thrilling finish. Caracalla was one of the best horses ever owned by M Boussac, and he had previously won our Gold Cup at Ascot. M Boussac had 112 horses in training in his two stables, the Écurie Pharis and the Écurie Djebel at Chantilly, named after two of his famous horses.

Most people were somewhat in awe of Marcel Boussac, France's most successful industrialist, but I received nothing but kindness from him, and when François de Brignac told him that I had had some difficulty in securing a press ticket on one occasion, he saw to it personally that I was granted a permanent French press pass.

Although my financial position was sounder than ever before, currency was a problem on every visit to France as my business allowance from Kemsley Newspapers did not pay for the luxuries which make Paris and Deauville just that little bit different from Bradford and Margate. I had heard that Georges, at the Ritz, was delighted to give 600 francs for a pound, as opposed to the 500 given by the banks, but as there were any number of Nosey Parkers at London Airport who were in the habit of searching passengers before allowing them on board the aircraft, I decided to take eight one-pound notes in each shoe. This added more than an inch to my height, and El thought that in future I should always carry my money in my shoes.

We had passed through the Customs, and were walking to the aircraft when El burst out laughing, and on looking down I saw that a pound note had worked itself up from the heel of my shoe and was protruding over the end of my trousers. I looked round in terror, but there were no Customs officials trailing me.

Rae Johnstone often helped me out, as he needed pounds on his frequent visits to England, but on one occasion, following an expensive evening in the casino at Deauville, I was desperately in need of £100. Rae had a friend going to Paris that evening, who agreed to take my cheque for £100 and secure me 600 francs to the pound on the black market. When the best part of a week had elapsed and there was still no sign of Rae's friend I became uneasy, but Rae insisted that he was responsible for my £100, which was typical of him. When his friend returned with my cheque uncashed he explained the situation to me. There were, he said, Treasury spies everywhere, and he dared not cash a cheque made out in sterling. It transpired that the British Treasury had started a blitz on those who broke the currency regulations, even for the smallest amounts, and had Rae's friend cashed my cheque I should not only have lost my £100 but should have been fined at least £200 into the bargain. This was one of the luckiest escapes of my life, and Rae came to the rescue by lending me sufficient money to tide me over till the end of my stay in France.

Although I have travelled extensively, France is the only European country I know intimately, though only the turn of a card stood between me and an intimate knowledge of Copenhagen and a Danish girl who lived there.

I was staying in Monte Carlo with a girl friend, and one afternoon she decided not to accompany me to the Sporting Club for my pre-dinner session at the tables.

Sitting alone at the long bar was a most attractive girl, who readily accepted my offer of a glass of champagne, and in the space of a few minutes we were chatting away like old friends. Girls one meets alone at casino bars usually have a hard luck story, but having got that off her chest, she proceeded to paint a most glamorous picture of her native Copenhagen, pronouncing the third syllable with a very long A.

Over a couple or perhaps three more glasses of champagne, she suggested that I should return there with her, as soon as we could get seats on a plane. I could stay at her apartment, where we would make a lot of love, and in the evenings she would show me the night life in the 'gayest city in the world'. She was very attractive and the project delighted me, but, as usual, there was the problem of currency. This, however, was dismissed with the words, 'We will win it at *chemin de fer*.' So I gave her the equivalent of £20, which she lost in the twinkling of an eye, but having forked out another fiver I stood behind her while she turned it into approximately £120. Every time she won she would give me a dazzling smile and exclaim, 'One step nearer to Copenhagen.' It was now a case of £240 or nothing, but as you may have guessed it was the Belgian industrialist who called Banco, and not the Danish girl who dealt the cards, who got the nine.

I have often wondered what would have been the outcome had the hands been reversed, as I was so enchanted with Miss Copenhagen that I have not the slightest doubt I should have flown away with her to her home town, where I should have stayed till my money ran out. The winner, of course, was my girl friend, who was waiting in our hotel to be taken out to dinner.

# 20 *The post-war racing scene*

Gordon Richards was succeeded as champion jockey by Doug Smith, who held the title in 1954, '55 and '56, and after Scobie Breasley had intervened in 1957 he was again champion in '58 and '59. Doug retired at the end of the 1967 season, and is now a highly successful trainer with eighty horses in his two yards at Newmarket. Throughout his long career there was never a suspicion of scandal connected with his name, and he was a worthy successor to the greatest champion of them all.

Racing owes a great deal to men like Gordon and Doug in that the public knew that by backing their mounts they would be sure of getting a run for their money. Doug was always most helpful to the press, realising that it was to a jockey's advantage to be able to tell his own story of what took place in the course of a race. I have been accused of being afraid to speak my mind when it appeared that a jockey had ridden a bad race, to which my reply has been that though he may have appeared to do so from the Press Stand, I decline to criticise a man until I have heard his side of the story and that of the other jockeys riding in the race. Hence my frequent visits to the weighing-room door in order to have a word with the jockeys on their way to ride in the next race.

The racing journalist carries a far heavier load of responsibility than his colleagues who write on other forms of sport, by reason of the colossal sum of money which is involved in every race. There is no point in excusing a cricketer, who has thrown away his wicket, or a footballer for missing a goal. No money is directly involved and the chances are that they will redeem themselves before the game is over. But if I had accused a jockey of throwing away the Derby I would not only have jeopardised his career, but I would also have condemned him in the eyes of the millions who had backed his mount, who would be only too happy to find a scapegoat for their failure to back the winner. A mistake in a big race is a catastrophic and irreparable blunder, and I should hate to pile on the agony for the unfortunate jockey.

Twice I have defended a jockey who was alleged to have ridden a bad race in the Derby. The first occasion was in 1934, in which Rae Johnstone on the favourite Colombo was baulked and finished third to Windsor Lad, ridden by Charlie Smirke, and Easton, the mount of Gordon Richards. I was certain that Colombo did not really stay 1½ miles, and the fact that he did not get a clear run racing down to Tattenham Corner was to his advantage, in that it gave him time to get his second wind. In no circumstances would Colombo have beaten Windsor Lad, a view which was shared by Smirke, with whom I watched the film of the race that evening at the party given by the Maharajah of Rajpipla. This view was not, however, shared by Colombo's owner, Lord Glanely, who soon afterwards dispensed with Rae's services.

The second occasion on which I thought a Derby jockey was most unfairly accused was in 1950, in which Mr Woodward's Prince Simon, ridden by Harry Carr, was beaten by a head by M Boussac's Galcador, ridden by Rae Johnstone, who in contrast to his experience sixteen years earlier was lauded to the skies. In my opinion Harry did everything humanly possible on a colt lacking in finishing speed and if Rae, on a very fast colt, who barely stayed 1½ miles, had waited a little longer, Galcador would have won more convincingly.

When I arrived on the racecourse the following day, I was told that Captain (now Sir Cecil) Boyd-Rochfort, trainer of Prince Simon, wanted to see me. If the message had come from some trainers I would have thought I was in for a rocket, but Cecil had been a friend of mine from my early days in Fleet Street, and I knew him to be not only one of the great trainers in turf history, but also one of the fairest men. When I met him outside the weighing room he said, 'I want to thank you for your article in this morning's *Sporting Chronicle* about my jockey Carr. It coincides exactly with my reading of the race and I have sent a copy of your paper to Mr Woodward in America.'

Neither Harry nor I were considered likely by our colleagues to succeed at the jobs which, in point of fact, we held down till our retirement. When Harry, who had ridden largely in the North, was appointed in 1947 first jockey to Captain Boyd-Rochfort's stable, for which the King was chief patron, a famous jockey, who had a higher opinion of his own ability than that of his contemporaries, described the appointment as 'a bleeding liberty', though at whose expense he did not specify. Big-head went on to proclaim that Harry wouldn't last the month out, but when, after a serious illness as the result of wasting, Harry retired, he had been the royal jockey for fifteen years.

I am not suggesting that my appointment was in any way comparable with Harry's, but at Lincoln, on the first day of publication, I overheard the following conversation between two elderly colleagues. 'So the *Sporting Chronicle* has started up again.' 'Yes and they have appointed Quinny Gilbey as Kettledrum. I'd like to bet evens he'll be out on his ass before the month is out.' During my career in Fleet Street, my prognostications were all too often wide of the mark, but never by as much as twenty-one years.

I am proud to say that I never once missed a deadline, though the fear of doing so still haunts my dreams, and my friends of both sexes were unanimous that I was hell to be with until my story was in the hands of the editorial department. This particularly applied when I was abroad, and on one occasion I spent a ghastly hour, and saw to it that El, who was with me in Paris, shared my anxiety and frustration.

The race I was covering was for the Prix de l'Arc de Triomphe and I had arranged, as always, for the London office to put through a call for 6.30 p.m. Nothing happened, and at 7 p.m. I tried to put a call through to London, without success. At that time the telephonic communications between England and France were still pretty dicey, and it was seldom that both ends of the conversation were audible. Having given up all hope of getting my story over, I was wondering how the Editor would fill the front page at the last moment, when at 7.30 my call came through. In reply to my query as to what the hell they had been up to since 6.30 p.m.

I was informed that that was the time in London, Great Britain having reverted to Greenwich Mean Time in my absence.

I was indebted to that entertaining and highly controversial journalist Tim Fitzgeorge-Parker of the *Mail* for preserving my unblemished record in July '65.

A couple of days before the race for the Prix Robert Papin was due to be run at Maisons-Laffitte, Jeremy Tree told me he was sending over our leading two-year-old Double Jump for this race and I decided to cover it, though I could not tell the office where to call me, saying I would ring them around 6.30. I hadn't realised that the Post Office go-slow measures in operation at that time would interfere so drastically with foreign calls, and I was horrified when I was told that there was a three-hours' delay. I had the hell of a good story to tell: on a sweltering hot afternoon, when it seemed that heavyweight Jeremy Tree would melt before our eyes, Double Jump, ridden by Jimmy Lindley, became the first English-trained horse to win a major event in France for seventeen years, and he did it with three lengths to spare.

Tim Fitzgeorge-Parker, having telephoned his story, kindly told the *Daily Mail* office to ring Thomson House and ask them to try to get through to me at the Hotel George V. This they managed to do, but it is experiences such as this which make newspaper reporters old before their time.

When Harry Heywood was satisfied that the *Sporting Chronicle* was firmly on its feet, he asked me if I could find someone with an extensive knowledge of breeding to succeed the late Professor Robertson, whose articles had been so widely read in pre-war days. I answered, without hesitation, 'I know the very man; John Hislop.' 'Do you mean the amateur rider?' Heywood asked me, looking somewhat dubious. 'Yes, I do,' I replied; 'his knowledge of the Stud Book is on a par with that of Lord Rosebery and the Aga Khan.' John was asked to write a specimen article, and the following day received a telegram seeking permission to publish the article, and engaging him to write a weekly article on breeding.

When John left to join the *Sporting Life*, his place was taken by Peter Willett, already on the staff of Kemsley Newspapers, one of his jobs at that time being to understudy me as Kettledrum. He succeeded me on my retirement, and since he stepped into my shoes the *Sporting Chronicle* has continued to increase its circulation.

My own knowledge of breeding was confined to my practical needs, and I have never pretended to be an expert on this highly technical subject. From a study of a horse's pedigree I could arrive at a reasonably accurate conclusion as to what its best distance might be, though, as I have already stated, all racing theories are composed of many shades of grey, and nothing stands out in black and white.

If a lifetime devoted to racing should leave one with one quality it is humility; not even the most self-opinionated individual could fail to be chastened by the daily reminders of his fallibility. Men, like John and Peter, with their vast knowledge of this esoteric subject, are well aware of this, and the most they can promise is that provided a breeder has sufficient money, time and patience, his theories will produce a very good horse indeed in the course of the next three or four generations.

Peter Willett and I usually stayed at the same hotels, when racing in the North, and with his sense of humour and knowledge of racing he has been a delightful companion. During my illnesses in the early sixties he wrote most of my articles as well as his own, which must have severely taxed even his capacity for hard work. For the past twelve years I have stayed with him at Yateley for the Royal Ascot meeting, and his eldest son David is my godson.

In the autumn of '46 the *Sporting Life* announced that they were running a competition during the forthcoming National Hunt season on the naps of the twenty-five leading journalists. One point was awarded for an even money winner, 2 points for a 2/1 winner and so on. A winner at 2/1 on earned half a point. The prize was £100 plus a challenge cup.

Steeplechasing has figured very little in this book for the reason that I always took my holiday in the winter, and as I worked a seven-day week I was entitled to a long one. In addition to six or seven weeks in the winter I usually took a fortnight in August or September, but even so I put in more man hours per year than those who worked a five-day week.

Only sadists, who enjoy killing animals, and masochists, who get a kick from discomfort, can find much to enjoy in an English winter; as I am neither, the first week in January could not come round quick enough, when I would take off for a country in which the sun was reasonably certain to shine, though I have the reputation of bringing bad weather wherever I go. Once, when Romie and I arrived at Biskra, an oasis in the Sahara Desert, the rain was pouring down and the inhabitants were kneeling in the mud. When Romie was told that they were praising Allah for this priceless gift of rain, the first for seven years, she announced, 'Allah be damned, it's my bloody husband.'

The winter of 1946/47 was the most severe for many years, and throughout my skiing holiday at Davos, no racing took place. When I left I was a couple of points behind Eric Rickman (Robin Goodfellow of the *Mail*), and we were several points ahead of our nearest rivals. When racing was eventually resumed, the form bore no relation to what it had been before the hold-up, but I was fortunate enough to nap a winner just when I needed it most. Incidentally, it was one of the luckiest winners I have ever tipped, as the hot favourite was trotting up when he fell base over apex at the last flight leaving my selection, a 5/1 chance, well in front of the rest of the field. and winning me the Cup, £100 and the delight of my Editor.

Only half a length prevented my winning the competition for the second time running. When the last race of the season, the Manchester November Handicap, came along, I was still in the running, and I napped Sir Eric Ohlson's Star of Autumn, a 25/1 chance. Eric had backed him at 33/1, and laid me £200/£6 so, with the prize, I stood to win £300. As so often happened, the race was run in a fog, and when the horses reappeared Star of Autumn and Regret were lengths ahead of the remainder, but Regret, who was in receipt of 23 lbs from Star of Autumn, was the narrow winner.

The Manchester November Handicap had never been my lucky race, but ten years later the luck changed. My nap selections had done well and were showing a good profit after Great Rock had won the Northumberland Plate at 10/1 and Ballymoss the St Leger at 8/1, but I struck a losing run, and when I went to Manchester for the final three days of the season I was well in the red.

On the first day, however, I napped a 9/2 winner, and it occurred to me that I might still bring it off if I could find a long-priced winner. Trentham Boy, at approximately 10/1, was no use to me, but on entering the Midland Hotel I ran into Peter O'Sullevan, and over a drink he told me that Ryan Price had gelded a horse named Polar Lodge, and that, after the operation, owner Mr Nat Cohen, had changed its name to Chief Barker.

The horse had not run for over five months, but in a recent gallop he had beaten the pants off his stable companion Gold Wire, who had the same weight to carry the following day. 'How about that for a good outsider?' Peter asked me, and the words were hardly out of his mouth before I had dashed off to Kemsley House, where I told them to kill my original story, while I sat down and wrote a new one, giving a confident vote to Chief Barker.

The only fly in the ointment was that at the time of going to press no jockey had been found for him. If a boy claiming the 7 lbs allowance could be found, Chief Barker would carry only 6.5, but with so many of the runners carrying featherweights where was a boy of this weight to be found.

Late that evening Ryan Price was informed that Woodruffe, who trained a few horses at York, had a capable lightweight boy called Dennis Walker, and he promptly engaged him.

I had never seen Walker ride, and when he emerged from the weighing room, with the thirty-nine other riders, he was so small that he appeared to be all colours and cap, and it seemed impossible for this tiny tot to steer a horse, standing over 16 hands, round this tricky 1½-mile course in a large field. Later, I discovered that Dennis stood 4 ft 2 ins and weighed several pounds under five stone.

The visibility was surprisingly good for Manchester in November, and Chief Barker, one of the best away, was never out of the first three. Diminutive Dennis sent him into a clear lead after entering the straight, but there was still a long way to go, and I doubted whether he would have the strength to keep this big horse balanced and fully extended all the way to the winning post.

My fears seemed well founded when Peter Robinson, on Spaceman, went three-quarters of a length to the good, less than 100 yards from the winning post. The race seemed all over, but Dennis and Chief Barker were not done with, and fought back like a couple of tigers, with the result that it was Chief Barker's nose which was in front at the only place that matters. The three minutes' suspense, while the photograph was being developed, seemed like hours, but it showed that Chief Barker had won by just over an inch. Without the photograph the judge must have given a dead heat.

The Clerk of the Course, Mr Frith, presented me with the photograph which hangs in my bedroom. Chief Barker's offside was smothered with white paint as the result of his being forced into the rails, so had the verdict gone the other way he might have got the race on an objection, though I doubt whether I would have survived a further half-hour's suspense while the Stewards were arriving at their verdict.

The drama, however, was not yet over as Dennis could not reach Chief Barker's girths in order to remove the saddle, and by the rules of racing nobody was allowed to do it for him. A chair or an up-turned bucket was the obvious solution, but at that moment Chief Barker was announced over the loud speaker as the winner, and his stable lad, in his excitement, seized Dennis by the waist and held him at arm's length while he unbuckled the girths. Walker's future appeared bright with promise, but his fine riding on the last day of the season was forgotten by trainers when the next season opened, and I cannot remember his riding another winner.

Chief Barker's starting price was 33/1 and left me with a profit on the season of £27.13.0. I had napped 75 winners and a 109 losers, and my nearest rival showed a profit of £12. I should never have napped Chief Barker had it not been for Peter O'Sullevan's last-minute information, but strangely enough he did not tip him, though he had a fiver on him which I had not.

Everyone who reads the *Daily Express* and owns a television set knows Peter for his highly entertaining articles and for his outstanding brilliance as a race reader, but only his close friends know of the kindness and consideration for others which lie beneath that sophisticated exterior. I also finished second on three occasions in this competition – to Gimcrack (Norman Pegg) of the *Daily Graphic* in the National Hunt season of '47 and 48, to Gimcrack (John Rickman) in '61 and to The Scout (Clive Graham) of the *Daily Express* in 1964. John's success provided the Rickman family with their revenge for my defeating his father seventeen years earlier. John and Peggy Rickman are very good friends of mine and on the three occasions on which I was narrowly beaten I could not have finished second to nicer people.

Sir Max Aitken gave a dinner at the Écu de France to the senior members of the staff of *Express* newspapers to celebrate Clive's success, and kindly invited me. Most of us were called on to make a short impromptu speech, and when it was my turn I said that although I was disappointed at my narrow defeat by my old friend Clive, I now thought it was the best possible result, as had I won there would have been no party.

True to the traditions of Sir Edward Hulton neither Lord Kemsley nor Lord Thomson believed in 'spoiling' members of their staff, for fear, I presume, they might be emboldened to ask for a rise. A journalist's position in the nap table is largely a matter of luck, and is in no way a criterion of his merits as a writer or as a judge of racing. A pin is just as likely to find you a long-priced winner as the most conscientious journalist, and the competition is invariably won by someone who, more by luck than judgement, has tipped a winning outsider. This being so, it is illogical that journalists should set such store by their position in the competitions run by the *Sporting Life* and the *Sporting Chronicle*, but worry they do, and so much so that these competitions were responsible for the early death of one of my colleagues and have taken years off the lives of several others. I do not know whether I worried more when I was near the top of the table, with a good chance of winning, or near the foot, with a good chance of finishing bottom.

Next to Chief Barker, my longest-priced winning nap was the grey horse Nicolaus Silver in the Grand National, at 28/1, though it did not win me the competition. I dined with Peter O'Sullevan at the Adelphi on the evening before I had to make my selection, and he tells the story against himself of how he spent two hours trying to convince me that Nicolaus Silver had no chance and that I was crazy to go for him. But in racing, one has to be a bit obstinate at times, and if one doesn't stick by one's own judgement one has no right to one's job.

My friendship with the Carr family (Harry, Joan and their daughter Anne, now Mrs Joe Mercer) has given me much pleasure in various parts of the world. I have told how one of Harry's colleagues doubted his ability to hold down the job of first jockey to the reigning monarch, and other members of Captain Boyd-Rochfort's stable, and the start of his career at Newmarket was inauspicious, to say the least of it. In the spring of the year following his appointment, his leg was smashed when he was forced up against the rails in a race at Birmingham and it took so long to heal that he missed the ride on Black Tarquin in the St Leger. Ridden by Harry's close friend, Australian Edgar Britt, this magnificent coal-black horse was an easy winner in the colours of Mr William Woodward.

Early in '54 Cecil Boyd-Rochfort was confident that in Lady Zia Wernher's Meld, a daughter of Lord Derby's great stayer Alycidon, he trained a filly destined for the highest honours, but before she could run she split a pastern, and any idea of training her for the valuable two-year-old races had to be abandoned. She ran twice in the autumn, winning a small race at Newmarket so impressively that her name was entered in most people's books as a likely classic winner.

Meld's first race as a three-year-old was the One Thousand Guineas, which she won convincingly. So Harry had at last won a classic race, but this was only the beginning. When winning the Oaks, Meld was magnificent, beating Ark Royal, a filly good enough to win nine Oaks out of ten, by six lengths.

She was put by for the St Leger, in which she would, of course, be opposed by the best colts. In the late summer of '55 the worst epidemic of coughing in living memory swept through the stables, and in the week before the St Leger, Meld and two others were the only members of Boyd-Rochfort's stable unaffected.

She left for Doncaster in blooming health, but when the assistant trainer George Archibald entered her box on the morning of the race, he heard the dreaded sound. Her temperature was well above normal, but as she seemed well enough in herself he kept his mouth shut. She did not cough while being saddled, but half-way through the race Harry realised that all was not well with her. But Meld had a heart as big as herself, and she fought on to beat Miss Dorothy Paget's Nucleus, ridden by Lester Piggott, by three-quarters of a length.

As the winner of three classics, Meld took her place among the immortals, and I have no hesitation in nominating her as the best filly of my time. We have only to cast our minds back to the last time we had flu to appreciate how Meld must have felt throughout the race for the St Leger. She was a very sick filly by the time she arrived home at Newmarket, but the results of her strenuous efforts in the face of adversity had no lasting effects on her constitution; in 1963 she had a foal by Charlottesville, who Lady Zia called Charlottown. Three years later he won the Derby, ridden by Scobie Breasley.

In 1958 Captain Boyd-Rochfort seemed sure to win the Derby with Sir Humphrey de Trafford's Alcide but less than a week before the race he pulled a muscle and could not run. Just to show what a good thing he would have been for the Derby, he gave Harry Carr his second success in the St Leger, winning by eight lengths. A year later Sir Humphrey and Cecil Boyd-Rochfort received consolation for the tragic mishap to Alcide when Parthia won the Derby beating Fidalgo ridden by Harry's son-in-law Joe Mercer.

For years, Harry had had to undergo severe privations in order to keep his weight down, and when in 1964 he was taken seriously ill for the fourth time in five years, he decided to hang up his boots. As his weight is now around twelve stone this decision was unquestionably a wise one.

I felt very honoured when Doug Smith asked me to make the speech proposing Harry's health at the farewell dinner given by his fellow jockeys at the Savoy at the end of the season.

Unfortunately Doug was not present, having sustained a serious accident in a six-furlong race at Liverpool in almost the last race of the season. His mount fell, and over twenty horses galloped over him, kicking him around as if he were a football. His life was in danger for more than a week, and we all thought that his career as a jockey was over. But this lovable little man, although nearing his fiftieth birthday, came back the following season to ride as brilliantly as at any time in his career. We hear a great deal about the dangers of the Grand National, but I consider it a far less perilous race than one over the six-furlongs course at Liverpool in a big field.

Jamaica, Majorca and Paris are three of the places I have enjoyed myself in the company of the Carrs, and on my retirement Harry wrote the following letter to my Editor Bill Clarke for publication in the *Sporting Chronicle*.

'I am quite certain that with the retirement of my very good friend Quinny Gilbey, racing has lost one of the great journalists of all time, and all who know him, and no doubt hundreds who don't, will agree with me. If Quinny couldn't say anything good about a person he never said anything bad. I know his articles will be sadly missed as they were such good and interesting reading. I am sure all his many friends will join me in wishing Quinny the happiest of retirements which he so richly deserves.'

Next to Meld I regard Petite Etoile as the best filly I have seen. She, like Meld, won the One Thousand Guineas and the Oaks, but she was not started for the St Leger. In the Coronation Cup, as a four-year-old, she defeated the Derby winner Parthia.

The Noel Murless–Lester Piggott association, which ended in 1966 when Lester chose to ride as a freelance, is one of racing's most glamorous success stories, and Lester's decision to terminate it at the end of a season in which Noel Murless had his best ever string of two-year-olds was surprising to say the least.

Noel Murless made a great start as Master of Beckhampton. by saddling Sir Percy Loraine's Queenpot to win the One Thousand Guineas, but he soon discovered that this large remote stable with its own gallops was not a financial proposition, and he moved to Warren Place, Newmarket. He has never regretted this step. Since he moved to Newmarket Noel has beaten every record in respect of stake money, and has gone on to beat his own record, much as Gordon used to do as a jockey. Even though the purchasing price of the pound continues to depreciate I cannot believe that his record of £259,000, set up in 1967, will ever be beaten, unless the stakes are materially increased in the years to come.

Every year Noel and Gwen invited me to stay a night before the beginning of the season, and it was a thrilling experience to go round evening stables, and be introduced to 70 horses, every one of which was bred in the purple.

Like his predecessor, Fred Darling, Noel Murless does not suffer fools gladly, but if he considers a question is sensible and justifiable, he will go to an infinity of trouble to answer it. He rarely bets himself, and runs his horses for the benefit of his owners, and not for his acquaintances to bet on.

Laconic Lester, in common with most people who converse in infrequent monosyllables, is not an easy man to get to know well, and I cannot pretend that I am one of the few who have succeeded. I recognise him to be as straight as a die and one of the great jockeys of all time, but as to what goes on behind that poker face I haven't a clue.

What little he has to say is said deliberately, and anyone meeting him for the first time might think that this denoted a slow-working brain. This could not be wider of the mark; Lester, with his lightning reflexes, not only has a quick brain, but is capable of making an accurate appraisal of the prospects of the horse he is to ride and of the possible dangers to him.

Lester was one of the most sensationally successful infant prodigies since Frank Wootton arrived from Australia with his father, Richard Wootton, in the first decade of the century. Like the youthful Frank, Lester was apprenticed to his father, but unlike old man Wootton, ex-jumping jockey Keith Piggott was no disciplinarian, and this was to land his son in trouble in the years to come.

I do not think that Lester can have been more than thirteen when I first saw him ride a winner. The race was at Newbury, and Lester's mount, after leading into the last furlong, began to tire. But instead of going for his whip right away, as ninety-nine boys out of a hundred would have done, he gave his mount an easy, and having got its second wind, the horse ran on to regain the lead and win by a neck.

It was a staggering piece of riding on the part of one so young, and convinced me that sooner or later this child would become world famous. In the years to follow, Lester's most formidable opponent was himself; having been allowed to do as he liked from the day he was born, he thought he could continue doing so on the racecourse.

There was nothing vicious about his behaviour, though from time to time it involved his fellow riders in danger, and to a lesser extent himself. Time and again, in his desperate eagerness to win, he would resort to tactics which evoked the displeasure of the Stewards and was punished by fines and terms of suspension, the longest being the result of an alleged offence at Ascot when riding Never Say Die, the colt on which he had won the Derby at the age of 18.

Never again did he fall foul of the Stewards on account of reckless riding, and he went from strength to strength. His suspension cost him the winning ride on Never Say Die in the St Leger, and a present of approximately £1,200. This must have been a bitter blow, as from his earliest days Lester has had a finely developed appreciation of the value of money.

Although he had ridden 1,015 winners in this country by the end of 1961 he had not yet realised his full potential. He rode many brilliant races, but was inconsistent, and was also too free with his whip. Sometimes he would wave his whip with such Gallic abandon that one might have thought that one was watching one of the less distinguished French jockeys.

But in recent years Lester has developed into an artist who goes for his whip only as a last resort. Throughout a race he has his mount well placed, beautifully balanced, and ready to challenge when he considers the moment for action has arrived, while there has never been a more powerful finisher.

George Moore, who succeeded him as first jockey to Murless, is one of the greats, a superb horseman and a great jockey, accomplishments which are by no means synonymous.

I first met George Moore and his beautiful wife Iris at Alec Head's house at Chantilly. Alec was training for the Aga Khan, and George was stable jockey. I had telephoned my story on the French Derby from Alec's house and was trying, unsuccessfully, to hire a car to take me to Le Bourget, when George, who was riding in England the following week, offered me a lift. Owing to engine trouble our flight was delayed three hours, but the time passed quickly in the company of these friendly Australians, and when we arrived at London Airport in the middle of the night I returned the compliment by driving them in my car to the Dorchester. Moore did not return to this country in 1968, and he was succeeded as first jockey to Murless by the brilliant 19-year-old Scottish jockey, Sandy Barclay.

Australian jockeys have enjoyed fantastic success over here in the post-war years, the most successful of all being Scobie Breasley. He was thirty-seven when he had his first ride in this country, incidentally, on a winner, and he had already toyed with the idea of retiring, but England and English racecourses suited him, and he was riding as well as ever when he retired at the end of 1968 to take up training.

Scobie and May Breasley became friends of mine soon after their arrival, and I have had some wonderful times with them in Barbados, where Scobie has built himself a lovely house. I was with them the day they chose the plot of land, and I was in the motorboat with May the morning that Scobie first tried his hand at water-skiing. More than twenty times he assumed the perpendicular as the motorboat surged forward, only to fall backwards, but at the end of what must have been one of the most frustrating hour's of his life, he ordered the driver of the motorboat to be back at 2 p.m.

Tenacity of purpose such as this deserves to be crowned with success, and in the space of a few days Scobie was quite an expert. Jockeyship, however, requires another quality besides determination, and Scobie was a 'natural', without which no man achieves greatness. Is George Moore better than Lester Piggott, and how do they both compare with Scobie Breasley, and are they all that superior to Jimmy Lindley, Joe Mercer, Ron Hutchinson, Geoff

Lewis and Bill Williamson? I do not pretend to know the answer to that one, but I do know that there has never been a better judge of pace than my old friend Scobie from Wagga-Wagga.

Bobby Jones, perhaps the greatest of all golfers, wrote 'All that man can do is to beat the people around at the same time that he is. He cannot win from those who came before, any more than he can from those who come afterwards.' These words apply equally to horses. It was said of both triple crown winner Bahram, and Tulyar, winner of the Derby, St Leger, Eclipse Stakes and 'King George', 'he was the best of a bad lot', but a champion can do no more than beat those opposed to him, and it is a characteristic of a top-class horse not to win by more than is necessary.

Where jockeys are concerned, it is impossible to arrive at a decision as to who is the best, even among contemporaries, as they are dependent on the horses under them for their success. Nevertheless, the old adage that a jockey cannot come without his horse is often forgotten, and a jockey is unfairly blamed because his mount could or would not go any faster.

No story of the post-war years would be complete without a reference to Charlie Smirke, though his name was a household word long before Hitler invaded Poland. Apprenticed to Stanley Wootton, he was an infant prodigy, though he did not ride in public at such an early age as Lester Piggott. Stanley was a stern disciplinarian but even he found this cheeky Cockney boy a bit of a handful.

The two Charlies, Smirke and Elliott, were betting in hundreds before they needed to shave, and the Stewards were gunning for them. Elliott secured a lucrative engagement in France, where he rode with brilliant success for many years for Marcel Boussac. Smirke was not so lucky, and was warned off for an offence of which I have always believed him innocent.

It was at Gatwick that Charlie Smirke rode his last race for nearly seven years. His mount, Welcome Gift, was considered such a certainty that he was almost unbackable. No bookmaker wanted to lay him which they would have done had they thought the race was bent. I remember the betting very well as I tried to back a horse belonging to Geoffrey each way at 20/1, and no bookmaker would let me.

Welcome Gift was left at the post and Charlie Smirke was warned off for making no attempt to start. The horse was subsequently sold to a rich Hindu and arrived in Bombay, where I was acting as a Stipendiary Steward to the Western India Turf Club. In his first three races he declined to go near the starting gate, and it was only after the starter Colin Gulliland had spent hours humouring him under the gate that he consented to take part in a race.

The year following his return to the saddle Charlie Smirke won the Derby on Windsor Lad and two years later he won it for the Aga Khan on Mahmoud. After the war, he again won the Derby for the Aga Khan on Tulyar and for Sir Victor Sassoon on Hard Ridden.

Possessed of the bouncy arrogance of the complete extravert, Charlie Smirke was not everyone's cup of tea, though no one could deny him his expertise, any more than they could that of his less assertive friend Charlie Elliott. I have met few men who possessed such implicit faith in their own ability, and I do not think that it ever entered Charlie's head that he could ride a bad race. Although many people found this self-assurance irritating, I would hesitate to say it was misplaced. The brash Cockney kid who could do everything just a little better than the next fellow gloried in his self-created image, but there was another side to his character. He was ever ready with a helping hand for those down on their luck, and must have given away thousands. When I was taken ill in Jamaica he and his wife Ruth were the first people to visit me with fruit and flowers. He was also extremely hospitable, so much so that he refused to allow anyone else to pay for a drink.

He holds two records, unique in my racing experience – he was the first jockey, who betted heavily, to retire a rich man, and he was the only jockey who wasted drastically for years on end without ruining his health.

Harry Wragg retired from the saddle at the end of 1946, but his fame as a jockey lives on as the man who brought sanity back to the race for the Derby. In the early 'twenties Steve Donoghue seemed unbeatable in our premier race, and told the world that the secret of his success was that he always had his horse in the first three at the top of the hill (a mile from home) or as soon afterwards as possible. The result was that approximately thirty jockeys rode like madmen, apparently oblivious to the fact that thirty into three won't go. Young Harry Wragg from Sheffield had other ideas, and though he, like all the other jockeys, had a great respect for Steve's jockeyship he thought that Steve's recipe for success was a load of nonsense. He decided to try and win the Derby by adopting waiting tactics, and he was successful on Felstead in 1928 and Blenheim in 1930.

Unlike many jockeys who become trainers, Harry Wragg was an immediate success in his new profession, and he has for many years now been one of our leading trainers, winning the Derby in 1961 with Psidium, ridden by the French jockey Roger Poincelet for Mrs Arpad Plesch. Harry has always been a theorist and he has refused to accept blindly the formulas for success handed down to him, which he considers outdated. Immensely painstaking, he has made an exhaustive study of American methods, many of which he has adopted with success at Newmarket. Born with a first-rate mental equipment, he has employed it to the best advantage, both as a jockey and as a trainer.

Although the Irish have been winning the Grand National since long before my time, they enjoyed comparatively little success over here on the flat before the war. Since the war, however, three brilliant Irish trainers in Vincent O'Brien, Paddy Prendergast and Mick Rogers have achieved fame and, to a large extent with horses owned by wealthy Americans, have won all five classic races, and most of our other great races as well.

Racing enthusiasts will argue till kingdom come as to who was the greatest trainer, but there can only be one opinion as to who was the most versatile. I first met Vincent O'Brien at Leopardstown when I was spending Christmas 1946 with Peter and 'Obbie' Fitzwilliam in Ireland. He had just won a Novices Chase with a very nice horse called Cottage Rake. Knowing that Fulke Walwyn was in the market for a promising young chaser, I asked Vincent his valuation of the horse. '£10,000' was his immediate reply, at which I retired discomfited. Vincent was, of course, absolutely right, as Cottage Rake subsequently won three Cheltenham Gold Cups on the trot. Furthermore, this remarkable young man won three Champion Hurdles in succession with Hatton's Grace and three Grand Nationals, also in succession, with Early Mist, Royal Tan and Quare Times. Turning his attention to flat racing, Vincent won the Derby with Larkspur, the St Leger, Coronation Cup, Eclipse Stakes, 'King George' and Prix de l'Arc de Triomphe with Ballymoss, the One Thousand Guineas with Glad Rags, the Oaks with Long Look and Valoris, and many other important races as well. In 1968 he won the Two Thousand Guineas, the Derby, and the Washington International with Sir Ivor, ridden in all his races by Lester Piggott. A man of great charm, Vincent is as well turned out as his horses.

Paddy Prendergast has been a friend of mine for many years, and luncheon at Paddy's before the Irish Derby is a function not readily forgotten. Paddy combines the spontaneous good fellowship typical of the Irishman with one of the shrewdest brains in the business. He is a wonderful judge of a horse, from foals to elderly stallions and broodmares, and most of his winners have been bought by him at public auction as yearlings.

Ragusa, owned by Jim and Meg Mullion, is the best colt he has trained and after finishing third in the Derby he trotted up for the Irish Derby, 'King George', and English St Leger, and as a four-year-old won the Eclipse Stakes. Paddy's best filly was Noblesse, who won the 1963 Oaks in a canter at 11/4 on.

I have enjoyed many good times with Paddy, the most hilarious being the dinner party he gave at the Grosvenor Hotel at Chester on the evening of the Chester Cup, which he had won with Larry Gelb's Credo, who had been my nap. The hospitality was on the most lavish scale, rendered even more lavish by a telephone call from the winning owner who was in Rome, insisting that Paddy and his guests should drink a case of champagne at his expense to celebrate Credo's victory. Paddy is a born raconteur and that evening he excelled himself.

Some idea of the strength of the Irish opposition these days can be gleaned from the fact that Paddy Prendergast was leading trainer in England in 1963, '64 and '65 and Vincent O'Brien in 1966.

Beaverbrook Newspapers have always been fortunate in their racing journalists, and in addition to Clive Graham and Peter

O'Sullevan the *Daily Express* has another expert in Old Etonian Charles Benson. He has not yet received the opportunities he deserves, but they will come.

The *Sunday Express* has a first-class combination in Tom Forrest, who covers most of the flat racing, and Dick Francis, who gives his readers the benefit of his expert knowledge on steeplechasing. Dick, an ex-champion jockey, will always be remembered as the partner of Queen Elizabeth the Queen Mother's Devon Loch, who collapsed fifty yards from the winning post when leading in the Grand National. Dick has since established himself as one of the most successful writers of thrillers in the country. They are all written with a background of racing, but thousands who enjoy his books have never been on a racecourse. They are extremely well written and I always enjoyed reviewing them. Today, when I have to pay for them, I still look forward to the publication of another book by my friend Dick, a man of many qualities, one of them being that he is a most congenial companion.

Both *The Times* and the *Daily Telegraph* are doubly represented. Michael Phillips in the South and Jim Snow in the North give racing a most comprehensive coverage in *The Times*, and this go-ahead democratic newspaper, so different from 'Auntie *Times*' of my young days, permits them to use their own by-lines. Peter Scott and John Lawrence cover racing with equal efficiency in the *Daily Telegraph*. Peter is young as racing journalists go, but his knowledge of his subject is astronomical and he is known as the Walking Encyclopaedia. Peter is the only person I know who manages to read every daily racing article, but I managed to read sufficient to appreciate what a very high standard has been achieved by my colleagues in a branch of journalism which was a bit of a joke until well into the 'twenties. Arthur Salter, a successful tipster, Tim Fitzgeorge-Parker, a highly controversial and entertaining journalist and all-rounder, and Julian Simcox represent the *Daily Mail*. John Rickman, prince of TV interviewers, with a vast fan mail (80 per cent of it from females), and Norman Pegg are a formidable combination in the *Daily Sketch*, as are Bob Butchers and Dick Ratcliff in the *Daily Mirror* and Lionel Cureton and Don Cox in the *Sun*.

As regards commentators, Julian Wilson, son of the distinguished journalist Peter Wilson, is highly professional in the manner in which he gets people to talk about themselves. Few racing men are very articulate, and sometimes it must be like trying to get blood out of a stone. Julian, having modelled his style on that of Peter O'Sullevan, is also a competent race reader. Still young, he has a great future.

Tony Cooke, a friend of mine of great charm, is the hardest worked of the racecourse commentators. He delights viewers not only by the accuracy of his commentaries but also by the way in which he takes viewers into his confidence and gives each one the impression that he or she is the only one that matters.

I have always regarded international rivalry as constituting the spice of racing, but it was not until the aeroplane became the accepted means of transport for racehorses in the early 'fifties that it was possible to stage a race in which horses from every country in the world could compete with one another. Needless to say, it was an American, John Schapiro, from Baltimore, a distinguished businessman and President of the Boston Metals Co., who took advantage of the shrinkage of the size of the earth's surface to stage a race of $1\frac{1}{2}$ miles on Laurel Park Racecourse (a grass track) in Maryland, which he called the Washington International.

It was a courageous enterprise, but it immediately caught the imagination of owners in every part of the globe, and the race has gone from strength to strength. Our only success was with Wilwyn in the inaugural event in 1952. The race has been won eight times by the U.S.A., five times by France and once each by England, Ireland, Venezuela, and Australia. The Russian horse Aniline finished third in 1965 and second in 1966. The Washington International is not only a great race, magnificently staged by Schapiro, the most imaginative of all racing impresarios; it is also an international occasion. A live wire if ever there was one, this most likeable of men has done more to promote good relations between the United States and the rest of the world than all the politicians in Washington, and France showed her appreciation of him by making him a Chevalier de Mérite Agricole of France for his pioneering of international horse racing.

No chapter on my profession would be complete without a tribute to the Press Association, to whom every journalist, and none more than myself, owes a debt of gratitude. With an article of never less than 1,500 words, and often a great deal more, to turn out every day, it was impossible for me to glean every item of news that was going. Hardly a day passed when I was not indebted to 'Fairy' Fairchild, Dai Davis or some member of the P.A. staff for some item that I should otherwise have missed. On the rare occasions on which I did not go racing I was entirely dependent on the Agency reports for what had taken place. Geoffrey used to say that I wrote a more colourful article from the P.A. tape, embellished by my own imagination, in the news room at Thomson House than when I was an eyewitness.

It would be invidious for me to draw comparison between the respective merits of those with whom I worked in the racecourse press rooms all over the country, and on occasions in Ireland and France, but I hope I shall not give offence when I say that I derive my greatest pleasure from reading the articles of my friend John Lawrence.

The standard of racing journalism has improved out of all knowledge since I first joined the press. In those days few members of the racecourse press could have got a living at any other job, but today a large proportion of my ex-colleagues could have made a success of any profession they had entered. As the son of Lord Oaksey, it is not surprising that John has a first-class brain, which has fortunately remained unimpaired despite the number of occasions he has fallen on his head in his role as our most successful amateur rider.

Sunday is now a day much looked forward to by those who like reading intelligent articles on racing, as opposed to those devoted solely to tipping. In addition to John's article in the *Sunday Telegraph* one should never miss Roger Mortimer's article in the *Sunday Times* and Richard Baerlein's in *The Observer*. All these men are Old Etonians, which goes to show that a public school education is no longer the handicap it was when I first entered a racecourse press room.

# 21 *The last lap*

Pondering over the events of the past sixty years, I have arrived at the conclusion that the best years of my life have been the last twenty. This, I hope, will prove a pleasant surprise to the young people of today who are convinced that life worth living ends at forty.

My war had been a singularly cushy one. My flat had suffered no damage from bombs, though one morning, when I was still in bed after working on night shift, a V2 fell on Chelsea Hospital, a couple of hundred yards away, inflicting a number of casualties on residents or passers-by. Hundreds of windows were shattered but mine remained intact.

Although it was a long time before the wartime restrictions were removed it was good to be alive in a country at peace, and again I was lucky. I had been offered the job I had always hoped might some day come my way.

'What about your illnesses? They can't have been much fun,' a friend asked me recently, after hearing me enthuse over the post-war years, but you can't win all the time.

Ever since I had collapsed on the floor of the gymnasium at Sandhurst, I had suffered from what can be loosely described as indigestion, and in 1948 the doctors decided that I must be operated on for the removal of a dimeticulum. This was brilliantly performed, but it didn't happen to be what I was suffering from, and my operation was comparable with pulling out the wrong tooth, but much more uncomfortable and expensive, though, amittedly, not so serious as the amputation of the wrong leg.

The following year, Sir Victor Negus told me he thought he could relieve my discomfort by stretching the passage leading to my stomach, under an anaesthetic, but he emphasised that this would not effect a permanent cure. Thanks to Sir Victor, I enjoyed twelve years of comparative comfort before I suffered a complete breakdown in health, necessitating three major operations in the space of a year, and three for the removal of ulcers from my left eye. When I was convalescent I was asked if I had been frightened of the proximity of death, but if one is in pain, or suffering acute discomfort, all one craves is oblivion, and one is not choosy as to what form it takes.

As to the existence of God, my heart and my head have been at war with one another ever since I was old enough to question the authenticity of what I had learned at my mother's knee. While my heart yearns to believe, my head is full of scepticism, with the result that I am what Sir Norman Birkett once described as a Christian agnostic.

What does it matter if a man believes that Jesus Christ was the Son of God or the greatest human being that ever lived? Am I a worse citizen by reason of the fact that I do not believe that he fed 5,000 hungry people on a few loaves and small fishes or that he raised Lazarus from the dead? His crucifixion still remains the supreme sacrifice, whether he was God or man, and no one has yet found a flaw in his teaching.

So long as we believe that Christ died an agonising death as an example to mankind and we endeavour to follow his teaching in our association with our fellow men, I do not think that the rest of our beliefs have any bearing on our lives.

Christ condemned hypocrisy, and I should be an arch-hypocrite if I were to stand up in church and recite the Apostles' Creed. I do, however, respect the views of those who can do so, meaning every word, and I think I envy them as well. Faith, however, is not something you can acquire – you either have it or you haven't, and I do not believe that the haves are any more virtuous than the have-nots.

I believe with all my heart that no one on earth has the right to treat another as less than human and that everyone on earth has the right to dignity, freedom and the pursuit of happiness. I believe that cruelty, whether directed against a human being or an animal, constitutes a far worse crime than dishonesty – a view which is not shared by the lawmakers of this country, dire penalties being inflicted on the thief while those guilty of diabolical cruelty to children and animals often get away with a fine. I believe in equal opportunities for all men, and that racialism, which is of course a refined form of cruelty, is a deadly sin.

I believe that the greatest criminals of all are those responsible for the waging of wars, and with the passing of the years since those bloodthirsty days in 1914 my realisation of the insane futility of the nations setting out to exterminate one another has convinced me that if I were to stick a bayonet into the belly of a complete stranger, simply because those governing our respective countries had failed to come to terms, I should be guilty of murder. Nationalism is unimportant, but being a human being is a wonderful thing. I therefore believe that Internationalism, which is working out most successfully in Antarctica, is the only solution to the world's problems, and I hope that it will come before the world has been blown to bits as the result of the heads of state of the most powerful nations pressing a button at the same time.

Universal freedom of thought and action should be the aim of all governments. Discipline for discipline's sake frustrates and makes rebels of us. Self-discipline should be the aim of all individuals. Throughout history the Heads of both Church and State have employed measures which have been the negation of freedom.

When I was at Eton I received nine marks out of ten for an essay on what the world would be like in the twentieth century if Jesus Christ had not been born. On this hypothetical question I really went to town, painting a lurid picture of a gruesome world peopled by savages, had not Christ preached the Gospel of peace and goodwill. I made no mention of the fact that at that very moment we were engaged in the bloodiest war of all time, and that in every town and village boys were being taught to hate their neighbours and to look forward to the day when they could kill them. Neither, of course, did I refer to the fact that some of the worst atrocities have been committed by Christians in the name of Christianity on fellow Christians whose mode of worship did not conform with their own.

Today we have the Lord's Day Observance Society so obsessed with the letter of the Fourth Commandment that they will fight tooth and nail to prevent God-fearing, hard-working people from indulging in harmless pleasures on Sunday. If these busybodies, whose activities antagonise the faithful and the faithless alike, were honest with themselves, they would never read Monday's paper. I speak feelingly on this subject, having spent more Sunday afternoons than I can remember in a News Room.

I am not in the least ashamed of my morals, believing that in order to commit a sin one must do harm to a fellow being, and I like to think that those with whom I have broken the Seventh Commandment derived some pleasure from it.

One man's religious beliefs are another man's superstitions. Some years ago, when I was in Ceylon, our guide pointed with reverence to a scar near the summit of a mountain, and informed us that it was made by Buddha's foot as he took off for heaven, at which a fellow tourist exclaimed in a loud voice, 'How preposterous!' In an equally loud voice I expressed the view that it was no more difficult to believe than the story about Christ turning water into wine. This was received in shocked silence, followed by mutterings in which the word 'blasphemy' occurred several times.

The story of my operations might be of interest to readers of the *Lancet*, but apart from saying that for several months in 1963 I lost the desire to go on living, so acute was my discomfort, I have no intention of inflicting on others my tale of woe.

Tigie and Tom Nickalls are old friends of mine, and in May 1963 Tigie wrote to me telling me of a doctor in Zürich who had cured the daughter of a friend of hers, after they had given up all hope. So on the day Relko won the Derby, I flew to Zürich. A week after my return I went to stay with Marjorie and Peter Willett for Ascot, though I did not resume work for another month. From that time, till the day I retired, I did not miss a day's work through ill-health.

I received countless acts of kindness while I was in the shadows, and one in particular remains in my memory. Unable to swallow, I was fed intravenously for several days, but in order to build up my strength to undergo an operation, I was urged to eat solid food at the earliest possible moment, and when Peter O'Sullevan visited me one evening I was trying to force down some tough fish. Next morning Peter arrived, bringing me some delicious smoked salmon, which may not have been what the doctor ordered, but constituted the first enjoyable meal I had had for weeks. In order to convince me that he had gone to no trouble on my behalf, Peter told me he had dropped in on his way to Kempton, to which I replied that if he thought that St Thomas's Hospital lay between Chelsea and Kempton his knowledge of London must be on a par with his sense of direction in Paris.

This referred to an incident in Paris several years earlier. We had spent an enjoyable evening, and Peter, who was staying at the Ritz, offered to drive me to my hotel in the 16ème arrondissement near the Étoile, explaining that he knew a short cut which would save at least a quarter of an hour. At the end of that time we arrived in such an ill-lit quarter that it was impossible to decipher the names of the streets from the car. On disembarking, I found we were in the rue de Rome at which I am alleged to have said, 'I knew we were bloody well lost, but I did hope we were still in the right bloody town.'

One of the advantages of increasing age is that one lives in awe of fewer and fewer people, till one fine day one discovers that one doesn't give a damn for anybody. Lord Rosebery has always shown me much kindness, and I have spent many pleasant days lunching with him at Mentmore and going round his stud, but I was only one of many who found him awe-inspiring. I therefore felt very proud of myself on the day that I realised that while I retained my respect for this country's youngest octogenarian, my fear of him had evaporated.

Another source of satisfaction to me was my friendly association with my Editor, Bill Clarke, which, as the years went by, developed into a real friendship.

We had little personal contact as the *Sporting Chronicle* is published in Manchester and I lived in London. Except when I was racing in the North my articles were either telephoned to or handed in at the London office, from which they were teleprinted to Manchester. This state of affairs precluded last-minute consultations, though we talked on the private line several days a week. In common with all the best Editors, Bill was not in the habit of throwing bouquets, but, far more important, he never referred to it when I was suffering one of those inevitable runs when one can't tip a winner.

As I had always been on tenterhooks as to whether I might have missed some story the other boys had got, I was surprised, at the presentations made to me at Thomson House by the board of Thomson Newspapers and my colleagues on my retirement, to hear that I was regarded as a phlegmatic individual, and that any irritation I had evinced from time to time was the result of a colleague either sitting in the seat which I had occupied for years, or moving a sheet of my copy.

Of all my colleagues, the man with the keenest sense of the ridiculous was John O'Neill, whose job is the very responsible one of returning the Starting Prices for the *Sporting Chronicle*. The price of every horse we back at Starting Price is determined by the representatives of the *Sporting Life* and *Sporting Chronicle*. John O'Neill and Bob Watson are the leading representatives of the *Sporting Chronicle*, and Geoffrey Hamlyn and Doug Newton for the *Sporting Life*.

Of all the kind things which were said and written about me when I said goodbye, the following letter to the Editor of the *Sporting Chronicle*, from John O'Neill, gave me most pleasure.

'With Quinny's retirement the Race Course Press Room has lost a great character as well as a great racing journalist. Quinny Gilbey's dry wit and his forceful language, when he felt strongly on any subject, have for long delighted his colleagues, none more so than myself. I have always envied him his remarkable powers of concentration. Once he had begun writing he would carry on, even if everyone else in the Press Room was talking at once, apparently completely oblivious of the hubbub. Only once did I see him lose his detachment. This was just after Nicolaus Silver had won the Grand National in 1961, and winning owner Mr Vaughan, trainer Fred Rimell and jockey Bobby Beasley had been brought into the Press Room to be interviewed.

'Reporters and photographers from all over the British Isles, and other parts of the world, crowded in, and in their eagerness to get as close as possible climbed on to the table at which one lone figure sat scribbling away – Quinny. He had napped the winner, and thus had all the gen about it, and had no need to join the questioning throng.

'He ignored the jostling crowd until some of them got perilously close, and one man was actually standing on Quinny's copy. The table was swaying, and this was too much, even for Quinny. He rebuked the owner of the nearest pair of legs in a few well-chosen but unquotable words, adding "I don't mind you standing on the table, but there's surely no need to bloody dance on it." Then he resumed writing.'

One has only to live long enough to be considered a bit of a character, and, if one stays too long, to become an object of pity. All too often had I heard a colleague described as 'a poor old chap', who should have turned it in years ago, to be tempted to stay on till I had to ask a colleague what had happened.

As I grew older I read a race less accurately, but this was largely owing to my remaining at my desk until the horses were at the post, thereby allowing myself no time to check the colours. As Michael Seth-Smith, Bob Haynes and the other racecourse commentators give such an accurate description of the races I was well content to let them do the job for me.

I forget who it was who wrote, 'There is nothing so infinitely pathetic as the evening of a great reputation', but though I never rated my reputation in that category I think that everyone who can afford to do so should get out while he is still capable of performing his task unaided.

From 1963 onwards, however, I was so overjoyed at being restored to health that I worked harder than at any time in my career. Bill Clarke often urged me to take a day or two off, but I usually refused. It was not that I thought that my substitute might let me down, but having believed that I should never work again, I did not want to take time off from what was not only my job, but also my way of life.

I cannot leave the subject of my job without expressing my appreciation of Max, my telephonist, who was not only 100 per cent reliable, but was a charming companion. I have described how I fussed about my work, but when it was in Max's hands it was as good as on the Editor's table.

At the time I was appointed Kettledrum, Cyril Luckman, a great journalist who had been the Scout of the *Daily Express* for donkey's years, was on the point of retiring, and though his pen was as agile as ever he found the climb to the top of the Stand, six times a day, too much for him. He would therefore remain in the Press Room, and ply me with questions on my return, and I found it infuriating when as the result of his interrogation of me he would write a better article than I did.

For years we had sat opposite one another at a narrow table on the Rowley Mile course at Newmarket. He had friends in the black market and would arrive with his dispatch case full of food. By the time the first race was run pieces of pie, legs of chicken and salmon mayonnaise had encroached on to my copy. But he was such a kind man, always inviting me to share his luxuries, that I had not the heart to remonstrate with him.

One of the old school, he still wrote with a pen and ink, and one day he gave vent to a wail of anguish on opening his case. The stopper of his ink bottle had come out, saturating his pies and other delicacies with ink. Although he had a great sense of humour he did not think it all that funny when I exclaimed 'Now I know what a black pudding looks like.'

It was Cyril who introduced Peter O'Sullevan to the *Daily Express*, so his fame lives on. Clive Graham succeeded Cyril as the Scout. Cyril was not an easy man to follow, but the *Express* Racing Service has risen to new heights as the result of the joint efforts of Clive and Peter, a wonderful combination, both on the air and on paper. My brother Geoffrey was responsible for Clive joining the *Express*. Whilst still at Eton, Clive convinced Geoffrey that he was not only an infant prodigy, but one who was likely to train on, a promise which he has fulfilled up to the hilt.

There is no way of measuring the hand of fate, and assessing how much we owe to it, but we all know that events which can alter the entire course of our lives can result from a trifling incident.

In December 1957, Bobby and Sybil (now Sir Robert and Lady) Kirkwood asked me to a cocktail party with dancing, which they were giving for their debutante daughter Roberta in the penthouse at the Dorchester, and had not Roberta cut my dance, and had I not at that moment seen an old friend Rupert Belville, sitting by himself, I should never have met Maggie, and it is unlikely that she would be alive today.

I was sailing on the *Alcantara* for South America on my annual holiday in a few days' time, and when I told Rupert this he said that a charming friend of his was travelling on the same ship as far as Lisbon, and that he would tell her to get in touch with me. He did not mention her name, and I forgot all about her till I found a note in my cabin from someone called Maggie Marks, asking me to have a drink with her in the second-class bar.

I thought, at first, that she was probably married to one of Messrs Spencer's partners, but dismissed the idea as improbable, as if she were, what was she doing in the second class? On my arrival in the second class, with a note accepting Mrs Marks's invitation, I was pushed into a cabin by a stewardess, where I was greeted by the spectacle of the longest and best pair of legs I had ever seen. Their owner was recumbent on the lower berth, reading aloud to two small boys on the upper berth.

'Sorry about this,' she said, pulling her dress down till the hem of it was no more than six inches above her knees, while I also apologised for bursting into her cabin without knocking. On meeting her in the bar I discovered that the rest of her, and she was very tall, was up to the standard of the legs.

She agreed to join me again after she had put her sons to bed, and we were still talking and drinking whisky in a secluded corner of the bar when closing time was announced at 1.30 a.m. We found that we had many friends in common, and I had met her sister Virginia, who was still married at that time to the Marquess of Northampton. More important, we seemed to think alike on most subjects, including marriage, and most important of all I found her devastatingly attractive. As we had each been married twice we considered that sufficient, and I felt that as my marriage to Romie had failed it was most unlikely that a subsequent one would succeed.

Maggie's husband worked for United Press in Lisbon, but her marriage was nearing the last stages of disintegration, and she was not looking forward to the reunion. As we said goodbye she promised faithfully to be on the quay on 23 January when the *Alcantara* docked at Lisbon on our return journey.

True to her word, Maggie met the ship on my return, and we dined in Lisbon, and drank green wine. I found her even more attractive than on our first meeting, but she was suffering from a very bad cough, and though she made light of it it seemed to me imperative that she should return to London as soon as possible, and be examined by a specialist.

She explained that this was out of the question as her husband would not agree to her going back to London so soon after her return to Portugal, and in any case she could not afford it. I insisted that she come as my guest and the vision of that tall figure emerging from the Customs at London Airport six weeks later will always remain with me.

I had arranged to pay my annual pre-season visit to the French stables at Chantilly the following week, and Maggie thought that four days in Paris together sounded the greatest fun. But before we set off she visited a lung specialist, and on our return she found his report stating that she was suffering from tuberculosis in both lungs.

A month in a London hospital was followed by six months in the King Edward VII Hospital at Midhurst, from which she was discharged, cured. I had spent all my spare time with her at Midhurst, but though she knew that there could be no happiness for her in Lisbon she insisted on returning there at the end of the Christmas term, accompanied by her eldest boy, who was at school in England.

Before she went we spent ten wonderful days in Rome, followed by four hectic days in Paris. As we were both inveterate sightseers we were so tired at the end of each day in Rome that only once did we sample the 'Dolce Vita' after dark. This was, I think, the best holiday of my life, though it was spent under the shadow of Maggie's departure.

In January, I went on my annual holiday to Barbados. The M.C.C. were touring the West Indies, captained by Peter May, and as the guest of my Barbadian friends I found Maggie's absence easier to bear. I spent the days on the beach, in the sea, or watching cricket, and returned to England in a happier frame of mind.

A few weeks after my return from the West Indies Maggie walked into my flat unheralded. She had come to London to see her specialist, and had intended leaving again without seeing me, but the temptation to come and say hello was too strong, and here she was. It so happened that, once again, I was on the point of leaving for Paris on a racing story, so she came with me, returning direct to Lisbon at the end of our stay. I did not see her again till August, when we spent a few days together in Gibraltar and Tangiers, but in October she arrived in London, having finally parted from her husband.

The divorce was far from amicable, and the opposing solicitors had been so zealous in their determination not to miss a trick that their petition read like a brochure for a Cook's Tour – London, Paris, Rome, Florence, Cortina, Venice, Tangiers, Gibraltar and Eastbourne all figuring in their plea for the dissolution of the marriage.

One of my happiest experiences, in recent years, has been the return into my life of my eldest son, Robin, whom I had only seen once since he was a small child. When Robin was seventeen, I received a message through the son of a friend who was in his house at Eton that he would very much like to see me. I was also informed that Betty and her husband had changed his name to Wellesley before he went to his prep school (Ludgrove) or was old enough to have any say in the matter. This came as a shock to me, but I was too excited at the prospect of meeting my son for the first time for twelve years to grasp the fact that his mother and stepfather had not only deprived Robin of his father during his formative years but had also robbed him of his name.

I made no reference to this when we met for lunch at a Windsor hotel, which Robin has since told me he enjoyed as much as I did. Little did I think at the time that a further sixteen years would elapse before we had our next meal together.

He had by then been elected to Pop, and was in the XI. When I met him in the pavilion at Lord's before the Eton and Harrow match I realised that something was wrong, but I refrained from questioning him. I was desperately keen that he should do well in this all-important match and that his concentration should not be broken by the problem of divided loyalties.

He went in first and made top score in each innings. Seated on top of the pavilion, I applauded every run, and my friends must have marvelled at my enthusiasm for a boy who did not bear my name. It was a strange experience – paternal pride and indignation vied with each other. Lord Rosebery summed up my feelings in a nutshell when he compared them with those of a man watching a horse which he had bred win the Derby carrying his bookmaker's colours.

A few weeks later Robin wrote telling me that he could not see me again. The letter had been dictated by his stepfather, who had informed him that he would never have him in his house again, or allow him to see his mother, if he associated with his father.

I am not, by nature, a vindictive man, in fact, so far as I know, I have no enemies, though by this I do not mean I consider myself universally popular. Gerald Wellesley is dead, but this does not lessen my contempt for a man who deprived me of my son for thirty years.

My other son, Anthony, was married in Paris in the autumn of 1958, and the Gilbeys and the Brinckmans celebrated it with two dinner parties, a luncheon party and a visit to the Crazy Horse. The airline pilots were threatening to go on strike, so we travelled to Paris by train and boat. It was a very long time since I had made the Channel crossing, and I had forgotten how unpleasant it was, but we had an excellent luncheon on the train.

On the night before the wedding Naps Brinckman gave a dinner party at Maxim's, the bride's mother, who was not present, stood us luncheon at the Grand Véfour, and I gave a dinner party at Fouquet's. Luckily the strike was settled, and we were able to fly home, as I would have dreaded a Channel crossing after all that food.

I had written a weekly article for the *Empire News* for seventeen years, so one might have thought that I would have been informed that it was about to fold up. But the first I heard of it was when I read about it in the *Daily Express* on Wednesday, when I was about to collect material for my next Sunday's article.

Although I did not receive a handshake composed of even one of the baser metals, or a week's salary in lieu of notice, the demise of the *Empire News* was one of the more fortunate episodes in my career. On the following day Frank Butler, Sports Editor of the *News of the World*, telephoned me asking me to write a weekly article, at the same time making an appointment for me to lunch with the Editor, Mr Stafford Somerfield, the following week.

Thus began a happy association, which continued until my retirement. When I informed Mr Somerfield of the salary I had received from the *Empire News* he thought I was joking. Taking into account feature articles, I earned over four times the amount during my six and a half years with the *News of the World* that I would have done had I still been working for the *Empire News*.

Retirement, like death, is something which happens to other people. Unlike death, however, it provides one with a pleasing diversion as one pores over brochures and maps, working out an itinerary which had always been a couple of weeks too long to be fitted into an annual holiday.

In the summer of 1965 I came to the conclusion that the time was approaching for me to make way for a younger man, and though I could not imagine what life would be like with no daily deadline I felt that if I was to derive full enjoyment from my leisure I must get out while I still had my health and strength.

Although my job had become my way of life I was fortunate in having many other interests which I had been unable to indulge in for the past twenty years. It was therefore agreed that I should retire at the end of the 1966 flat racing season.

I count myself the most fortunate of men, as few people have derived so much fun, directly and indirectly, from their job, and it was for this reason that Romie suggested I should call this book *Fun was My Living*.

I cannot pretend that when the Derby of 1966 came along I viewed with complacency the fact that it was the last Derby I should describe, or that I did not sometimes panic as the weeks flew by and the dreaded day drew nearer and nearer, till I was on the train for Haydock Park for the final meeting of the season.

I have seldom been racing on a colder day, and as I tried to get some feeling into my fingers, I realised that instead of being full of self-pity I should have been thanking my lucky stars for my countless blessings.

I detested the English winter, and in three weeks' time I would be boarding the S.S. *Orsova* bound for Trinidad, Cartagena, Panama, Acapulco, Los Angeles, San Francisco, Honolulu, Fiji, New Zealand, Sydney and Melbourne.

What the hell had I got to bellyache about? On my return I could go racing every day for free for the rest of my life if I was so minded, thanks to the good offices of my friend Geoffrey Hamlyn.

I therefore got to work and wrote my final article, napping Peter O'Sullevan's Be Friendly to win the last big race of the season, the Vernons November Sprint Cup. As it was my last ever nap I announced to my colleagues in the Press Room, 'I've gone for Be Friendly, and mark my words he'll win.' Peter quoted me in the following day's *Daily Express*, adding some very kind words of his own on my career. Be Friendly had proved himself a brilliant two-year-old, and as I had not a very high opinion of our older sprinters I thought he had an outstanding chance, and I selected Green Park, another two-year-old, to be second.

Although I had conquered my unjustified feeling of self-pity, saying goodbye to people one has worked with for years, and for whom one has a deep affection, is an intolerable strain, so I decided to skip the final day, and watch the big race at home on television.

When Be Friendly, at 15/2, drew away from Green Park, with his race won a furlong from home, with commentator Peter O'Sullevan sounding as composed and unemotional as if the horse belonged to a stranger, I envied him his self-control. But there wasn't anyone to see, except my dachshund, and she was asleep on my knee.

But it was far from being the end of my career. On the first day of the big Ebor meeting at York in August Peter Walwyn came up to me and said, 'I'm sorry I haven't got a horse suitable to run in your race.' 'What race?' I asked. 'The Quintin Gilbey Stakes of £1,000 – to be run at Kempton on September 22nd,' he replied. 'Listen, Peter,' I answered. 'Racing people have been trying to pull my leg for over forty years, and though I may be fairly gullible I'm not falling for that one.' Peter assured me that he was deadly serious, but it was not till he showed me the race and its conditions, in black and white, that I believed him, and then I pinched myself to make sure I wasn't dreaming.

The race was over a mile, and was open to three-year-olds and upwards. There were forty-five entries, but as often happens in a non-handicap for a worth-while prize (it was the principal event of the day), it cut up and only four horses went to post. This was disappointing but it produced a thrilling finish between The Ambion, a three-year-old filly, ridden by Scobie Breasley, and the grey six-year-old Birdbrook, the mount of Ron Hutchinson, Scobie's mount getting the verdict in a photo finish by a neck.

When the race first appeared in the Calendar Scobie told me that he was determined to win it. He did not know at that time what he would ride, and after Sir Gordon had withdrawn his two entries he readily accepted the mount of Sir William Dugdale's filly, who was trained by Atty Corbett.

From my point of view it could not have been a better result as owner, trainer and jockey are all friends of mine. Racing had never before honoured a living journalist in this manner, and my heart was full of gratitude, though my colleagues expressed the view that an even bigger compliment was paid me by a stranger who asked me in the paddock whether I had put up the £1,000 stake money.

Bill Clarke wrote me the following letter when I received the Derby Award, shortly after I had retired. 'Honours are coming to you thick and fast, so again my congratulations on your latest achievement in being selected as Journalist of the Year. It is indeed an honour richly deserved, and I am proud to think that it was achieved during my reign as Editor.'

Lord Derby was prevented by illness from making the presentations to Mr Jim Joel, owner, Noel Murless, trainer, Major Leslie Petch, racecourse official, Doug Smith, flatrace jockey, Josh Gifford, steeplechase jockey, and myself, racing journalist, his place being taken by Lord Boothby. Bob and I were contemporaries at Eton, and when he said in his speech that we had been friends for sixty years he was not exaggerating by all that much.

I think that my story should contain some tips which may prove of value to those who have not been around quite as long as I have. Although I was moderately successful as a tipster you would be well in the red if you had backed all my selections on a level stake. I have already explained that as the result of the efficiency of the Bookmakers' Intelligence Service, the Betting Tax and consequent weakness of the market it is more difficult to win money by betting today than ever before. I nevertheless believe that the several publications by Timeform Limited of Halifax, allied to some work on your own behalf, should enable you to show a profit at the end of each season.

All Timeform publications are the brain children of my friend Phil Bull, whose flaming red beard, now nearly white, has been as conspicuous a landmark on our racecourses as the Bushes at Newmarket. The reason that followers of these publications show a profit is that Phil employs a large and highly competent staff which covers every meeting in the country. A journalist can only be in one place at a time and therefore has to sum up the prospects of a number of horses he has never seen.

Another invaluable publication is the Raceform Notebook for which Johnny Sherratt, the best race reader I know, is the chief contributor. Commentating and race reading are not synonymous, as so many people think. The commentator describes events as they occur, while the man who reads a race for a publication has to store up all the incidents in his mind till he reaches his desk.

Retirement is a subject on which I also feel competent to give a tip. I believe that the two ingredients essential to happiness are a clear conscience and a diversity of interests.

Readers may not think that my conscience troubled me all that much over the years, but when life is no longer competitive the tempo slows down and one can consider one's course of action from the point of view of other people and not entirely from self-interest.

Although I loved my job, retirement opened the door on a

vista of new experiences with the opportunity to please myself for the first time in my life.

Those who are too lazy or too bored to avail themselves of their new-found freedom fade away, and deserve to do so.

At the risk of boring one's friends one should enthuse at the prospect of visiting some new place or re-visiting a country one has longed to see again. I travel a lot though I find life in England to be just as much fun as it was at any time in my life. My colour TV set is a never-ending source of pleasure and I am not ashamed to admit that when I am at home I watch telly on an average twenty-four hours a week. Motion pictures are better than ever before, and there are half a dozen first-class plays now running in London.

My only complaint about present-day entertainers is that they have contrived to extract all the melody from their music, replacing it with a series of sounds, unrelated to one another, and offensive to the ear.

My addiction to the 'box' has one draw-back in that it plays hell with my reading, and no fewer than six books I long to read remain unopened by my bedside. Three dailies, three Sundays, with their voluminous supplements, plus *Private Eye* once a fortnight, monopolise my time, and the days are never long enough. Non-addicts are apt to think that senility has already caught up on me, when in response to an invitation to dinner I ask my would-be hostess if she is out of her mind or does she not know that it's the 'Forsyte Saga', 'Civilisation' or 'The Trouble Shooters'.

Don't fuss about your health but appreciate your limitations. Don't try anything more strenuous than golf, and if you don't play golf, walk. I am certain I should have packed up years ago had I not walked several miles a day, for which I have to thank my dogs. I hesitate to offer advice about indoor sports, except to say that every churchyard has its complement of optimists who have gone before their time as the result of kidding themselves they were as good as ever.

By and large the clergy do their level best to accomplish the impossible, and two of the finest men I know are my cousin, Mgr Alfred Gilbey, a Roman Catholic, and the Reverend Bob

Wickham, a Protestant and an ex-headmaster of Twyford School.

What shocks me about the priesthood of all denominations is its hypocrisy over the Sixth Commandment. From our earliest childhood we are told that to kill constitutes the greatest sin of all, that we should love our neighbours as ourselves, and that we should turn the other cheek. But no sooner have the governments of two countries fallen out than the priests of both countries rise in their pulpits and pronounce it to be a Holy War, and that it is our duty to kill those against whom we have no personal animosity and, for all we know, are dutiful sons, loving husbands, and fond fathers.

This book was already in the hands of my publishers when I received a letter from an old friend suggesting that I should name the personal acquaintance whom I consider has rendered the greatest service to humanity. I unhesitatingly name the late Sir Benjamin Rycroft. Ben Rycroft operated on me on three occasions for the removal of an ulcer from my left eye, a simple straightforward affair, if any operation in which the margin of error is a fraction of a millimetre can be so described. We became friends; he liked to listen to my shop while I was, of course enthralled by his.

Some readers may recall an operation he performed in front of the television cameras for the transplant of the corneas from the eyes of two deceased persons to those of two women, one aged thirty who had been blind from birth, and the other, middle-aged, who had been blind for thirty years. The programme had been recorded a month earlier, and at the end of it we were introduced to the two patients. The bandages had been removed that morning and both could see. It was one of the most moving experiences of my life, and I straightaway wrote to Ben offering him my eyes when I had no further use for them. He wrote me back a charming letter saying he could not accept my offer as my eyes were susceptible to ulcers.

I am still in love with life, but as the shadows grow longer it would be a consolation to know that the eyes which have served me so well would bring happiness to someone who had been less fortunate. To walk on the moon is man's most spectacular achievement, but a man must be inspired by God to give sight to the blind.